# PERCEPTION AN

This book offers a provocative, clear, and rigorously argued account of the nature of perception and its role in the production of knowledge. Walter Hopp argues that perceptual experiences do not have conceptual content, and that what makes them play a distinctive epistemic role is not something that they share with beliefs, but something that sets them radically apart. He explains that the reason-giving relation between experiences and beliefs is what Edmund Husserl called "fulfillment" – in which we find something to be as we think it to be. His book covers a wide range of central topics in contemporary philosophy of mind, epistemology, and traditional phenomenology. It is essential reading for contemporary philosophers of mind and phenomenologists alike.

WALTER HOPP is Assistant Professor of Philosophy at Boston University. He has published articles in numerous journals including the *Canadian Journal of Philosophy*, the *European Journal of Philosophy*, and *Husserl Studies*.

# PERCEPTION AND KNOWLEDGE

*A Phenomenological Account*

WALTER HOPP

*Boston University*

CAMBRIDGE
UNIVERSITY PRESS

CAMBRIDGE UNIVERSITY PRESS
Cambridge, New York, Melbourne, Madrid, Cape Town,
Singapore, São Paulo, Delhi, Mexico City

Cambridge University Press
The Edinburgh Building, Cambridge CB2 8RU, UK

Published in the United States of America by Cambridge University Press, New York

www.cambridge.org
Information on this title: www.cambridge.org/9781107646988

First published 2011
First paperback edition 2013

*A catalogue record for this publication is available from the British Library*

ISBN 978-1-107-00316-3 Hardback
ISBN 978-1-107-64698-8 Paperback

*To Maita*

# Contents

*Acknowledgments*                                            *page* ix
*List of Husserl's works*                                          x

Introduction                                                      1
1  Content                                                        7
  1.1  Contemporary uses of 'content'                   8
  1.2  Two arguments for mental content                12
  1.3  A Husserlian account                            27
  1.4  Conclusion                                      36
2  Experiential conceptualism                                    37
  2.1  Motivating experiential conceptualism           40
  2.2  The argument from conditions of satisfaction    43
  2.3  The argument from perceiving-as                 47
  2.4  The argument from the perception of categorially
     structured objects                 60
  2.5  The argument from perceptual identification     73
  2.6  The argument from horizons                      76
  2.7  Conclusion                                      80
3  Conceptualism and knowledge                                   81
  3.1  McDowell's position                             82
  3.2  Brewer's account                                92
  3.3  Conclusion                                     101
4  Against experiential conceptualism                           103
  4.1  Detachable contents                            103
  4.2  The argument from knowledge                    106
  4.3  The argument from intentionality               115
  4.4  The demonstrative theory                       118
  4.5  Some arguments against the demonstrative theory 119
  4.6  Conclusion                                     129
5  Conceptual and nonconceptual content                         130
  5.1  Nonconceptual content                          130
  5.2  Conceptual content                             141

|       | 5.3   | The argument from horizons revisited | 146 |
|       | 5.4   | Conclusion | 148 |
| 6     | **The contents of perception** | | 149 |
|       | 6.1   | The relational view | 149 |
|       | 6.2   | The relational view and hallucination | 152 |
|       | 6.3   | Further considerations against the relational view | 161 |
|       | 6.4   | A defense of moderate disjunctivism | 172 |
|       | 6.5   | Conclusion | 189 |
| 7     | **To the things themselves** | | 190 |
|       | 7.1   | Epistemic fulfillment | 191 |
|       | 7.2   | Other kinds of fulfillment | 201 |
|       | 7.3   | Departures from Husserl | 206 |
|       | 7.4   | Epistemic fulfillment and knowledge | 210 |
|       | 7.5   | Conclusion | 224 |

| *Bibliography* | 226 |
| *Index* | 242 |

# *Acknowledgments*

I have presented much of the content contained in this work in previous talks, discussions, and courses, and owe an enormous debt to all of those whose comments and criticisms have helped me develop my arguments. I am especially grateful to all of my colleagues in the Department of Philosophy at Boston University for their support, the Boston University Humanities Foundation for providing me with a semester of funding, and the Boston University Center for Philosophy and History of Science, the Husserl Circle, the American Philosophical Association, the Department of Philosophy at the University of Manitoba, the California Phenomenology Circle, the Philosophical Psychology Lab at Harvard University, and the Department of Philosophy at Seattle University for allowing me to present my work.

I am also indebted to a number of teachers, colleagues, and students for helping me develop my ideas on these topics over the past several years, including but not limited to: Michael Barber, Klaus Brinkmann, Vaughn Cartwright, Colin Cmiel, Steve Crowell, Sean Culleton, John Drummond, Andreas Elpidorou, Jason Ford, Aaron Garrett, Charles Griswold, George Heffernan, Ryan Hickerson, James Higginbotham, Jaakko Hintikka, Burt Hopkins, Sean Kelly, Victor Kestenbaum, Manfred Kuehn, Janet Levin, Steven Levine, David Liebesman, Claudio Majolino, Ed McCann, John McHugh, Ronald McIntyre, James Mensch, Dermot Moran, Thomas Nenon, Jake Quilty-Dunn, Ethan Rubin, Ben Sherman, Michael Shim, Charles Siewert, David Woodruff Smith, Nate Smith, Susanne Sreedhar, Daniel Star, Carolyn Suchy-Dicey, James Van Cleve, Gideon Yaffe, and Jeff Yoshimi. I am especially grateful to Dan Dahlstrom, Brian Glenney, Dave Kasmier, and Dallas Willard for reading and providing feedback on portions of this work. Finally, I would like to thank the reviewers of this manuscript for their comments.

# Husserl's works

APS     2001. *Analyses Concerning Passive and Active Synthesis.*
        A. J. Steinbock, trans. Boston: Kluwer Academic Publishers.
        *Analysen zur passiven Synthesis. Aus Vorlesungs- und
        Forschungsmanuskripten, 1918–1926. Husserliana* vol. XI.
        M. Fleischer, ed. The Hague: Martinus Nijhoff, 1966.

CM      1977a. *Cartesian Meditations.* D. Cairns, trans. The Hague:
        Martinus Nijhoff. *Cartesianische Meditationen und Pariser
        Vorträge. Husserliana* vol. I. S. Strasser, ed. The Hague: Martinus
        Nijhoff, 1962.

Crisis  1970b. *The Crisis of European Sciences and Transcendental
        Phenomenology: An Introduction To Phenomenological Philosophy.*
        D. Carr, trans. Evanston IL: Northwestern University Press. *Die
        Krisis der europäischen Wissenschaften und die transzendentale
        Phänomenologie. Eine Einleitung in die phänomenologische
        Philosophie. Husserliana* vol. VI. W. Biemel, ed. The Hague,
        Netherlands: Martinus Nijhoff, 1976.

EJ      1973. *Experience and Judgment.* L. Landgrebe, ed. J. S. Churchill
        and K. Ameriks, trans. Evanston IL: Northwestern University
        Press.

FTL     1969. *Formal and Transcendental Logic.* D. Cairns, trans. The
        Hague: Martinus Nijhoff. *Formale und transzendentale Logik.
        Husserliana* vol. XVII. P. Janssen, ed. The Hague: Martinus
        Nijhoff, 1974.

Ideas 1  1982. *Ideas Pertaining to a Pure Phenomenology and to a
        Phenomenological Philosophy. First Book: General Introduction to a
        Pure Phenomenology.* F. Kersten, trans. The Hague: Martinus
        Nijhoff. *Ideen zu einer reinen Phänomenologie und
        phänomenologischen Philosophie. Erstes Buch. Allgemeine Einführung
        in die reine Phänomenologie. Husserliana* vol. III. K. Schuhman,
        ed. The Hague: Martinus Nijhoff, 1976.

*Ideas* II    1989. *Ideas Pertaining to a Pure Phenomenology and to a Phenomenological Philosophy. Second Book. Studies in the Phenomenology of Constitution*. R. Rojcewicz and Schuwer, trans. Dordrecht: Kluwer Academic Publishers. *Ideen zur einer reinen Phänomenologie und phänomenologischen Philosophie. Zweites Buch: Phänomenologische Untersuchungen zur Konstitution. Husserliana* vol. IV. M. Biemel, ed. The Hague: Martinus Nijhoff, 1952.

*IL*    2008. *Introduction to Logic and Theory of Knowledge: Lectures 1906/07*. C. O. Hill, trans. Dordrecht: Springer. *Einleitung in die Logik und Erkenntnistheorie. Husserliana* vol. XXIV. U. Melle, ed. The Hague: Martinus Nijhoff, 1984.

*LI*    1970a. *Logical Investigations*, 2 vols. J. N. Findlay, trans. London: Routledge & Kegan Paul. *Logische Untersuchungen. Erster Teil. Prolegomena zur reinen Logik. Text der 1. und der 2. Auflage. Husserliana* vol. XVIII. E. Holenstein, ed. The Hague: Martinus Nijhoff, 1975. *Logische Untersuchungen. Zweiter Band: Untersuchungen zur Phänomenologie und Theorie der Erkenntnis. Husserliana* vol. XIX. U. Panzer, ed. The Hague: Martinus Nijhoff, 1984.

*PCIT*    1991. *On the Phenomenology of the Consciousness of Internal Time (1893–1917)*. J. B. Brough, trans. Dordrecht: Kluwer Academic Publishers. *Zur Phänomenologie des inneren Zeitbewusstseins (1893–1917). Husserliana* vol. X. R. Boehm, ed. The Hague: Martinus Nijhoff, 1966.

*PICM*    2005. *Phantasy, Image Consciousness, and Memory*. J. Brough, trans. Dordrecht: Springer. *Phäntasie, Bildbewusstsein, Erinnerung (1898–1925). Husserliana* vol. XXIII. E. Marbach, ed. The Hague: Martinus Nijhoff, 1980.

*PP*    1977b. *Phenomenological Psychology*. J. Scanlon, trans. The Hague: Martinus Nijhoff. *Phänomenologische Psychologie. Vorlesungen Sommersemester, 1925. Husserliana* vol. IX. W. Biemel, ed. The Hague: Martinus Nijhoff, 1968.

*TS*    1997. *Thing and Space*. R. Rojcewicz, trans. Boston: Kluwer Academic Publishers. *Ding und Raum. Husserliana* vol. XVI. U. Claesges, ed. The Hague: Martinus Nijhoff, 1973.

# Introduction

Right now you are probably in a position to perceive the weather outside. Take a closer look. Now close your eyes or turn them elsewhere and merely think about the weather outside. Entertain various propositions about it. Now reflect on the difference between those modes of being conscious of the weather. I think it's obvious, first, that there is a pronounced phenomenological difference between the two experiences. To see the weather conditions, to determine perceptually that it is sunny, for instance, requires that you undergo one of a certain range of perceptual experiences. You can merely think about the weather, however, no matter what you are perceiving. You can do so whether your eyes are open or closed, whether you perceive an open book or the contents of your refrigerator. The difference in epistemic worth of the two experiences is equally profound. Merely thinking that it is sunny, say, does not give one a reason to believe that it is. Seeing that it is sunny, on the other hand, provides an excellent reason to believe that it is.

The distinction between merely thinking about something emptily and having it bodily present in perception is arguably the most important distinction in both the theory of intentionality and the theory of knowledge. Despite assurances to the contrary by a few influential philosophers, there can be no serious doubt that perceptual experiences can and do provide warrant or justification for beliefs. Understanding *how* they do that is one of the most important undertakings in epistemology. One of the most significant barriers to understanding how perceptual experiences justify beliefs is that a fairly recent but durable dogma of epistemology is at odds with some basic facts about perception. On the one hand, ever since Wilfrid Sellars's attack on the "myth of the given," there has been a widespread conviction among epistemologists that reason-giving relations can hold only among mental states whose intentional contents are conceptual or propositional, since only contents of that sort can bear logical relations to one another. If so, then the contents of perceptual states must be conceptual. On the other hand, there are several good reasons – conclusive reasons, I will argue – for thinking that perceptual experiences have a fundamentally different sort of content from beliefs. If so, then reason-giving relations do not hold solely among mental states with conceptual content. The challenge for any such view is to provide an account of how perceptual states can stand in reason-giving relations with beliefs.

Meeting that challenge is the ultimate aim of the present book. The principal thesis I set out to defend is that the reason-giving relation between perceptual states and beliefs is, to borrow Husserl's terminology, one of *fulfillment*. It is a platitude that beliefs are oriented towards truth. But beliefs are also oriented towards the *consciousness of truth*. No better fate can befall a belief than for the person who holds it to justify it, not on the basis of other propositions, but on the basis of a sufficiently rich perceptual encounter with the objects and states of affairs that it is about. That is what happens in fulfillment: we *find* the world to be as we *think* it to be and, when that occurs, we are conscious of a match between the proposition or truth-bearer believed and its truth-maker. Furthermore, although the *objects* of perception and belief are often, and in the case of fulfillment must be, identical, they have fundamentally different sorts of *contents*. There is no conceptual content such that believing or entertaining it is necessary or sufficient for undergoing a particular perceptual experience. Accordingly, the relation between perceptual experiences and beliefs is fundamentally different from the relation between beliefs and other beliefs.

In developing and defending this thesis, I argue for a Husserlian theory of mental content, one which sharply distinguishes mental contents such as concepts and propositions from their corresponding objects such as individuals, properties, events, relations, and states of affairs (Chapter 1). I then (Chapters 2–3) examine a number of arguments in favor of experiential conceptualism, according to which the intentional contents of perceptual states are conceptual, and I argue that all of them are flawed. I also argue (Chapter 4) that not only are there decisive phenomenological reasons to reject experiential conceptualism, but that, far from making the reason-giving link between experience and belief intelligible, as virtually all of its proponents claim, experiential conceptualism is utterly incapable of explaining why perceptual experiences play such a distinctive and privileged role in the production of knowledge. Perception is neither knowledge nor belief, and what makes perceptual experiences play such a distinctive role in knowledge is not some feature that they share with beliefs, but something that sets them apart, quite radically, from them. I then (Chapters 5–6) provide an account of conceptual and nonconceptual content and argue, in opposition to the view that perceptual states lack content altogether, that perceptual experiences possess two kinds of nonconceptual content. Finally (Chapter 7), I present a modified version of Husserl's theory of fulfillment, distinguish some of its varieties, and argue that it provides a very compelling account of how the nonconceptual contents that figure in perception can justify empirical beliefs.

I have said that the following investigation will be largely phenomenological, so I owe the reader a brief characterization of what I take phenomenology to be. 'Phenomenology' traditionally designates both a discipline with a distinctive subject matter and method, and a certain historical-philosophical tradition unified by a shared concern with the philosophical works of some of that discipline's founding members, especially Edmund Husserl. The more closely one adheres to Husserl's own conception of the subject matter and methods of phenomenology – methods he attempted to articulate often and voluminously, and which became increasingly bound up with his distinctive brand of "transcendental idealism" – the less philosophical work will strike one as genuinely phenomenological, particularly work by those who do not self-consciously identify with the historical tradition. If, however, one turns to the phenomena themselves, such as the nature of consciousness, meaning, intentionality, rationality, knowledge, perception, and so forth – the very things that Husserl was attempting to get into view via his method(s) – then one will find that a great deal of phenomenological work, including some of the best and most important, has little, perhaps nothing, to do with the tradition stemming from Husserl. That is how I see things, and it is how I believe Husserl – who was always ready, as we should all be, to "bracket" Husserl – might have seen things too. (Obviously 'phenomenology' did not primarily designate a historical tradition for *him*.) Many of the most important and exciting debates relevant to phenomenology today take place both inside and outside the phenomenological tradition.

Part of my basis for thinking so is that so many debates center around claims towards which anyone concerned with investigating what Husserl and his followers investigated must take some position. If you are interested in intentionality, you cannot be indifferent to whether a given version of internalism or externalism about mental content is true, for instance. Another reason for thinking so is that a great deal of philosophical work on consciousness, perception, and intentionality meets the minimal conditions to qualify as phenomenological. Those conditions, I believe, are the four that Charles Siewert identifies as constitutive of 'plain phenomenology.' You are doing plain phenomenology, says Siewert, if (1) you make and explain mental or psychological distinctions, (2) show why those distinctions are theoretically important, (3) rely on a source of first-person warrant, and (4) do not assume that first-person warrant derives from some source of third-person warrant (Siewert 2007: 202). Many people who have never read a paragraph of Husserl are undoubtedly doing plain phenomenology.

Of course, Husserl was doing that too, and was quite a bit better at doing it than just about anybody before or since. In the best of all possible worlds, those doing phenomenology today would also be involved, in some way, with the historical-philosophical tradition stemming from Husserl, since Husserl and his followers, as I hope to show, have a great deal to teach us. That Husserl's works lie completely off of so many contemporary thinkers' radar has a number of plausible sociological explanations – the fact that his seminal *Logical Investigations* wasn't translated into English until 1970, for instance, did not help matters – but no good philosophical ones. Even incorporating a few of his basic distinctions, to say nothing of his detailed analyses, could transform a number of contemporary debates. But in hoping for a world in which phenomenological inquiry is carried out, exactly what is one hoping for? And why should we hope for that when there are so many other, possibly more promising, approaches to under-standing the mind?

Beginning with the second question, provided that phenomenology actually can teach us something about consciousness, there is really no chance of *not* hoping for a developed phenomenology, since the concern with under-standing consciousness is something with which we, the thinking conscious, are simply saddled. No reasonable person could deny that there are other methods of investigating mental phenomena, and that those methods have yielded and will yield very impressive results. Cognitive psychology and cognitive neuroscience have produced a wealth of valuable knowledge, and will produce much more. On the other hand, most reasonable people would also agree that conscious experience is something rather than nothing, and manifests itself to us in a distinctive way. Whatever the ultimate metaphysical story concerning consciousness turns out to be, there can be no serious doubt that we are confronted with our own conscious experiences in a way that differs entirely from the manner in which we are confronted (or not) with our own nervous systems, brains, and behavior. For many other approaches to the mind, conscious experiences are theoretical entities postulated to explain certain observable data. For the phenomenologist, they are the data.

So what, then, is phenomenology? Corresponding to any object of which one is conscious, of any type whatsoever, there is a distinctive sort of experience in which precisely *that* object is represented or presented to one in precisely the way that it is. Having a headache, perceiving a bird in flight, playing a comprehending part in a wedding ceremony, and firing electrons at a detector screen all involve carrying out certain conscious acts and, with the possible exception of the first, presuppose a broad range of other occurrent mental states and background knowledge and abilities. Phenomenology, as I understand it, is the discipline whose business is to determine the definitive properties of *types* of conscious experiences and the sorts of relationships that conscious experiences have to one another by examining them as they present themselves from a first-person point of view. It is an ontology of consciousness, whose data are conscious experiences as they present themselves, and which are treated as potentially repeatable types rather than individual episodes – much in the way that a chalk figure on the board is an illustration of an ideal type rather than the principal theme of a geometrical investigation. And insofar as phenomenology is an ontology of consciousness, its main task is to discover *necessary* truths concerning consciousness and specific types of conscious experiences. The phenomenologist is more interested in such claims as that every conscious act is essentially self-intimating, that it is impossible to lie to oneself intentionally, or that any perceptual experience is necessarily inadequate to its object, than in the fact that Mahler's music reminds Jones of his grandpa. Again, many philosophers outside of the phenomenological tradition assert and argue for such claims as well.

It should be clear that there is more to phenomenology than a description of the merely sensuous or qualitative aspects of experience. There are no distinctive sensations or qualia that characterize making a logical inference. But there is, still, a distinctive phenomenological character to making an inference – part of that character consisting in the very fact that it possesses no distinctive sensuous feel – by whose means it can be identified and distinguished, from a first-person point of view, from other sorts of experiences. The differences between inferring something and, say, being jealous or understanding a sentence are manifest from a first-person point of view, and manifest themselves in a different way from the way they manifest themselves from a third-person point of view. Similarly, there is a phenomenological difference between believing and desiring, and between wondering whether it will rain and wondering whether it will snow, between thinking of the number two and thinking of the number three. The subject matter of phenomenology is broader than the phenomenal aspects of conscious experience.

Finally, Husserl characterized phenomenology as a presuppositionless science. I have serious doubts about the possibility of such a science. But

I do think that phenomenology, at its best at least, is characterized by a deep respect for the obvious and a corresponding unwillingness to allow it to be obscured or falsified in the service of advancing theories and worldviews. While the phenomenologist might wind up having something important to say about important metaphysical doctrines such as physicalism or dualism, such results should emerge, if they do, from an unbiased examination of conscious experiences themselves. A phenomenological description of consciousness should remain as uninfluenced as possible by any desire on the part of the one doing it to make consciousness turn out to be the way his favored metaphysical or scientific theory says it must be. If the phenomenologist concludes that qualia don't exist, for instance, this should be because he has provided a tolerably clear characterization of what qualia are supposed to be and examined whether any mental states have them, not, for instance, because qualia have no place in the desert landscape he wants the world to be.

I very much doubt that phenomenology can accomplish everything Husserl thought it could. I do, however, think that in phenomenological reflection conscious states and many of their properties stand before us in person, and that we should take the phenomena – any phenomena – that stand before us in that way with the utmost seriousness. In the following work I hope to discuss some of those phenomena, and address some important questions in the philosophy of perception and epistemology on their basis. I should, finally, make it quite explicit that despite my heavy reliance on some of Husserl's ideas, this is not intended to be, primarily, a work about Husserl, and nor does it aspire to be compatible with many of his signature theories. It is about perception and knowledge, and in investigating those phenomena, I am quite frankly co-opting what I find most valuable in Husserl for my own philosophical purposes.

# CHAPTER I

## *Content*

Thorstein Veblen wrote, "Except where it is adopted as a necessary means of secret communication, the use of a special slang in any employment is probably to be accepted as evidence that the occupation in question is substantially make-believe" (Veblen 1994: 157). The term 'content' definitely qualifies as a piece of special slang in philosophical discourse, which can, it is true, sometimes veer into the make-believe. But contents, properly understood, are not make-believe; they are what beliefs, and many other spectacular things, are made of. The purpose of the present chapter is to provide a broad characterization of what mental content is, and a few arguments that at least some mental states have it. I will focus on the contents – if any – of perceptual states in subsequent chapters. I will, finally, argue that Husserl's early theory of intentional content provides the most satisfactory philosophical account of the relationships among intentional experiences or acts, their objects, and their contents.

Many mental states and acts, including perceptual ones, possess intentionality; they point beyond themselves towards something else, their objects. Intentionality, according to Husserl, is "the own peculiarity of mental processes 'to be the consciousness *of* something'" (*Ideas 1* §84: 200). The car that I perceive is one thing, and my act of perceiving it is quite another. The car is black, weighs a bit over a ton, and can hold five passengers. It is not an event, and it is not of or about anything. My experience of the car, on the other hand, is not black, does not weigh anything, and cannot hold any number of passengers. It is an event, and it is of or about something – namely the car.

Other types of mental states and acts exhibit intentionality as well. My belief that grass is green is about grass's being green, which is a state of affairs, not a belief. My desire for more free time is directed towards my having more free time, which is not itself a desire – I am already stuck with that. Some philosophers hold that all mental states have intentionality. Others hold that only mental states and acts have intentionality. Both positions are far from evident. Certain mental states like pain, dizziness, and general, nonspecific feelings of anxiety are often taken to be counter-examples to the first claim. And it is clear that some things besides mental states, such as words and paintings, are about other things. A defender of the second claim might modify his view to say that only mental states possess *intrinsic* or nonderived intentionality in the face of such apparent counter-examples. In any case, these controversies will not detain us. What is clear is that many conscious experiences, including perceptual experiences and thoughts, do possess intentionality. They are directed onto or aimed at something distinct from themselves.

Distinguishing between acts and their objects, as Thomas Reid recognized, prevents a good deal of bad metaphysics: we cannot blithely move from claims about the ontological status of one to claims about the status of the other. But it does not get us very far. Not only does it fail to resolve such issues as whether different kinds of experiences have different kinds of contents. It does not even establish that mental states have *content* at all.

It might seem odd to suggest that experiences might not have content, since it is difficult to find any major figure in the contemporary discussion who does not characterize the intentionality of experiences in terms of their possession of content. Pick up any work on perception, intentionality, or the philosophy of mind, that has been written in the last several decades, and the chances are that it is bristling with 'contents'. But this unanimity is apparent only, since there is hardly any term in philosophy more ambiguous than, and less frequently clarified than, the term 'content'. Sometimes it is used to designate the *object* of a mental state or concept – what that mental state or concept is about. Jesse Prinz, for instance, says that "those things to which [concepts] refer, I call their intentional contents" (Prinz 2002: 4). Gendler and Hawthorne write: "Some contents, it seems, we perceive *directly* (say, that such and such is red)" (Gendler and Hawthorne 2006:11). Alan Millar appears to hold the same view: "The content of a belief is what would be the case if the belief were true" (Millar 1991a:10). M. G. F. Martin expressly identifies contents and objects: "It is common to talk of beliefs as being conceptual. This involves a commitment to the idea that the objects of belief, their contents, have a significant structure" (M. G. F. Martin 2003: 238).

Just as often as the term 'content' is used to designate what a mental state is about, however, it is also used to designate something else. Contents are often held to be something like Fregean senses or modes of presentation, which determine which object a mental state is about and (sometimes) the manner in which it is about it. Adrian Cussins, for instance, writes: "The term 'content,' as I shall use it, refers ... to the way in which an object or property or state of affairs is given in, or presented to, experience or thought" (Cussins 2003: 133). David Woodruff Smith (1989: 8), whose account I will follow somewhat closely, writes, "The content is the 'mode' of presentation, the conceptual or presentational structure of the experience itself." For anyone who thinks that propositions are contents, and that they are composed of Fregean senses or concepts rather than objects and properties, drawing a distinction between contents and objects would seem mandatory, on pain of holding the view that the only objects of thought are propositions, senses, and concepts.

Some authors even appear to use the term 'content' to mean *both* the object that a mental state is about and some other thing, distinct from that object and the mental state whose content it is, which is about something other than itself. Michael Huemer suggests that contents are possible states of affairs:

My statement, "The cat is on the mat," is a kind of representation: it represents a certain possible state of affairs, a state consisting in the cat's being on the mat. That possible situation – the cat's being on the mat – is called the "content" of the representation. (Huemer 2001: 52)

He also writes that an important class of representational states which he calls "apprehensions" "represent their contents as actualized" and that the content of a desire is "the state one wants to come about" (Huemer 2001: 53). All of this suggests that contents are the things that mental acts are about. When I say that the cat is on the mat, what else could be the object that I am talking and thinking about than the cat's being on a mat? But he also says that in order to be aware of x, one must apprehend it in the right way, where this means, among other things, that "the nature of x must correspond, at least roughly, to the content of the apprehension" (Huemer 2001: 54). So here it looks as though we are to distinguish the nature of x – x's being white, or being large, or being to the left of y – from the contents of the apprehension, otherwise the question of their corresponding to one another could not arise. He also characterizes representational contents as "aspects" of perceptual experience, where perceptual experiences are "the purely internal states that are involved in all perception" (Huemer 2001: 65). Because such states and their aspects are purely internal, they could have just the content they have even if the corresponding object of the perceptual state did not exist. Finally, he claims that contents are "abstract" (53). But not all of the objects of consciousness are abstract.

"Representational contents" now appear to be something distinct from the objects of mental states; instead of being the things which are *represented*, they are now given the job of *representing* those things.

John McDowell also appears to equivocate on the term 'content' – with important consequences, as we will discover in Chapter 3. He writes:

> *That things are thus and so* is the content of the experience, and it can also be the content of a judgement . . . So it is conceptual content. But *that things are thus and so* is also, if one is not misled, an aspect of that layout of the world: it is how things are. (McDowell 1994: 26)

Here it seems that the content of a true or veridical thought – that things are thus and so – is identical with the object of the thought, namely a certain state of affairs. McDowell also, however, claims that "[C]onceptual contents that are passively received in experience bear on, or are about . . . the world" (McDowell 1994: 39). Contents now emerge as bearers of aboutness, something which could not be said of just any object or state of affairs that a mental state is about. Neither a cat, nor a mat, nor the state of affairs consisting of a cat's being on a mat, is about anything, while the contents of mental states intentionally directed upon them, including the (Fregean) proposition that a cat is on a mat, are.

Gilbert Harman, for his part, writes, "Our experience of the world has content – that is, it represents things as being in a certain way" (Harman 1990: 34). This suggests that the content of the experience is something "in" the experience that does the representing, and this suspicion is at least partially borne out when he writes, "the content of the experience might not reflect what is really there" (Harman 1990: 34). He also describes certain contents as "not correspond[ing] to anything actual," where this is plausibly read as being about something that does not exist. But then he describes Ponce de Leon's search for the Fountain of Youth as having an "intentional *object*." And he describes a picture of a unicorn as having an "intentional *content*," apparently, given the obvious similarities between the two cases, using the phrases "intentional object" and "intentional content" synonymously. Finally, he says that when we paint or imagine a unicorn, the "content is not actual." This again suggests that by 'content' he means 'object', for it is surely possible otherwise that the content of such an experience could be perfectly actual even though the object of that experience is not. If we, for instance, were to treat the contents of thoughts as meanings of the sort that belong to sentences, then it is perfectly conceivable that a content would exist without "corresponding" to anything in the world. All false sentences have such meanings, for instance, but those meanings, and their tokens, are every bit as actual as those of true sentences. So are paintings of Zeus and maps of Middle Earth.

Christopher Peacocke offers an explicitly ambiguous definition of content: "Henceforth I use the phrase 'the content of experience' to cover not only which objects, properties and relations are perceived, but also the ways in which they are perceived" (Peacocke 2001: 241). Robert Hanna follows suit: "Broadly speaking, the mental content of an animal's conscious mental state is *what* that state refers to or describes, and *how* it does so" (Hanna 2008: 42). And this despite the fact that, first, the things perceived and the ways in which they are perceived are categorially different things and, secondly, that they are related differently to an act of perceiving. A thing such as a tree is an individual, has bark, and might be blowin' in the wind, whereas the way a tree looks is a property, is shareable by many other things, including non-trees, doesn't have bark, and isn't even the kind of thing that can blow in the wind. And when one perceives a tree, the object is precisely the tree, not the way the tree is perceived. Just as we can climb trees but cannot climb the ways we climb trees, so we perceive trees, not ways in which we perceive trees.

Tim Crane goes out of his way to distinguish the content and the object of a mental state:

[W]e should distinguish the propositional content of an experience – the way it represents the world as being – from its intentional object . . . If I see a rabbit, the rabbit is the intentional object of my experience. My experience may also have the propositional content that there is a rabbit running through the field. But I do not see such propositional contents or propositions; I see rabbits and fields. (Crane 2006: 136)

But even this is not quite adequate. In the first place, the phrase "the way it represents the world as being" is ambiguous. When I believe that Socrates is wise, is the way my belief represents the world as being identical with the state of affairs that Socrates is wise? Or is it identical with the way in which I represent Socrates as being wise? There are other ways of representing that same state of affairs. Using his own example, one could merely think that the rabbit in question is running through the field as opposed to perceiving it running through the field. The phrase in question does not make it clear whether "the way" in question is a way of the world or a way of mindedness. Second, it is unclear whether Crane uses the phrase 'propositional content' to designate the state of affairs whose constituents, in this case, include the rabbit and the field through which it is running, or a bearer of aboutness whose constituents are concepts, Fregean *Sinne*, or something along those lines. Certainly the rabbit must be distinguished from both. If Crane means the latter, then his point is well taken: in perceiving (or thinking about) a rabbit, the object of one's mental state is the rabbit, not a Fregean sense or concept. If, however, by 'propositional content' he means the state of affairs, then his point is mistaken. The distinction between the rabbit and the state of affairs of which it is a constituent does not, in the case like this where the state represents a rabbit running through a field, mark a distinction between what a mental state is about – its object – and something else. If I am conscious of a rabbit running through a field, what I am conscious of in each case, as an *object*, is an entire state of affairs (*LI* 5, §17: 579; Smith and McIntyre 1982: 6–9). When I believe that a rabbit is running through a field, although the rabbit is *among* the objects that my belief is about, it would radically underdescribe my belief to say that it is about the rabbit. It is also about the rabbit's activity, running, and where that activity is taking place, in a field. And if my perception represents the world as being a certain way, then that way, and not merely some proper subset of the objects and properties that constitute that way, is the object of my perception. Otherwise, obviously, it would not represent that way, but only some of that way's constituents.

Michael Thau has perhaps the most remarkable view of all. On his view, belief is a relation to a proposition, which is "a structured entity that contains things that determine which object it represents and which properties that object is represented as having" (Thau 2002: 83). Thau also assures us that, in one sense of the term 'belief', a belief just is a proposition: "propositions – the things we believe – are, in some sense of the term, themselves beliefs . . . That is, it's natural to think that a subject's belief just is the thing that he believes" (Thau 2002: 59). This seems odd, but not entirely so: you and I can have the "same belief," in *some* acceptable sense of 'belief'. But then we learn that propositions, which are the representational contents of belief – they are what people believe – are identical with what those beliefs represent: "a belief's representational content just is what it represents" (Thau 2002: 132). But a belief's representational content is a proposition, and propositions are beliefs. So beliefs, on this view, represent themselves. But the object of my belief, when I believe, say, that New York is crowded, is not about something, while my belief is.

## 1.2  TWO ARGUMENTS FOR MENTAL CONTENT

So what on earth is mental content? Is there even such a thing? And if there is, how is the content of a mental act related to (1) the act whose content it is and (2) the object of that act? It is not at all obvious that we need mental contents at all, and some philosophers have denied that we do. For instance, one might hold that a mental act is individuated in virtue of being (1) the general sort of mental act it is (imagining, perceiving, conceiving, and so on) and (2) the object that it is of. I will call this the "spotlight view" of intentionality. Russell provides one of the clearest statements of the view. "At first sight," he writes, "it seems obvious that my mind is in different 'states' when I am thinking of one thing and when I am thinking of another. But in fact the difference of object supplies all the difference required" (Russell 1984: 43).

The spotlight view cannot be true of all mental acts, given the things that we do in fact think about. First, there are plenty of mental acts whose objects do not exist. Thoughts directed towards the god Jupiter and Santa Claus, for instance, are about things that do not exist. So are thoughts directed towards the greatest prime number and the philosopher who criticizes all and only those philosophers who do not criticize themselves. So are all false thoughts. The belief that the moon is made of cheese and that Mount Everest is balmy are about whole states of affairs. They represent certain portions of the world as being a certain way. And yet the balminess of Everest and the cheesiness of the moon do not exist. Yet all of these thoughts and beliefs are different from one another. They give rise to different behaviors, inferences, and beliefs. They are compatible and incompatible with different sets of propositions. But the nonpresence of all of those nothings cannot add up to a difference in behavior, inferences, and beliefs, and logical role. As Husserl puts it, "Objects that are nothing in a presentation are also unable to create differences among presentations" (*LI* 5, §25: 603). Whatever it is that explains how a mental state is about the god Jupiter or the greatest prime number or the fact that Mount Everest is balmy cannot be the objects of those acts, since those objects do not exist.

Furthermore, many mental acts that do have existing objects only have them contingently. The thought that Mount Everest is cold represents an existing state of affairs, and therein consists its truth. But its identity does not depend upon, and so cannot be partially constituted by, the object it is about. It would be exactly the thought that it is if it were false. Finally, even when we merely think about, conceive, or imagine something that does exist, it is not *present* to the mind in a way required to make that thought the determinate thought that it is. When I merely think about Moscow from my Boston office, the object of my thought, Moscow, is not present to me in the way that a perceived object is. It neither exerts any causal influence on this particular act of thinking (even if it figures in a causal account of my general capacity to think of it), nor is it a constituent of it (even though it is a constituent of what my thought is *about*). Something besides the object must, in such cases, account for the fact that a given act is directed upon its object. In the case of many types of mental acts, including those (1) which are about nonexistent objects, (2) which only contingently depend upon the existence of their objects, and (3) whose objects neither exert a causal influence upon nor are constituents of them, there must be something besides their objects that accounts for their identity and determinate intentional direction.

The ability to embrace nonexistent and impossible objects in thought (and possibly in perception) is, I will admit, something of a mystery. I am not trying to solve that mystery, but merely to report it. In any case, that would only qualify as an objection if there were very good reasons for thinking that there are no mysteries, a claim that is put into considerable doubt by, among a thousand other things, the fact that we can think about nonexistent objects. The price for denying this mystery, moreover, is at least as high as accepting it. If Timmy hopes that Rudolph the Red-Nosed Reindeer lands on his roof tonight, what existing object could plausibly be taken to be the object of his hope? One is tempted to start with the obvious culprit, Rudolph, and claim that he is really an idea in the child's mind or an abstract object of some sort. Both claims are quite unbelievable. First, nothing "in" Timmy's mind, nor anything abstract, could possibly qualify as what he is thinking about when he thinks about Rudolph; as confused as he might be, he does hope that one of his ideas or an abstract object will land on his roof tonight. What he hopes will land on his roof is a reindeer that is identical with Rudolph, and this thing does not exist, either in his head, in the actual world, or in an abstract realm. As Husserl puts it, discussing his "presentation" of the god Jupiter,

This intentional experience may be dismembered as one chooses in descriptive analysis, but the god Jupiter naturally will not be found in it. The 'immanent', 'mental object' is not therefore part of the descriptive or real make-up of the experience, it is in truth not really immanent or mental. But it also does not exist extramentally, it does not exist at all. (*LI* 5, §11: 558–9)

Furthermore, Timmy is mistaken in supposing that Rudolph lands on roofs, but his error is not on a level with, say, supposing that numbers are sad. Supposing that something exists when it does not, on the other hand, is not a category mistake at all – existence or Being is not, as both Aristotle and Kant knew, itself a category, and the things which do exist might not have existed. This helps explain why when you tell a child that Rudolph does not exist, what you say is true, whereas if you tell him that his idea of Rudolph does not exist, or that an abstract object like the number 2 does not exist, what you say is false.

Even if Rudolph does exist, this does not entail that what Timmy hopes for exists. What Timmy hopes is that the world is configured in a certain way. And no matter what one takes Rudolph to be, it is certain that the world is not going to be configured to suit his hope. And here the hope of finding a suitable existing object is even more fruitless than before. The roof upon which Timmy hopes Rudolph will land is precisely his *roof*. He does not hope that his idea of Rudolph lands on his idea of the roof, or that an abstract Rudolph lands on an abstract roof, or any permutation of the above. He hopes Rudolph – let him be an idea or an abstract idea or whatever – will land on his roof. And he won't.

One might be tempted to think that the object of Timmy's hope is a proposition rather than a (nonexistent) fact. After all, Timmy hopes *that Rudolph will land on his roof*, and the proposition that Rudolph will land on his roof does exist. That proposition is also, let us suppose, *what he believes*. Similar solutions might be thought to work for other propositional attitudes. *What I think* when I think that grass is white is the proposition that grass is white, and that does exist. But this is a mistake. As Wayne Davis points out (Davis 2003: 317), there is an important difference between the following types of sentences:

(1)  S is thinking the thought "p".
(2)  S is thinking of (about) φ.

When the former claim is true, the existence of p is entailed by S's act of thinking it. You cannot think that Mount Everest is warm if the thing you think, the proposition or thought that Mount Everest is warm, does not exist. The proposition is, in this case, what Davis calls a "relational object" (Davis 2003: 318). When (2) is true, on the other hand, the existence of φ – the "intentional object" – is not entailed by S's act of thinking about it. Davis's distinction between relational and intentional objects is quite similar to the distinction, as I will understand it, between contents and objects. Sentences like "S thinks that__," "S desires that__," and even "S sees that__" do not function in the way sentences like "S sees__" or "S thinks about__" do. When I see an apple, what I see – the apple – is the object that my act of seeing is about. But when I think that an apple is on the table, what I think – the proposition that the apple is on the table – is *not* the thing I am thinking about.[1] The object is the fact, the apple's being on the table. The sentence

---

[1] Compare this point with Twardowski's (1977: 12 ff.) remarks about the verbs "to paint" and "to present." "To the verb 'to present,' there correspond – in a similar fashion as to the verb 'to paint' – first of all two things: an object which is presented and a content which is presented. The content is the picture; the object, the landscape" (1977: 13).

(3) S thinks that p
functions much like
(4) S says "A."

*What you say* when you say "Snow is white" is a sentence, or perhaps the proposition it expresses, but *what you talk about* is not a sentence or a proposition. And *what you think* when you think that you are rich is the proposition that you are rich. But what you think about is not a proposition. We talk with, not about, sentences. We think with, not about, propositions (compare Fodor's remarks on modes of presentation in his *Concepts* (1998: 18)).

Now, with Timmy's hope in mind, let us see why the object of his hope – and of propositional attitudes generally – is not a proposition. Let us take a broadly Fregean view of the make-up of propositions (leaving aside his view of empty names). On this view, propositions or *thoughts* are composed of senses or (non-Fregean) concepts. And those things exist. But this gives the wrong object. When Timmy hopes that Rudolph lands on his roof, his hope is not *about* any entity composed of concepts or any entity that is itself about something. It is about something composed of Rudolph, a roof, and an event of the type *landing on*. Furthermore, Timmy's hope – his particular act of hoping – is about the very same thing that the proposition itself is about. But the proposition is not about itself. Neither, therefore, is his act of hoping. To claim that Timmy's hope is about a Fregean proposition is no more plausible than claiming that his thoughts about Rudolph are about the concept of Rudolph. He does not hope for a thought or a concept, or that they be related to constitute a proposition. He has already got those, and they already do.

Consider, then, a Russellian view of propositions, according to which the proposition that Rudolph will land on the roof contains Rudolph, the roof, and the activity of *landing on* as constituents. A Russellian account need not identify this proposition with the (nonexistent) fact that Rudolph will land on the roof. Rather, as Russell himself and, more recently, Jeff King (2007) have held, the constituents of the proposition might be related differently from those of the fact. The proposition consists of Rudolph, Timmy's roof, and the activity of *landing on* bound together by some relation that *does* hold of them. For instance, on one possible development of King's view, Rudolph, the roof, and the activity of landing on are related to one another in virtue of the fact that the words 'Rudolph', 'will land on', and 'the roof' are themselves related in a distinctive way to form the English sentence "Rudolph will land on the roof" and denote, respectively, Rudolph, the activity of *landing on*, and the roof. The details are, for my purposes, unimportant. Let us just suppose that (1) Rudolph does exist, (2) he will never land on Timmy's roof, and (3) there is some proposition-generating relation R that *does* hold among Rudolph, the roof, and the activity of *landing on*. While this might work as an account of propositions, it does not work as an account of the things we typically think about and hope for. What Timmy hopes for is Rudolph's landing on his roof. He does not hope that Rudolph, his roof, and the activity of landing on are or will be related by R. Timmy will not settle for a proposition, and neither, for the most part, will any of us.[2] I might be related to the property of being filthy rich by R, but what I desire, if I desire to be filthy rich, is not that. I want to *be* filthy rich. Furthermore, provided that this view maintains that the proposition that Rudolph will land on the roof is about something, it faces the same problems as the previous account. The proposition is supposed to be about something other than itself. But Timmy's act of hoping is not about something that is in turn about something.

Any account that provides something less than a worldly fact as the object of Timmy's hope will mutilate the phenomenology of his hoping. Timmy's desire does not terminate in an idea or a proposition. Nor is Timmy hoping for *two* things, one of which is a *representation* of the thing we would normally say he hopes for; he already has a representation of it. As Husserl says, "If, e.g., we make a statement, we judge about the thing it concerns, and not about the statement's meaning, about the judgement in the logical sense" (*LI* 1, §34: 332). The "thing it concerns" is the state of affairs, not the proposition. If Timmy thinks "That Rudolph will land on my roof tonight is delightful," it is the state of affairs, not the proposition – whether Fregean or Russellian or Kingian – that he holds to be delightful. He could just as well have thought "The landing of Rudolph on my roof is delightful" – here the proposition falls away, but the state of affairs remains (*LI* 5, §33: 623).

Moreover, the introduction of intermediaries that do exist as the objects, or at least the "immediate" or "direct" objects, of mental acts does nothing to solve the original problem. The question "How can a thought be *directly* of what does not exist?" is exactly no more or less difficult to answer than the question "How can a thought be of what does not exist?" The introduction of intermediaries just pushes exactly the same problem back

---

[2] Reinhardt Grossmann writes that "it simply flies in the fact of commonsense to assert that the false belief that Desdemona loves Cassio consists entirely in 'thinking' separately of Desdemona, Cassio, and loving, without having any state of affairs before the mind. To put it differently, if this state of affairs were not before the mind, then there would simply be no belief that Desdemona loves Cassio and, hence, we could not have a false belief" (translator's introduction to Twardowski 1997: xvii).

one step. Either this intermediary is directly about what does not exist or it is not. If it is, then it is possible for something to be directly about what does not exist, and the intermediary becomes superfluous. If, on the other hand, it is not directly about what does not exist, then either it is not a bearer of aboutness at all, or it is about yet another intermediary. If the latter, then a vicious regress looms. And if the former, then it does nothing to explain how the thought or experience is about what is not. If my thinking terminates in a proposition (or fact) whose constituents exist and are related to one another in the way I think them to be, or if my perceptual experience terminates in a sense datum which exists and has the properties I perceive it to have, then I am precisely not related, either perceptually, intentionally, or in any other way whatsoever, to what does not exist. Introducing "immediate" objects of thought to stand between us and what is not does absolutely nothing to illuminate how intentional acts can be of what is not (Willard 1967: 517).

The spotlight view is, perhaps, capable of accommodating the fact that there are mental states with nonexistent objects – the image here might be of a spotlight shining into a void. What it cannot do is individuate those mental states correctly. According to it, the thought that Rudolph has a red nose and that the god Jupiter has a red nose must be the same thought. The content view, on the other hand, does have the resources to individuate objectless mental representations. What makes a mental state whose object does not exist the mental state it is – what gives it its intentional direction – is its *content*. The thought about Rudolph differs from a thought about the god Jupiter because they have different intentional contents. The content of the first includes an individual concept which is *of Rudolph*; the content of the second includes an individual concept which is *of the god Jupiter*. And it is in virtue of "having" such contents – more on this "having" below – that the mental states are what they are.

A second argument for contents is that mental states that are about the same object can differ from one another in phenomenologically obvious and epistemically relevant ways. John Perry can coherently believe that John Perry is spilling sugar in the supermarket without believing that he is spilling sugar, provided he does not believe that he is John Perry (Perry 1979). A person can coherently believe that Superman flies while denying that Clark Kent does. One can coherently deny that he (the man by the window) is Jones, even when he is Jones. Two utterances of 'that' might both refer to the same ship (Evans 1982: 84) or the same electrical wire (Campbell 2002: 84–5) but it is nontrivial – perhaps a matter of life and death – to learn that *that* (pointing to one end of the wire) is *that* (pointing to another). Someone might know that silver conducts electricity without knowing that the element with forty-seven protons in its nucleus has lots of free electrons, despite the fact that both propositions designate the same state of affairs. And, of course, there are many cases in which we are unsure of very important identities and differences. It is trivial that brains are brains and that minds are minds, but that minds are brains, or that they are not brains, are quite obviously nontrivial propositions. Mental states are not individuated, as the spotlight theory requires, by the objects they are about together with the psychological mode (judging, hoping, etc.) in which they are thought about.

It is important to note that this is not an argument that any linguistic terms, whether names or predicates, have Fregean senses, rather than individuals and properties, as their semantic values. The claim that we must distinguish contents and objects in the case of thoughts does not by itself entail anything about the semantic values of terms of a language. A Millian or neo-Russellian account of the semantic value of names, for instance, is compatible with the view that our consciousness of individuals is accomplished by means of contents. On Scott Soames's view, for instance, the meaning or semantic value of a term is the information that is "*invariantly* asserted and conveyed across contexts involving competent speakers" (Soames 2002: 68). The information invariantly conveyed by the sentences 'Superman can fly' and 'Clark Kent can fly' is identical: each asserts, of Superman, that he can fly. It does not follow that this semantic value is identical with the intentional content that a speaker has in mind when it is uttered or understood, however:

A competent speaker/hearer who is familiar with a particular proper name or natural kind term can typically be expected to associate it with a substantial amount of descriptive material in the form of pictures, images, stereotypes, descriptions, and so on. Because of this, the totality of information the language user associates with sentences containing the name or natural kind term will vastly outstrip what the theorist recognizes as the semantic content of the sentence. (Soames 2002: 70)

Soames continues by adding: "semantic claims about the expressions of a language are not claims about the individual psychologies, or states of mind, of language users" (Soames 2002: 71).

Extruding such things as Fregean senses or modes of presentation from the semantic value of an expression is not the same as extruding them from the intentional contents of mental acts that are involved in understanding that expression on a given occasion. As Evans puts it,

It is not only coherent but actually quite plausible to maintain, in the case of ordinary proper names, that they are not associated with any particular way of thinking of their referents. Full competence with such an expression would seem to be exhausted by knowing which object it is the name of. (Evans 1982: 69)

But in crediting someone with such knowledge, we must also credit him with some determinate way of thinking of the object, even if that determinate way of thinking is irrelevant from the point of view of the semanticist and is only sufficient, but not necessary, for knowledge of the expression's meaning. This is also Husserl's view. While Schultze may be given in many different "presentative content[s]" the name 'Schultze' "goes on performing the same significant role, always naming him 'directly'" (*LI* 4, §3: 496). Nevertheless, some presentational contents or other are necessary for our ability to present Schultze to ourselves, despite their variability. "Using the proper name significantly, we must present to ourselves the subject named, in this case the definite person Schultze, and as endowed with some definite content or other" (*ibid.*). The meaning of a name is simple, argues Husserl, but grasping such a meaning "necessarily presupposes a wider intentional background of content" (*LI* 4, §3: 497).

It is also worth noting that many neo-Russellian views in semantics effectively deny the spotlight theory of intentionality by incorporating modes of presentation of their propositions. Since neo-Russellians, in stark contrast to Russell himself, allow ordinary objects like Istanbul and Bertrand Russell to figure as constituents of such thinkable and knowable propositions, it is exceedingly plausible that such "propositions," along with their constituents, must be given via different modes of presentation. According to Nathan Salmon, for instance, the reason Lois Lane can hold different attitudes towards the propositions expressed by 'Superman can fly' and 'Clark Kent can fly' is because belief is a three-part relation holding between a believer, a proposition, and a way of taking that proposition. Lois believes the proposition that Superman can fly when she takes it by means of the sentence 'Superman can fly,' but not when she takes it by means of the sentence 'Clark Kent can fly.' These different ways of taking the proposition are not, however, semantically relevant. This proposal clearly requires there to be a many–one relation between modes of presentation or "propositional guises" (Salmon 1989: 246), on the one hand, and "propositions" on the other, which is precisely to deny the spotlight view with respect to these propositions. But unless the neo-Russellian wants to make modes of presentation intermediary objects standing between propositions and acts of thinking – a most unattractive option, especially if propositions themselves are construed as intermediaries between us and the world – this comes very close to maintaining the content view advocated here.

Third, the claim that something like Fregean senses are the intentional contents of thoughts does not commit us to a descriptive theory of those thoughts, that is, a theory according to which mental contents directed towards individuals are definite descriptions that uniquely pick out those individuals. This is clear from the fact that endorsing a Fregean view of the semantic value of names does not commit one to descriptivism about those names.[3] The supposition that it does is an example of what Wayne Davis calls the "Frege–Mill dichotomy," the idea that "either names have a descriptive meaning or they have no sense at all" (Davis 2005a: 232). As Davis notes, this plainly does not exhaust all options: such thoughts might have noncomposite, indefinable, simple senses, and names might express such senses.

This is not to deny that there is something right about descriptivism. One cannot think about something without thinking of it as propertied in some way or other. I cannot, for instance, entertain demonstrative thoughts about that table in front of me if I am not aware of at least some of its features. "But this insight," as Jason Stanley points out, "in no way requires that we ignore the non-descriptive element inherent in true demonstrative reference" (Stanley 1997: 564) – or in any other form of direct reference. You have to think of New York as being a certain way in order to think about it. If, in using the name 'New York', you are talking about something which, as far as you know, might be a city, a dance move, or a hippopotamus, then you are not thinking of New York, but exploiting an established referential device to produce utterances with a conventional meaning – one which, in this case, escapes you (Evans 1982: 69). Despite that, it doesn't follow that you will thereby think of New York descriptively, as *just whatever* has the properties you think it to have. I think of Nineveh as the capital of Assyria, and that is about all I know about it. But my concept of Nineveh is not my concept of the capital of Assyria. I can keep Nineveh in mind and alter the properties I conceive it to have, including the property of being the capital of Assyria. As Husserl puts it, "a proper name . . . names an object 'directly'. It refers to it, not attributively, as the bearer of these or those properties, but without such 'conceptual' mediation, as what it *itself* is" (*LI* 6, §5: 684). It is compatible with this that one cannot be aware of what an object itself is without being conscious of some of its features. Ultimately, the difference

[3] See Dummett (1973: 111–12); Evans (1982: 18); Smith and McIntyre (1982: Ch. 8); Davis (2005a, Ch. 13).

between thinking of something directly and thinking of it as just whatever has such-and-such properties is phenomenologically evident. But thinking about something directly is not incompatible with thinking of it in some way or via some sense.[4]

It might be objected, however, that every difference in how two mental states depict the world is a difference in how they represent it as being. As we have already seen in section 1.1, such phrases as "modes of presentation" and "ways in which we think about an object," along with "ways objects are represented," "ways the world appears," and so forth, are ambiguous. On the one hand, they might designate the various ways in which the object is represented as being. On the other, they might designate the various ways in which the object is represented as being that way. Ronald McIntyre (1999: 437–8) illustrates this distinction by comparing the phrase "the way things seem to S" with "the way women were depicted by Degas." When we are asked to describe the way in which Degas depicted women, we might give two different sorts of answers. If we are interested in how he depicted them as being, we might say "as dancers." But if we are interested in the way he depicted them as being dancers, we might say "impression-istically." This is not a property of what is depicted, but a property of the depiction itself. A clear photograph might represent those same women as dancers, and not represent them *as being different*, yet represent them *differently*. In short, we must distinguish the *what* of a representation from its *how*.

If the spotlight view were correct, we could never make this distinction in the case of mental acts. And, the objection goes, all that the arguments have established is that the same objects can be represented as being different, not that they can be represented differently. In the case of mental states, every difference is a difference in what is represented. This is especially plausible in the case of perceptual experiences, which many, beginning with Moore, have alleged are transparent. As Harman puts it, "Look at a tree and try to turn your attention to intrinsic features of your experience. I predict that the only features there to turn your attention to will be features of the presented tree."[5] Things like books and maps and photographs are not diaphanous in this way. If one is asked to review, evaluate, or describe one, one will not simply describe what it is a representation of. What I would need to

---

[4] "The fact that one is thinking about an object in a particular way can no more warrant the conclusion that one is not thinking of the object in the most direct possible fashion, than the fact that one is giving something *in a particular way* warrants the view that one's giving is somehow indirect" (Evans 1982: 62).
[5] Harman (1990: 39). See also Moore (1951: 20, 25).

establish the falsity of the spotlight view is that mental states are analogous to other, conventional representations in that we can distinguish what is represented from how it is represented. But, the objection goes, it seems we cannot do that. If two mental states represent the world *differently*, that is because they represent the world *as being different*. It is only under those conditions, furthermore, that familiar mistakes about identity are intelligible. Even Frege seems to admit as much: "Comprehensive knowledge of the *Bedeutung* would require us to be able to say immediately whether any given sense attaches to it. To such knowledge we never attain" (Frege 1997a: 153).

Frege's claim is almost certainly true. If a person had comprehensive knowledge of silver, then he should be able to recognize that the sentence "silver is shiny" is true if and only if the sentence "the element with forty-seven protons in its nucleus is shiny" is true. What explains a person's ability to believe one and not the other, then, must be his ignorance of silver. He represents silver as being different in the two cases. But this does not show that two thoughts cannot differ in their how yet be identical in their what. The proposition that A is on top of B differs from the proposition that B is underneath A, since they contain different concepts as constituents. Nevertheless, the state of affairs that each is about is identical. Again, "The ideas *equilateral triangle* and *equiangular triangle* differ in content, though both are directed, and evidently directed, to the same object" (*LI* 5, §20: 588). Frege, according to some, individuates thoughts or propositions on the basis of their cognitive significance, where two thoughts differ in their cognitive significance if and only if it is possible to understand both and take different attitudes towards them. But sameness of cognitive significance is only a necessary condition for sameness of content.[6] If it were sufficient, then not only would many propositions containing different constituents wind up being identical, but every sentence that expresses a self-evident proposition – "1 = 1," "Red is a color," "Middle C is not a panda bear," "I exist" (to the person thinking it), and countless others – would express the same proposition.

The spotlight view might work as an account of perceptual states – we shall investigate that in Chapter 6. It likely does not work as an account of thoughts. And its shortcomings become very plain when we consider what is arguably the most important distinction among intentional acts: the

---

[6] As it is on Evans's "Intuitive Criterion of Difference" (Evans 1982: 18). Frege, however, suggests that it is both necessary and sufficient, provided that anyone who accepts A as true must "straightaway" accept B as true (see Frege 1997c: 299; also see Dummett 1994: 99–100).

distinction between those which are empty and those which are intuitively filled. By an "empty" intentional act I mean one in which the object that it is about is not intuitively present, either present in the flesh as in perception or even quasi-present as in imagination and imagistic episodic memory. An intuitively fulfilled intentional act is one in which the object intended is *presented*, either in the flesh, as in perception, or via a resembling image, as in imagination and imagistic memory. The implausibility of the spotlight view is apparent when we consider the unboundedness of thought principle (UTP):

UTP: Anything that can be perceived can be emptily thought about *directly*.[7]

One can perceive a forest fire, and one can merely think about precisely that forest fire. One can perceive that a certain dog is running. And one can think that that dog is running. If there are sense data, then they too can be merely thought about.[8] Moreover, anything that can be perceived can be thought about *directly*. I do not need to think of the car I just perceived as just whatever satisfies the description 'the car I just perceived'. Rather, I can entertain thoughts that are directly about it, thoughts that refer to it rigidly across different possible scenarios. But if mere thoughts can represent the world to be precisely the same way that perceptual states do, then the difference between thought and perception cannot be that the mind is directed upon different objects, as the spotlight view predicts. As Pietersma puts it, "When an intentional experience is characterized as 'empty', this term designates a character of that experience" (Pietersma 1973: 96). It is not a feature of the object of experience.

Let me now discuss several objections to UTP. The first that may come to mind is that perceptual consciousness is often richer and more fine-grained than mere thought. With respect to its richness, I don't just see my desk. I see my computer and my door and the stapler and lots of other things. With respect to its fineness of grain, I don't just perceive it as being brown. I perceive it as being a very determinate shade of brown, and so on for the other perceptible properties. But I cannot think of the world in such rich and fine-grained terms.

---

[7] See *APS*: 113: "Corresponding to every mode of intuition is a possible mode of empty presentation."
[8] Thanks to his spotlight analysis of intentionality, Russell is led to deny this. At the end of his second 1918 lecture on logical atomism, an audience member asked, "If the proper name of a thing, a 'this', varies from instant to instant, how is it possible to make any argument?" Russell responded: "You can keep 'this' going for about a minute or two . . . If you argue quickly, you can get some little way before it is finished, a matter of some seconds or minutes or whatever it may happen to be" (Russell 1985: 64–5). Thanks to UTP, we can adopt a more leisurely pace.

While both points are correct, for a wide range of cases at least, they do not entail the falsity of UTP. First, UTP does not attribute any particular powers to any class of thinking and perceiving beings. I am not claiming that porcupines or lampreys can entertain direct thoughts about everything they perceive, or that you and I can. UTP does not even entail that any actual things can think about anything at all. But if there are certain things that we cannot entertain empty direct thoughts about, such as fully determinate shades of color or the precise layout of a busy subway station, this is a merely contingent fact about the limitations of our powers of thinking, not a necessity grounded in the nature of empty thought contents as such. The mere fact that human beings cannot entertain direct empty thoughts that represent the world in the same gloriously rich way that experience does is no argument against UTP.

With respect to the richness of experience, if it is possible to think emptily about each of the items present to me perceptually – my desk, my stapler, my door, the distance between my desk and my door, and so forth – it should at least in principle be possible to think about all of them collectively emptily. The barrier to our doing so is not that some of the items cannot in principle be thought of emptily. If the distance between my door and my desk is three meters, then in thinking that my desk is three meters away from my desk I am representing *the same* distance that is given in perception. That is why I can assent to the claim that *that* (pointing at the gap) is three meters long, and that claim can be true. Nor is there, as a matter of necessity, some number *n* that marks the upper limit of what can be emptily thought of by any mind of any type. It is plainly a contingent fact about us that we can hold just so many objects in mind in mere thought, and there is almost certainly a bit of variation among individuals in this respect.

With respect to fineness of grain, it is a mistake to think that perceptual consciousness is necessarily of more fine-grained properties than empty thought. Not only can perceptual consciousness present us with merely determinate properties, but empty thought is very often much more finely grained than perception, as every good rationalist knows. I can think that an object is square without being able to perceive that it is – because, for instance, I can conceptually but not perceptually distinguish between a side's being 100 centimeters long and 101 centimeters long. I can think that something is a chiliagon, but while I can see a chiliagon, I cannot see *that* anything is a chiliagon. The distinction between fine- and coarse-grained representations is orthogonal to the distinction between empty thought and perception. "Empty intentions," writes Husserl, "can also be determinate."[9] To see just how different the distinction between representations of coarse- and fine-grained distinctions is from the distinction between thought and perception, just consider that as you move from the thought that Mount Everest is a physical object to the thought that Mount Everest is a mountain, that Mount Everest is a massive, snow-covered mountain, and so forth, you do not come any closer to perceiving it.

Another objection is that perceptual experiences present their objects as *bodily present* to the perceiver, and presents them as being located in an egocentric space whose zero-point of orientation is (typically) one's own body. They are also represented *as being perceived*. But again, it is possible to just think that an object is bodily present, that it is before one's eyes, that it is in contact with one's hands, and so forth. Right now I can think that my desk is bodily present, that the Eiffel Tower is bodily present, that Abe Lincoln is bodily present, and so on. It is also possible to merely think that any such object is located in one's egocentric space. I can think that the Eiffel Tower is over there, or up there, or back there. And while thoughts of this sort depend on the perceptual presence of the locations that are demonstratively referred to ("over there," "up there"), those locations themselves are identical with portions of objective space, and can also be merely thought of. Egocentric and allocentric space are not two spaces, but the same space differently given. If I want to get myself to the kitchen, it must present itself egocentrically at some point so that I can direct myself there. But when I want to go *over there*, I don't want to go *over there* instead of or in addition to the kitchen; I want to go *over there* because that *is* the kitchen. "Over there" might be 48°51′29″ north, 2°17′40″ east, and if so, then the perceptual experience whose content represents the Eiffel Tower as bodily present over there has, as its object, the same state of affairs as the thought which represents the Eiffel Tower as bodily present at 48°51′29″ north, 2°17′40″ east. This latter is a thought you have just entertained, wherever you happen to be. The world of perception is the same world that we think and talk about. But perceiving and thinking are completely different ways of being conscious of the world. Since they differ, and yet can take precisely the same objects, at least one of the members of any co-directed thought/experience pair is not individuated by its object alone. In Chapter 4 I will argue that the difference between perception and thought cannot be explained in terms of differences in their psychological mode either.

---

[9] *TS* §18: 49. See also A. D. Smith (2001: 285–6).

## 1.3 A HUSSERLIAN ACCOUNT

Does this force us to hold that we are never "immediately" aware of anything but ideas or mental contents? By no means. Something can be "present to the Understanding," to borrow Locke's phrase (Locke 1975: 721), without being its object. This becomes intelligible when we consider the way in which the content of, say, a book is related to the book itself and its subject matter. One can only take an analogy between books and conscious mental acts so far, but books do offer us a number of helpful ways of thinking about mental content. The content of a book is not, except in the case of a book that is about itself, identical with the subject matter of that book – what the book is about. For instance, the subject matter of Gibbon's *Decline and Fall of the Roman Empire* includes the fall of the Roman Empire and the antics of the individuals, institutions, legions, microbes, and unlettered hordes whose actions had some connection with it. Septimius Severus – the man himself – is part of the subject matter of Gibbon's classic. But he is not part of the content of the book. If you open it, you will not find him there. He is no more "present to the book" than he is "present to the Understanding." He is not present to anything anymore. He's dead. Or, to take another example, when a political advertisement informs you that "the So-and-Sos are responsible for the content of this ad," they do not, in general, mean that they are responsible for what the advertisement is about, such as a candidate or the need to reform health care (they usually blame their opponents for that). They are responsible for something else, namely the aboutness-bestowing features of the ad itself. The contents of the book (or ad) include the meanings of its words, tables, maps, illustrations, and so forth. It includes those features and parts of the book in virtue of which it is about its subject matter in the determinate manner that it is.

We can, finally, also distinguish the *vehicle* from both the content and the subject matter of a book. The normal vehicle for a book's content is, well, a book – printed pages bound together. The term "book" is ambiguous, designating both the content of a book and the type of vehicle that most typically carries it. But a book, in the sense of a unified body of content, can also be stored on a hard drive or a compact disc. It can be recited live. It can be retained in memory. These items do not differ in either subject matter or content, but in the vehicle that "carries" the content. Incidentally, that vehicles are said to "carry" contents also supports this interpretation, since things like ink marks, sound waves, and bits do not carry things like Septimius Severus, Rome, or the sorry state of health care. What they carry is *information about* such things.

How is the book related to its content? One might hold, as many have held when it comes to mental acts, that a book is "immediately" about its content, which is itself, in turn, about its subject matter. The content of the book is, on this view, its immediate *object*, such that the existence of a book calls into being two aboutness relations: that between the book and its content, and that between the content and its subject matter. Or, schematically, where the arrows stand for aboutness:

book → content → subject matter

But this is surely wrong. If asked "What is Gibbon's book about?", it is not even a half-truth to respond that it is about its own words and their meanings, its illustrations, maps, and so forth. There is nothing "in" the book, in any remotely acceptable sense of "in," which any sentence about Rome, Augustus, Diocletian, the Visigoths, and so forth could be taken to be about. When we read it, we read words, but we do not read about its words and their meanings. We are reading about Rome and its downfall. There is nothing, as it were, standing between the book and its subject matter, such that it must first be about that thing in order to be about Rome and its downfall. Moreover, it is difficult to see how one thing can be about another without having at least some intrinsic properties of its own in virtue of which it is about it. But what intrinsic properties, short of its possessing the content that it does, could account for the book's being the book that it is and being about the subject matter that it is about? The contents of the book are not mere relata of the already constituted book. Rather, the book depends, for its very being, on having the content that it does. The content of the book constitutes it, makes it up, renders it this book rather than some other one. It would not be *this* book if it had another content, that of, say, Wittgenstein's *Tractatus*.

But exactly how is the content of a book related to it? To answer this, we need to distinguish book types from book tokens. Gibbon's classic sits over there on my shelf, but this is just a copy. The book itself is of a different order entirely, not identical with this or that collection of physical symbols on paper or bits on a hard drive, but rather something that is realized in each of them. All such copies have their own individual parts or constituents. These are the *real* contents of each copy, the contents that belong to each copy individually, and arise and perish with them. Each copy also, however, instantiates common properties, in virtue of which each is a copy of the same thing. They all have the *same* content; each is about the same subject matter in the same determinate way. How is that possible? One way, to be sure, is that they are all about the same content. But we have already disposed of the view that books are about their contents. A more promising route is to say that the same content is *instantiated* in each copy of a book. On this view, then, we should regard the ideal contents of a book as among its properties, and, more specifically, as its aboutness-bestowing properties. The *ideal contents* of a book are those properties in virtue of which the book is about its subject matter in the determinate way that it is. Its *real contents*, by contrast, are the instantiations of those ideal contents – the word and sentence tokens in it, for instance.

And so we have the following to say about the relationship among books, their contents, and their subject matters. An individual book is about its subject matter, and nothing else. It is about that subject matter in a determinate way. And what makes an individual book about its subject matter in that determinate way is that it possesses a certain content. The individual book has its own, individual content – the meaningful word tokens, illustrations, and so forth making it up – which are instances of a shareable, abstract content. This abstract content is instantiated in each individual book of a common type.

The rough sketch just given of books mirrors, in many relevant respects, Husserl's account of intentionality in his *Logical Investigations*, and it is that theory that I will lay out and defend for the remainder of this chapter.[10] Husserl goes to great lengths to distinguish the intentional objects of acts, which he wisely urges should never be called 'contents', from their intentional contents (*LI* 5, §17: 580). According to his account of intentional content in the *Logical Investigations*, *every* intentional experience consists of two independently variable but non-separable abstract parts or "moments," a *matter* and a *quality*. They are moments, rather than pieces, in much the way that timbre, volume, and pitch are moments, rather than detachable pieces, of a tone. Husserl characterizes an act's quality as "the general act-character, which stamps an act as merely presentative, judgemental, emotional, desiderative, etc." (*LI* 5, §20: 586). The matter of an act is that feature that gives it its intentional directedness toward an object; it consists of both a *reference to* something, an "objective reference," and the manner in which that something is meant, what it is intended *as*, its "interpretive sense." The matter is "that element in an act which first gives it reference to an object,

---

[10] Husserl presents a more complicated picture of intentionality in his later works (*Ideas 1* §§87–135). There, he introduces something called the "noema" as a "correlate" of every intentional experience. I have too many problems, both textual and philosophical, with the noema to discuss here. See, for instance, Willard (1992). Fortunately, Husserl maintains that there is a parallelism between noetic and noematic contents, so most of what I say in what follows can, in principle, be translated into noetic, or act-based, terms.

and reference so wholly definite that it not merely fixes the object meant in a general way, but also the precise way in which it is meant" (*LI* 5, §20: 589). Elsewhere he characterizes it as "that moment in an objectifying act which makes the act present *just this object in just this manner*" (*LI* 6, §25: 737). Throughout what follows, I will use the term "content" to mean what Husserl means by "matter."

The distinction Husserl draws between the objective reference and interpretive sense of an act's content, it bears stressing, is not the same as Frege's distinction between *Sinn* and *Bedeutung*. The complete matter of an act, including its *reference to* an object, is contained in that act. But the *referent* of an act (Frege's *Bedeutung*) is, in general, not. It need not even exist. Nor are the interpretive sense and objective reference two components of the matter of an act in the way that matter and quality are. Not only are they not pieces of the matter, they are not even dependent moments. Rather, the distinction between the objective reference and the interpretive sense is that the latter is a determinate and the former a determinable feature of the matter itself. No act could simply have an objective reference without an interpretive sense, since no act could simply refer to its object without doing so in some way:

[T]here is not one piece of matter corresponding to an identical object, another to the differing mode of presenting it. Reference to objects is possible *a priori* only as being a definite manner of reference: it arises only if the matter is fully determined. (*LI* 5, §20: 589)

Two acts may share the determinable property of referring to Rome, and thereby have the same objective reference (to Rome), without sharing the determinate property of referring to Rome in way W. And no act which has a determinate sense could fail to have the determinable property of referring to, or being directed upon, something. As Peacocke puts it, "It would be wrong ... to regard the referential relations in which concepts stand as grafted onto a structure of concepts that can be elucidated without any reference to reference. Referential relations are implicated in the very nature of judgment and belief" (Peacocke 1992: 17).

Finally, according to Husserl, although matter and quality are two independently variable, and thus distinct, properties or moments of mental acts, they are not separable from one another. No mental act is *just* a judging or an imagining or a desiring; every such quality must be conjoined with a matter that provides it with a fix on something that is judged, imagined, or perceived. Similarly, no mental act is *just* an intentional directedness towards some object without being directed upon it in some way, e.g. judicatively, desiringly, etc. Even mere entertainings are act-qualities. Accordingly, no concrete mental episode consists solely of a matter or a quality.[11]

The matter of an act together with its quality jointly constitute what Husserl calls an act's "intentional essence" or, if the act in question imbues a linguistic expression with sense, its "semantic essence" (*LI* 5, §21: 590). The intentional essence of an act is as individual as that act itself. This is an act's real intentional content, and it is impossible for two numerically distinct acts to possess the same real content in common. And yet numerically distinct acts, whether those of an individual subject or of different subjects, can have the same ideal content. The real content of an act is an instance of a universal or type, and it is these types which interest the logician and the phenomenologist. Husserl says that a linguistic meaning, for instance, is an "ideational abstraction" of the intentional essence of an act (*LI* 5, §21: 590). And, as one would expect, Husserl says that ideal entities of this sort are *instantiated* in acts of consciousness:[12]

> The manifold singulars for the ideal unity Meaning are naturally the corresponding act-moments of meaning, the *meaning-intentions*. Meaning is related to varied acts of meaning ... just as Redness *in specie* is to the slips of paper which lie here, and which all 'have' the same redness. (*LI* 2, §32: 330)

While Husserl places acts of meaning and their constituent parts and moments – matters and qualities – in the mind in the most literal sense, he does not place meanings, in the sense relevant for logic, there. "My act of judging is a transient experience: it arises and passes away. But what my assertion asserts, the content *that the three perpendiculars of a triangle intersect in a point*, neither arises nor passes away. It is an identity in the strict sense, one and the same geometrical truth" (*LI* 1, §11: 285). Propositions and their constituents are "in" the mind as properties, not as parts, and not as intentional objects.

---

[11] Husserl's characterization of quality as the character which "stamps an act as merely presentative, judgemental, emotional, desiderative, etc." (*LI* 5, §20: 586; also *LI* 6, §27: 743) is extremely unsatisfactory. We are not given an insentional definition, nor are we given an exhaustive list of act qualities. Contrary to one interpretation, however, perceptual acts are *not* distinguished from mere beliefs by their quality. Not only does Husserl not say that perception is an act-quality, he makes it quite clear that intuitive acts generally (perception, imagination, imagistic memory) are not differentiated from one another by their quality or their matter (*LI* 5, §21: 592). Since an empty thought itself sits on a continuum of intuitiveness – its intuitive content is nil – the difference between an empty thought and a perception is not a difference in quality either. I will argue, however, that intuitive acts do have different matters than empty ones.

[12] Wayne Davis holds a similar view: "Ideas are event-types of a certain sort, specifically, thoughts or parts of thoughts" (Davis 2005a: 324). Also see Davis (2003, Ch. 15).

To sum up, then, Husserl's account specifies the relationships that hold among all of the following: (1) mental acts or intentional experiences, (2) real contents, (3) ideal contents, and (4) intended objects. The relationship that holds between (1) and (2) is that the latter are quite literally "in" the former: an intentional experience is partially made up of intentionality-bestowing parts, comparable to what Crimmins and Perry call "ideas" and "notions."[13] The relationship between (1) and (3) is that the latter are instantiated in the former; they are its intentional properties, whose instances are acts and, more specifically, those acts' intentional components (2). These ideal contents are "in" the mental acts, not as parts, but as properties. Finally, the "relation" between each of (1)–(3) and (4) is that of intentionality: the former are about the latter. My thought that snow is white, for instance, is about its object – the state of affairs of snow's being white – in virtue of its intentional components (2), which are in turn instances of intentional properties (3). Concepts and propositions, construed as shareable bearers of intentionality rather than as nonintentional properties and states of affairs, are paradigmatic intentional properties. When you and I think that snow is white, our mental states each instantiate the proposition that snow is white, along with its constituent concepts. The object of a mental act may be "in" it as either a part or a property, but need not, and typically will not, be. This entails that things like concepts and propositions can be predicated of mental states. We can predicate the concept of water of a mental state by saying things like "My belief is *of water*." We can predicate the proposition that water is wet of a mental state by saying something like "My belief is that water is wet."

Finally, although Husserl does not make the distinction himself, we can distinguish all of the intentional features, properties, and objects of a mental state from its *vehicle*. If, for instance, a robot and I are both thinking that silver conducts electricity, then our mental states have the same object and the same Ideal content, but different vehicles. The content of its mental state is instantiated in chips, while mine is instantiated in, let us suppose, neurons. If the robot then thinks about this state of affairs in some other way – via the proposition that element forty-seven has lots of free electrons, say – our acts still have the same object, different vehicles, and different contents. And if, at this point, a team of scientists were to replace my

---

[13] "Beliefs are structured entities that contain ideas and notions as constituents. Ideas and notions, like beliefs, are on our view concrete cognitive particulars" (Crimmins and Perry 1989: 690). They hold, however, that propositions are the objects of belief, rather than the universals of which beliefs are instances.

neurons with functionally equivalent computer chips, then my mental state and the robot's would share the same type of vehicle and object, but different contents. We can see, then, that the vehicles, contents, and objects can vary, in certain ways at least, independently of one another. This should be unproblematic: the referents, senses, and vehicles of linguistic expressions can vary in precisely analogous ways.

Russell and Frege each appear to have held views quite different from Husserl's. Frege consistently writes as though contents – senses and thoughts – lie on the object side of the act–object nexus, though his account is compatible with this not being the case. And Russell, as we have seen, maintains that everything lies on the object side, and expressly rejects the existence of contents altogether. In contemporary philosophy such an object-side analysis is virtually built into our vocabulary. Beliefs, judgments, and desires are attitudes *towards* propositions, and a mind's relation to concepts, propositions, and *Sinne* generally is that of "grasping."

Let me begin with an argument of Russell's that might seem to speak against Husserl's view:

> One man's act of thought is necessarily a different thing from another man's; one man's act of thought at one time is necessarily a different thing from the same man's act of thought at another time. Hence, if whiteness were the thought as opposed to its object, no two different men could think of it, and no one man could think of it twice. That which many different thoughts of whiteness have in common is their object, and this object is different from all of them. (Russell 1999: 71)

While it is trivially true that every act of thought is numerically different from every other, it does not follow from this that the *only* thing such acts can have in common is their object, as this passage strongly suggests. Rather, they can and must have shared properties in common. Instantiating the shareable intentional property of being *of-whiteness* explains how there could be many thoughts of whiteness. And even if one rejects this analysis, recognizing some shared properties of thoughts is mandatory. In particular, bare aboutness itself will have to be one shareable property. Otherwise, we would have to suppose that because acts of thought are all different, only one could have the property of aboutness. Clearly it will not help here to claim that aboutness is the common *object* of all mental acts. But if bare aboutness can be a shared property of acts, then so could being-about-x (in way W).

Frege, for his part, does not do much to clarify the relationship between senses and acts of thinking – he calls it the "the most mysterious of all" (Frege 1997b: 246) – but he consistently writes as though senses and thoughts are among the objects of mental acts. We "grasp" thoughts, and thinking is "the apprehension of a thought" (Frege 1994: 521). Treating senses, propositions, and so forth as the objects of mental acts might appear mandatory if we wish to account for their objectivity and the objectivity of the laws governing them. In particular, it might be thought that this is necessary to avoid psychologism, which I will understand to be the thesis that individual psychological episodes of thinking, judging, inferring, and so forth both (1) are the truth-makers for and (2) constitute the evidential basis of our knowledge of contents and the logical laws governing them.[14]

As we have already seen, there are very good reasons to reject the claim that Fregean propositions are objects, whether "immediate" or terminal, when we entertain thoughts with those propositions as contents. It should also, however, be clear that Husserl's account is perfectly consistent with his and Frege's insistence that ideal contents are objective. That ideal contents are instantiated in, rather than intended by, particular mental acts does not exclude their being shareable and ontologically independent of our psychological constitutions or any particular mental acts whose contents they are. Fodor, who may or may not be aware of the similarities between his and Husserl's account, expresses this point perfectly:

[T]o claim that MOPs [modes of presentation] must be *mental* objects is quite compatible with also claiming that they are *abstract* objects, and that abstract objects are *not* mental. The apparent tension is reconciled by taking MOPS-qua-things-in-the-head to be the tokens of which MOPS-qua-abstract-objects are the types. (Fodor 1998: 20)

Holding such a view does not, moreover, commit one to logical psychologism. It in no way follows from Husserl's (or Fodor's) position that psychological states are either the truth-makers of logical propositions, or the evidential basis of our knowledge of them. Just as the fact that the instances of geometrical types are physical entities does not entail that geometry is a branch of physics, so the fact that the instances of contents are psychological entities does not entail that logic is a branch of psychology.[15] And yet, if Husserl and Frege are right, in thinking anything whatsoever I am related to senses or concepts and propositions. If this relationship is not that of aboutness – and it isn't – then Husserl's account offers one of the only live alternatives.

[14] "Logical Psychologism is the view that the non-normative statements made by logicians are about, and draw their evidence from the examination of, the particular conceivings, assertings, and inferrings of particular persons – a range of facts commonly thought to belong to the science of psychology alone" (Willard 1977: 10).
[15] See, for instance, B. Smith (1989); Hanna (1993); Willard (1994); W. Martin (1999).

Of course, nothing I have said here decisively establishes that my mental state's having a content amounts to that content being instantiated in my mental act. There are quite a few determinate relations falling under the determinable *having*. But it is, I think, a promising account. First, we know that a mental state's having a content is not a matter of its being about it, so the most familiar mental relation of all, intentionality, cannot be it. Second, the instantiation model readily explains why a mental state's having a certain content is what makes it the mental state that it is. It is not as though mental states exist and then acquire their contents, as though their contents are something they could gain or lose. A mental state is a certain configuration of consciousness, and it would not be *this* configuration if it were not directed towards its object and related in various ways to these and those actual and possible mental states. And it is the content of a mental state – and the contents of others – that accounts for its standing in those relations. Instantiation of a property is an intimate enough sort of "having" to explain this. Finally, mental states do have properties, and it is in virtue of having those properties that they are directed upon the objects that they are. The instantiation model provides a very economical account of what those properties are: they are the very same properties that are expressed by that-clauses, capable of truth and falsity, expressed linguistically, and so forth. Fortunately, the account of conceptual and nonconceptual content I will defend in subsequent chapters does not depend on the truth of the instantiation model, but only upon some of its commitments, namely that contents are about things, that it is in virtue of "having" a content that a mental state is about what it is about, and that the content of a mental state is almost never its object. Nevertheless, I think the instantiation model is very likely to be true.

Finally, this might seem to be a mysterious or "magical" account of intentionality, according to which "mental representations necessarily refer to certain external things and kinds of things" (Putnam 1981: 15). Well, the theory is committed to precisely that claim. On the other hand, there is nothing magical about that, unless anything that cannot be explained in terms that leave intentionality out or reduce it to something else qualifies as magical. If there are such properties as being about water or being about Socrates, and if mental representations are individuated by their possession of such properties, then there is a perfectly acceptable sense in which mental representations, unlike configurations of clouds, patterns of paint, and possibly words (depending on how they are individuated), are essentially of what they are of. And there are such properties. It makes perfect sense to ask how a sense-perceptible sign like 'water' comes to be about water. And it makes perfect sense to ask how mental acts come to instantiate their intentional properties such as the property of being of water. But it does not make sense to ask how intentional contents themselves come to possess their intentional properties. They *are* intentional properties. The concept of water, unlike the word 'water', doesn't come to be about water via any process; it is intrinsically and essentially about water.[16] But what, exactly, is mysterious about that? How is being about water any more, or any less, mysterious than being water? And how is coming to instantiate a property like that any more or less mysterious than coming to instantiate the property of being watery?

### 1.4 CONCLUSION

Having achieved a tolerably clear and, it is hoped, workable conception of the differences among acts, contents, and objects of consciousness, the task now is to determine what sorts of intentional contents, if any, perceptual experiences have. Over the course of the next three chapters, I will examine arguments for and against the thesis that experiences have conceptual content.

---

[16] See Davis (2005a: 4): "For an idea to have the content water is for it to be the idea of water. The content of the idea is thus an intrinsic, essential property: it makes no sense to suppose that the idea of water should change its content, or to ask how it acquired this content."

# CHAPTER 2

# Experiential conceptualism

Thus far I have argued that at least some mental states have content, and have endorsed a broadly Husserlian account of what contents are, how they are related to the mental acts whose contents they are, and how they are related to their objects. Briefly, contents are intentional properties of acts, and are those properties in virtue of which acts are intentionally directed upon their objects in the determinate manner that they are. Nothing, however, has so far been said about whether perceptual states are among the mental states with intentional content and, if they are, what sort of contents they have. One idea, motivated by a number of different considerations, is that at least some, and possibly all, of the intentional contents of perceptual experience are conceptual contents. Over the course of the next three chapters, I will consider and reject two versions of what I will call 'experiential conceptualism' (EC). According to strong experiential conceptualism (SEC), all perceptual experiences necessarily have intentional content, and their intentional content is exclusively conceptual content.[1] That is, I will understand SEC to claim that the very same type of intentional contents that makes thoughts intentionally directed upon their objects is responsible for perceptual states being directed upon their objects. I will understand weak experiential conceptualism (WEC) as the position that all perceptual experiences necessarily have at least some conceptual content. SEC, but not WEC, is incompatible with the claim that perceptual experiences have nonconceptual intentional content. Since most of the actual defenders of experiential conceptualism are equally concerned with denying that perceptual experiences have nonconceptual content, SEC is not only the more interesting position, but the more broadly endorsed.

There are a lot of reasons why philosophers have adopted EC, and it is beyond the scope of this book to investigate them all. In the following two

---

[1] This seems to be the position A. D. Smith has in mind when he discusses conceptualism. See A. D. Smith (2002: 94–5).

chapters I will focus on two broad-ranging sets of considerations: phenomenological and epistemological. But before turning to the arguments, it is
necessary that we get at least some idea of what conceptual content is. At
this point I will not attempt to provide a phenomenological characterization
of conceptual content, since that, along with my characterization of nonconceptual content, will only make full sense and appear rationally motivated after the discussion that is about to ensue. For now, I will only assume
a few claims.

*Concepts are about things.* The first is that concepts are bearers of aboutness: they are of or about things other than themselves. The term 'concept'
has, as David Wiggins points out, two distinct senses. On the one hand, a
concept is "something with instances" that "belongs on the level of reference" (Wiggins 2001: 10). On the other hand, in its "Kantian" use, the term
'concept' is applied to something that belongs on the level of sense. Unlike
Wiggins, it seems rather clear to me that the latter, Kantian use is more
prevalent today. As Georges Rey puts it, "Concepts seem to be the very stuff
of which cognitions are made" (Rey 1999: 279) – and not the stuff out of
which the objects of cognition are made. "Traditionally speaking, concepts
are a person's means of representing objects in thought" (Burge 1977: 345).
I will therefore understand concepts and conceptual contents to be a type of
intentional content. Concepts, therefore, are certain types of intentional
properties whose instances are intentional acts.

From this it follows that concepts are not, in general, identical with
whatever objects, properties, categories, or essences they are about. There
are several good reasons to endorse this view anyway, independently of the
details of the Husserlian position advocated here. First, concepts are bearers
of aboutness, while categories, essences, and (nonintentional) properties are
not. Neither water, nor the property of being water, nor the essence of water
is about anything. The concept of water, on the other hand, is about water
(in the actual world and every possible world considered as counterfactual,
at least). And when we exercise the concept of water, what we are thinking
about is water, not the concept of water (Willard 1999; Davis 2003: 419).
Second, what it is to possess a concept is not what it is to possess an essence
or property. To possess the concept of red is to have the capacity to carry
out mental acts, with a certain character, that are about the color red. But to
possess the property of red is to be red. The same, of course, goes for
essences. Unless some thinkers are numbers, nothing that possesses the
essence *number* is identical with anything that possesses the concept 'number'. Third, some concepts, such as 'round square', are of properties which
could not possibly exist. But the concept 'round square' does exist, and is

realized in mental states every time someone entertains a thought in which it figures. Fourth, many concepts are individuated more finely than what they are about. The concepts 'water' and '$H_2O$' refer to the same stuff, but they are not the same concept. Fifth, all concepts are imperceptible, but many properties are not. I cannot see the concept 'red', but I can see red.

*The contents of belief and judgment are conceptual.* A further claim concerning concepts that seems to be widely agreed upon is that they are essentially involved in judgment and belief. Geach tells us that "Concepts ... are capacities exercised in acts of judgment" (Geach 1957: 7). And Peacocke (2001: 243) writes:

I shall be taking it that conceptual content is content of a kind that can be the content of judgment and belief. Concepts are constituents of those intentional contents which can be the complete, truth-evaluable, contents of judgment and belief.

If we understand propositions to be those truth-evaluable intentional contents to which Peacocke is referring, then concepts are constituents of propositions. Conceptual contents, then, are either concepts or wholes composed of concepts. And since the content, or matter, of a thought is independent of its quality or assertoric force, concepts are also constituents of questions, commands, doubts, and at least some "mere" thoughts. There are, to be sure, good reasons to reject the claim that all complete conceptual contents must be propositions. Consider, for instance, titles of books and chapters, labels on maps, road signs, and lists (Davis 2003: 176). Nevertheless, any conceptual content belongs to some syntactic and semantic category, and could be a component of a proposition.

*Linguistically expressible contents are conceptual.* Another widely endorsed thesis concerning conceptual contents is that any linguistically expressible content is conceptual. Alex Byrne writes, "Since everyone agrees that propositions expressed by sentences are of a kind that can be believed, linguistic content is automatically conceptual" (Byrne 2005: 234). And Peacocke writes that "any content that can be expressed in language by the use of an indicative sentence, including sentences containing indexicals and demonstratives, will be a conceptual content" (Peacocke 2001: 243). Linguistic expressibility, then, is at least a sufficient condition for conceptuality. I suspect that it is necessary as well.

Given this preliminary understanding of what concepts are, and provided there is any distinction to be made between contents and objects of consciousness, we can also distinguish the properties of being conceptual and the being conceptualized. Conceptuality, as I understand it, is not a property of an object of consciousness, unless of course that object itself happens to be a concept or a whole composed of them. Trees and rocks, for instance, are not conceptual. To say that an ideal content is conceptual is to say that it, or its constituents, are concepts. To say that a real content is conceptual is to say that it, or its constituent real contents, instantiate ideal conceptual contents. If the only type of content is conceptual, then the term 'conceptual content' is pleonastic. A conceptualized object, on the other hand, need not itself be conceptual. If I entertain the proposition that grass is green, then the content of my mental state includes the concepts 'grass' and 'green', and so is conceptual, while the object of my mental state, the fact that grass is green, is conceptualized. The content, the proposition that grass is green, is not conceptualized, however. To conceptualize it would require that I make it, the proposition, the object of another mental state whose content is both conceptual and directed upon it. And the state of affairs that grass is green is not conceptual, since it is not composed of concepts, but of grass and greenness. I think this distinction is quite obvious. To say that something is conceptualized by me implies that I am conscious of it as an object. But when I think that grass is green, and thereby employ the concepts 'grass' and 'green', I am not making those concepts themselves objects of my thought. I conceptualize grass and greenness *by means of* the conceptual contents 'grass' and 'green'. Finally, consider the term 'nonconceptual content' itself. It expresses a conceptual content. Everyone who understands the term possesses a concept that is about nonconceptual content, and nonconceptual content is, when they think about it, conceptualized. But nonconceptual contents are not, even when conceptualized, conceptual; the term is not an oxymoron.

## 2.1 MOTIVATING EXPERIENTIAL CONCEPTUALISM

Traditional empiricists, though differing among themselves about which sorts of things are perceived, and by which sense, agree that the list is astonishingly shorter than we would normally suppose. Hume, wondering whether we have any idea of substance, remarks, "If it be perceiv'd by the eyes, it must be a color; if by the ears, a sound; if by the palate, a taste; and so of the other senses" (Hume 1978: 16). Arguably even Hume could not confine the objects of perceptual awareness to those that would pass this austere test. But the guiding idea, I think, is plain enough.

It is difficult – though it has been done – to exaggerate the differences between the impoverished world of perception with which Hume presents us and the world as it is actually experienced. I can say with considerable confidence that I have seen all of the following: people, cars, fires, running animals, smiles, football games, weddings, and injuries. And none of those things is a color or a combination thereof. I can say with certainty that I have *seemed* to see such things, and that alone renders Hume's description phenomenologically inaccurate. It is, furthermore, no use to insist that Hume has successfully described how the world seemed to us originally, since that alone entails nothing about how it seems to us now. Phenomenologically, Hume's description is a nonstarter.

The world we experience presents itself as categorially structured, complex, and significant. It consists not merely, or even principally, of colored points, sounds, and odors, and still less is it a blob of undifferentiated sense-stuff. It is a world of kinds, relations, properties, events, processes, states of affairs, and substances. The principal objects of perception, those which anchor the world, are the things which endure through time despite qualitative change such as trees, houses, and people. We are aware of qualities, but typically not in isolation from objects; virtually any presentation of redness, for example, is also a presentation of something that is red. What strikes us first about objects is rarely their qualities, but their significance. We notice the screwdriver before we notice its color, just as we notice whether a face is hostile or friendly before we notice most of its other properties. Objects, moreover, do not appear as mere thises, but as this-suches, instances of multiply instantiable types and kinds – here the pen, there the houseplant, there the red color of the carpet. "[O]ur pregiven surrounding world is already 'pregiven' as multiformed, formed according to its regional categories and typified in conformity with a number of different special genera, kinds, etc." (*EJ* §8: 38). Commonalities, similarities, and differences among objects impress themselves on us as forcibly as redness and heat. Not only are we aware, perceptually, of the likenesses and unlikenesses of things, but the respects in which they are alike or unlike. Objects appear to be related to one another in multifarious ways – as cause and effect, as part to whole, as means to end, and so on. The perceptual appearances of parts depend on the wholes of which they are a part. The sound of a musical note depends on the phrase of which it is part, whose sound in turn depends on its place within a broader piece of music. Mona Lisa's mouth would appear differently if her eyes were smiling. Finally, many of the objects of perception seem to be ontologically independent of our acts of perceiving them, thinking about them, or talking about them.

Accepting this description of the world of perception has its price too, however. How can a world of such extraordinary richness be present to us, or even *seem* to be present to us, given the extremely limited character of our perceptual experience? After all, Hume didn't pull his list of perceptible properties from thin air; colors, sounds, and so forth are present with a constancy, a fullness, and a degree of certainty which is absent in the case of other sorts of objects. Speaking of a color with which he is acquainted, Russell writes, "I know the colour perfectly and completely when I see it, and no further knowledge of it itself is even theoretically possible" (Russell 1999: 32). But that is virtually never the case with external objects. When I take myself to perceive a barn, I perceive only a smallish portion of it. It might turn out to be a barn façade. But I at least perceive its color. It is even conceivable that I have never seen a barn, that every putative perception of one has been hallucinatory. But if I have seen anything at all, I have seen colors. Not only that, but even if we grant that the barn is perceived, my perception of it is so inadequate that an infinite number of comparable experiences would fail to exhaust it. It has a back, an inside, and a history in time. There are infinitely many points in space from which it could be viewed. It is composed of innumerable microphysical constituents. It has causal properties which, if they manifest themselves in perception at all, do so very differently than its color and shape do. Finally, what I strictly perceive, what is intuitively present to me, when I see objects like barns is simultaneously too rich and too impoverished to explain how I am conscious of them: too rich because every individual appears in a field of co-given objects, and too impoverished because any physical object is always more, and always given as more, than what is strictly presented perceptually. "[W]e see both more and less than what is sensorily given" (Gallagher and Zahavi 2007: 96).

This disparity between the aspirations and the achievements of "external" perceptual experiences prompts Husserl to say that their claim to "give us the object 'itself'" is "a mere pretension" (*LI* 6, §14b: 712), and even that perception "harbors an essential contradiction" (*APS*: 39). This last claim just isn't true, as we shall see, and nor is it Husserl's considered view. Rather, perceptual consciousness is always, at the same time, a consciousness that there is more to the perceived object than what is presented. Nevertheless, it does provide some motivations to embrace an empiricist view, since that view at least closes the gap between perception's aspirations and its achievements.

But we shouldn't close that gap. The kinds of objects that we perceive – cats, people, cities, buildings, football games, and symphonies, to name a few – are given imperfectly. We can perceive more than what can be adequately presented, and more than what is merely sensed. And if we accept that – and, as we'll see, even colors and sounds cannot be adequately presented – we must provide at least some account of how perceptual experience could lay hold of the kinds of things it seems to despite being so massively inadequate to them. To accommodate the phenomenology of perceptual experience, we must acknowledge a surplus of intentionality beyond that supplied by mere sensation. According to the conceptualist, this surplus is provided by concepts. In the sections that follow, I will examine several reasons to suppose that only experiential conceptualism can account for various phenomenologically discoverable features of perceptual experience.

I should add at once that EC, in some variety or other, is an enormously plausible theory, and even some of its most vocal critics admit that virtually all adult experiences do have conceptual content, and that at least some sorts of experiences can be influenced by, or are even impossible without, the possession of certain concepts. A. D. Smith, for instance, insists that "Concepts are simply irrelevant to perception as such" (A. D. Smith 2002: 95). Yet in the very next paragraph, he writes:

I in no way contest the enormously important role that conceptualizaton plays in the perceptual lives of adult human beings ... Nor shall it be denied that possession of a concept ... may affect the way something perceptually appears to you. (A. D. Smith 2002: 95)

This concession seems to rob his initial rejection of EC of much of its force. If concepts are irrelevant to perception as such, then no experience should depend, for either its existence or its character, on the exercise of concepts, which is just what Smith seems to deny. Smith clarifies his remark by saying: "what I mean is that they are irrelevant to what it is that makes any sensory state a perception at all; they are irrelevant to the intentionality of perception, to its basic world-directedness" (A. D. Smith 2002: 95). I take this to mean that although there are concepts the possession of which affect *how* an object perceptually appears, there is no sense-perceptible object or property which is such that concepts are necessary to explain the fact *that* it appears. So, for instance, although the way a computer appears to me might be affected by my possession of the concept 'computer', the fact that it appears at all does not depend on that. In what follows, I will argue that even this is too much of a concession to EC. Or rather, I will argue that while having certain perceptual experiences *might* entail that one possesses concepts, the contents actually operative in perception itself are never conceptual.

## 2.2 THE ARGUMENT FROM CONDITIONS OF SATISFACTION

One argument for EC is that because perceptual experiences have conditions of satisfaction, and therefore can be correct or incorrect, experiences must have propositions as their contents. And since propositional content is conceptual content, they must have conceptual content. Perhaps the clearest statement of the first part of this argument is due to Searle. As he puts it,

The fact that visual experiences have propositional Intentional contents is an immediate (and trivial) consequence of the fact that they have conditions of satisfaction, for conditions of satisfaction are always that such and such is the case.[2]

My perception of a yellow car, for instance, is satisfied if and only if there is a yellow car suitably related to me.

The first thing to note about this argument is that, if sound, it only establishes WEC; it comes nowhere near establishing that the only intentional contents of perception are conceptual. The second thing to note is just how nontrivial it really is. For what the argument assumes is that only propositional contents can be correct or incorrect. But this is not so (Burge 2003). An accurate map of the United States will depict Texas as being larger than Ohio. But it does not do so by expressing a proposition. Maps are not made of the right kind of stuff to express propositions. No map could *only* contain the information that Texas is larger than Ohio. In depicting their respective sizes, it will *also* depict their respective shapes and locations. And maps do not have negations: you cannot draw a map whose content is merely that Texas is not larger than Ohio (Millikan 2004: 93). Pictures are another good example. A portrait of Napoleon can be accurate or inaccurate, and it can depict how something is. But it does not express a proposition. If it did, it would have a negation. If something like a map or a picture, which to all appearances is a massively simpler representational vehicle than a perceptual experience, can manage to depict facts without expressing propositions or judgments, it is not at all obvious that perceptual experiences cannot do so without having them as contents.

Alva Noë presents a related argument, and it fares no better than Searle's. He writes:

Perceptual experience presents the world as being this way or that; to have experience, therefore, one must be able to appreciate how the experience presents things as being. But this is just to say that one must have concepts of the presented features and states of affairs.[3]

---

[2] Searle (1983: 41); see also Huemer (2001: 74).
[3] Noë (2004: 183). Also see (2004: 189), Porter (2006: 82–3), and Noë Peacocke (1983: 19–20).

Noë's argument proceeds as follows:

P1      If S has an experience that presents the world as being some way W, then he must be able to appreciate that the world is way W.

P2      If S is able to appreciate that the world is way W, then S must have concepts of the objects and features that constitute the way W.

C       Therefore, if S has an experience that presents the world as being some way W, S must have concepts of the objects and features that constitute W.

This argument has two flaws: first, it doesn't establish either version of EC, and second, it effectively begs the question against anti-conceptualism.

Beginning with the first point, one could be a devoted anti-conceptualist and endorse the conclusion of this argument. The mere fact that perceiving something entails that you have an ability to conceive of it does not entail that your perceptual experience itself involves exercising that ability. Anyone who has the ability to play the piano has the ability to drum his fingers on a table. It doesn't follow that when someone engages in the activity of playing the piano, he is drumming his fingers on a table.

Suppose we modify the premises of the argument in such a way that they entail:

C*      Therefore, if S has an experience that presents the world as being some way W, S must exercise concepts of the objects and features that constitute W.

Even so, EC does not follow. The fact that every perceived object is actually conceptualized in the act of perceiving does not entail that perception itself has conceptual content, since there is a competing explanation of why that is so (if it is so) that is both independently plausible and requires perception to have its own, autonomous intentionality, namely that I conceptualize something *because* I perceive it.

I think it is clear that Noë's argument is supposed to establish that perceiving *consists in* exercising certain concepts, and that is incompatible with anti-conceptualism about experience. As he puts it, "Perception is a *way of thinking* about the world" (Noë 2004: 189). So let us modify the argument appropriately to generate a stronger conclusion:

P1**    If S has an experience that presents the world as being some way W, then he appreciates that the world is way W.

P2**        Appreciating that the world is a certain way W *consists* (in part) in
            exercising concepts of W.
C**         Therefore, if S has an experience that presents the world as being
            some way W, S's experience consists (in part) in exercising
            concepts of W.

P1** permits of two readings, depending on what we take "appreciating"
to consist in. If we, following Noë, take "appreciating" to consist in *under-standing* or *thinking* that the world is way W, then P2** is extremely
plausible. However, P1** itself is highly contentious on that interpretation –
just as contentious as C** itself, in fact. No one who is not already
committed to some version of conceptualism would endorse it.

P1** permits of another interpretation, however, which is quite obvi-ously true, namely that in having an experience that presents the world as
being a certain way, S must be in a state that presents the world as being
that way. That is, S's "appreciating" that the world is that way, on this
construal, simply amounts to S's being in a mental state that is about it.
But if we interpret P1** in this way, P2** becomes highly problematic; it
claims that being in a mental state that (re)presents the world as being a
certain way is, at the very least, a matter of exercising concepts of that way.
But that, again, assumes precisely what is at issue. If everyone were
prepared to swallow that claim, then virtually everyone would also endorse
some version of EC.

The argument that perception has propositional or conceptual content
simply because it presents the world as being this way or that is, then,
inconclusive, unless and until it can be shown that conceptual content is the
only kind of content that can present the world as being this way or that.
This allows us to address another argument of Noë's as well. He argues that
because experiences and judgments can conflict, they can also accord with
one another, "and this," he writes, "would seem to show that they have the
same sort of content" (Noë 2004: 189). But this is wrong; the most it shows
is that they are capable of having the same kinds of *objects*. What makes
judgments accord or conflict with one another is that they are of states of
affairs that could or could not jointly obtain; the (broadly) logical compat-ibility of contents is parasitic on the *ontological* compatibility of their
intentional objects. But if the ontological compatibility of two states of
affairs is sufficient for the compatibility of contents directed upon them,
then all we need to explain why perceptual and judgmental contents can
conflict and accord is that they are of the same kinds of objects, not that they
have the same kinds of contents.

## 2.3 THE ARGUMENT FROM PERCEIVING-AS

A second consideration in favor of EC, and without doubt one of the most popular and convincing, is that all perceiving is "perceiving-as." What we perceive is always classified and conceptualized in some way. Indeed, despite all the vague talk of the "activity" or "spontaneity" of thought and conceptualization, it would require activity of a much more recognizable sort not to experience the world in this way. But obviously – or so it might seem – if every object of perception is conceptualized, then perception must always have conceptual content.

The fact that every object that is perceived is conceptualized does not entail that the *only* intentional content of an experience is conceptual, however. For while it is trivially true that if an object is conceptualized by S, then S is in a mental state with conceptual content directed towards that object, it does not follow that S is not also in a mental state whose intentionality is partially determined by a different, nonconceptual sort of content. That concepts pervade our experiential life does not show that any conceptual contents are sufficient for perceptual experience. At most, then, this argument supports WEC.

But it doesn't even entail that much. That all of the objects of experience are conceptualized, or even necessarily conceptualized, does not entail that perceptual experiences themselves have any conceptual content. There is a perfectly intelligible explanation why everything we perceive is conceptualized: when we perceive something, we always (or even necessarily) either (1) apply concepts already at our disposal to it, or (2) acquire new concepts of it in the course of perceiving it. Suppose that you see an aardvark as an aardvark – that is, that you see one, and that you apply the concept 'aardvark' to it. What is the best explanation as to why you, just then and there, employed the concept 'aardvark'? "Because you saw one" sounds like a start. Suppose further that the three-year-old kid standing next to you acquires the concept 'aardvark' at the same time. Why, just then, did that occur? The explanation "Because she saw one" also sounds promising. But in order for these explanations, or anything like them, to work as causal explanations, the experiences of seeing the aardvark must have been independent of your deployment, or the child's acquisition, of the concept 'aardvark'. The fact that every object of experience is necessarily conceptualized only entails that every total experience involving or containing a perceptual experience also has conceptual content. But if such total experiences exceed, in their contents, the perceptual experience proper, then it does not follow that every perceptual experience has conceptual content.

As H. H. Price said of this argument, it "only proves that nothing stands merely in the relation of givenness to the mind, without also standing in other relations: i.e. that what is given is always also 'thought about'" (Price 1950: 7).

This sort of explanation must be resisted by the conceptualist. The conceptualist must maintain that deploying concepts is at least partially *constitutive* of perceiving objects. Let us, then, turn to some actual varieties of EC and see how they hold up. The most extreme view that I am aware of maintains that perceiving just is a form of conceptualizing activity, namely judging. Simon Blackburn, for instance, writes:

The critics of "the given" have a simple, and strong, case. Experience cannot be regarded as an independent source of a conception of a fact – independent, that is, of the operation of judgment – for two reasons. The first is obvious: to see a situation as one containing or illustrating or displaying a fact is just to judge and interpret. (Blackburn 1984: 243)

Then so much the worse for critics of the given. If anything is obvious, it is that seeing a situation as displaying a fact is not just to judge. Just judging that the Mississippi is muddy is sufficient for judging that it is muddy, but it is hardly sufficient for perceiving that it is. Any account which construes perception as just judging, or as an inclination to judge, leaves one of the most central features, its presentational character, completely unaccounted for. In perception objects are present in the flesh. And judging is not even necessary for perceptual experience. To cite a well-worn example, my experience presents the lines of the Müller-Lyer illusion as unequal in length, but I do not judge them to be so.

Even the view that perception necessarily involves judging is phenomenologically incredible. It is very easy to persuade oneself that perception has the same sort of intentional content as judgments when one's paradigmatic instance of perception is visually attending to an already familiar sort of object and reporting, either to others or internally, what you see, and do so for the sake of doing just that. But this is not a paradigmatic case of perception. Most perceptual experiences do not have perception, or even knowledge, as their goal. Perception is more typically done in the service of action. "I do not perceive in order to perceive but in order to orient myself, to pave the way in dealing with something" (Heidegger 1985: 30). Most perceptual experiences are not visual, either, and even in the case of hearing, which is perhaps the second most "intellectual" of the senses, they do not seem to require conceptualization.

To see just how fundamentally different perceiving is from judging, just consider the experience of reading this page right now (Dretske 1969: 11). As you read, what are the propositional contents of your mental states? Well, in the first place, those that are expressed by the sentences on this page. In addition, you probably think various thoughts about those propositions, such as "that sounds right" or "that is ludicrous" or "so-and-so said that." But are you in the least aware of entertaining propositions about each of the sentences you perceive? How about each word? How about each letter? How about the various perceived portions of each letter? How about the white spaces in between each word and letter? You do perceive a great many of these things – and more – otherwise you couldn't read. But I very much doubt that you have made a judgment about, say, every horizontal line on each letter 't' in this sentence. Again, could you imagine trying to make a judgment about, say, every chord, every note, every timbre, every pitch, every volume, every phrase, every nuanced transition, that you hear when listening to Chopin's black key étude? Doing that, even if possible, would be quite a different achievement from listening to it. And it would almost certainly preclude your enjoying it.

A slightly less extreme, but hardly more plausible, view is the one put forth by, most famously, Norwood Hanson (1961) and Thomas Kuhn (1970). According to them, all perceptual experience is inextricably laden with theories and shaped by our concepts. "The Kuhnian conception denies the idea of pure experience. Hence, it denies that there is some neutral content which is not yet structured by any conceptual schemes. The conceptual schemes permeate everything. Whatever we perceive is already structured by our conceptual scheme" (Forrai 2001: 7). Disregarding Forrai's seamless transition from the claim that concepts structure experiences of objects to the claim that they structure the objects of experience – as though it were just obvious that if concepts shape my seeing of a cathedral they also shape the cathedral – what can be said in favor of such a claim? Kuhn, for one, tells us that, while a scientist may see something other than a pendulum when looking at a swinging stone, "the scientist who looks at a swinging stone can have no experience that is in principle more elementary than seeing a pendulum" (Kuhn 1970: 128). Again: "The duck–rabbit shows that two men with the same retinal impressions can see different things" (Kuhn 1970: 126–7). I agree with the latter claim, but that is no concession to EC, as we shall see.

Furthermore, I believe the phenomenon here has been misdescribed. Two individuals looking at, and having retinal impressions caused by, a single duck–rabbit figure ("*the* duck–rabbit") are not seeing two different things, and we all know it, and they probably do too. But how do we know this? Not, surely, by looking at others' retinal impressions. Our evidential basis for the claim that their retinal impressions are the same is that it is the same objective item which causes their visual experience, not the other way round. And our evidence for that is that we can see that it is the same objective item – which is exactly what it cannot be if Kuhn is correct. When we look at the duck–rabbit, we are perceptually aware that it is the same figure whose aspects shift. We are quite plainly conscious that the "ears" of the rabbity figure are identical with the "bill" of the duckish figure, that the slight notch on the back of the duckish figure's "head" is the "mouth" of the rabbity figure. If there were nothing more fundamental than seeing a rabbity or a duckish figure, it would be an open question whether the Gestalt shift was in fact a reality shift, a change in what is objectively before us. But it isn't an open question. That is what makes the figure remarkable: we would find nothing remarkable if we thought there were two figures present, since there is nothing remarkable about two different things look-ing like two different things. Or rather, we would find it remarkable that a drawing on paper could change with no apparent cause, but that would locate the remarkableness of ambiguous figures along a dimension com-pletely different from the one it's actually on. And, it hardly needs saying, the identity of the figure-as-rabbit with the figure-as-duck is something each of us knows on the basis of *our own* perception. But then it is false that in seeing the figure under different aspects we are seeing different things. If that were true, then we could not make the identification.

This argument does not just apply to the duck–rabbit figure, but to every putative case in which experiences of the same thing are also, in some other and presumably more important sense, experiences of different things. The scientist cannot, Kuhn says, see a swinging stone as something more fundamental than a pendulum. He could only see it as something else, but in an equally theory-laden sense, for instance as an object in constrained free fall. Even if we grant that a scientist could not help seeing it as a pendulum, it does not follow that he sees it *only* as a pendulum, or that his consciousness of that object essentially depends on his applying the concept 'pendulum' to it. If that were so, then it would be impossible for him to change his theory concerning that thing, the very thing he perceives. But he could. If, moreover, he took himself to be seeing a different thing upon adopting a new theory, then he would not feel rationally compelled to abandon the first theory. If the two theories or, in this case, perceptual states concern different subject matters – if they are "incommensurable" – then they would not conflict. But they do conflict, and they conflict in virtue of ascribing incompatible properties to the very same thing. And none of these points needs to be established from the transcendental point of view that

Kuhn, in open defiance of his own theory, permits himself to occupy. They are evident from our human point of view. The intelligibility of this example depends upon the fact that we are capable of seeing a swinging stone as either a pendulum or an object in constrained free fall, and that we recognize that it is the same thing that is seen in both cases. But if we can do this, then we can do exactly what Kuhn's argument attempts to establish cannot be done. As is so often the case with arguments for relativism, Kuhn's argument must get us to see beyond our own particular conceptual framework in order to convince us that we can't.

There are several other rather serious problems with Kuhn's view, problems shared by any view according to which perceiving requires subsuming a perceived object under some sortal or classifying concept. The first is that one can perceive something without knowing what kind of thing it is. To borrow an example from John Campbell, our descendants a millennium from now who discover a teacup need not know that it is a teacup, or even have the concept of a teacup, in order to perceive the teacup. Far from it – the unearthed artifact would, assuming our descendants are civilized enough to value knowledge of the past for its own sake, most likely be an object of deep curiosity and untamed speculation. But, as Campbell notes, "Given the intense discussion it receives, it would be absurd to say that our descendants have not managed to 'single it out'" (Campbell 2002: 71). Or, to borrow another example from Dretske, one can see a screwdriver without even having the concept of a screwdriver. As he puts it:

When we see D, although, normally, we frequently do identify what we see as D, and hence believe that it is D, this identification is not a necessary condition for our seeing D. This point is, perhaps, too obvious to labor. One can see a screwdriver without believing that what one is seeing is a screwdriver, without believing that there are any screwdrivers, without even knowing what screwdrivers are. (Dretske 1969: 7)

But if the thesis that classifying an object under a sortal concept is partly constitutive of perceiving that object is correct, then one could not perceive a teacup or a screwdriver without having the relevant concepts. Or, as A. D. Smith says, it is possible to wonder, of a perceived object, what in the world it is. If we could not perceive without classifying, then this would be impossible (A. D. Smith 2002: 112).

The second point is that, even when one does classify a perceived object, one can be grossly mistaken in one's classification without thereby failing to perceive it or suffering a hallucination or illusion. I might perceive something and classify it as a duck, only to learn on closer inspection that it is a decoy, which, given the nature of decoys, is supposed to happen from time to time. And I might mistake a distant tree for an even more distant man. If classifying an object by means of a sortal concept were essential to perceiving it, then in these cases where the object does not fall under the sortal in question, I could not take myself to be revising my beliefs about one and the same unchanged thing. I could not, that is, hold the object in mind and discover, of it, that it really is not a man but a tree. I would instead have to conclude one of the following: (1) that there is one object perceived at both t1 and t2, and it has transformed from a man into a tree; (2) that I perceived one object at t1 and a different one at t2; or (3) that at either t1 or t2, and possibly both, I did not perceive anything, but suffered a hallucination. But none of those is what I would conclude. I would change my mind about the very same thing. But to hold an object in mind while changing the sortal concepts one applies to it requires that one have cognitive access to that object that is independent of any of the sortal concepts in question.

It should be noted, moreover, that the plausibility of these examples in no ways depends upon adopting a third-personal perspective with respect to conscious content. If I see a spark plug and wonder what it is, and then find out, I will not take myself to be in the presence of a different thing, but to have found something out about the very same thing that was already before me.

A third reason for rejecting the view that sortal concepts are even partially constitutive of the object-directedness of perceptual intentionality is that our perception of an object can both cause and explain our application of a concept to it. Alan Millar presents the following example. Suppose that you perceive a black cushion-like object on a sofa. You realize, upon closer inspection, that it is a curled-up cat. Millar admits that when this recognition occurs, there is a phenomenal change in one's experience, but suggests that the phenomenal change is due to the fact that various features of the cat become more salient. And, he adds, "It seems quite plausible that this change in salience, far from being dependent on your recognizing the cat as a cat, actually explains how you came to recognize the cat for what it is" (Millar 1991a: 36). That is, the reason we apply the concept 'cat' to the object before us depends upon its being perceptually before us. But if that is so, then the application of the concept 'cat' cannot in turn explain how the object is perceptually before us. "There has to be something about the experiences which explains their being apt to trigger recognition and that cannot be something which is essentially dependent on recognition having taken place" (Millar 1991a: 37).

There are, then, several compelling reasons to reject the claim that exercising concepts, or at least sortal concepts, is necessary for objects such as teacups and cats to perceptually appear to us. This argument cuts against both SEC and WEC. But what of the much weaker claim that the possession of sortal concepts can affect the way objects perceptually appear? There are such cases. If, for instance, one learns of what appears to be a barn that it is a barn façade, it appears, or at least can appear, differently.[4] Note that I am using 'appears' in a phenomenal rather than, or in addition to, an epistemic sense. It does not just intellectually *seem to be different*, as it would, for instance, if someone were to correct our beliefs about its age or micro-physical structure. It also *appears differently*.

Top-down effects of concepts and beliefs on perception would only establish EC – and only the weak variety – if it could be shown that the effects in question were constitutive rather than causal (Alston 1999: 185). I think they are causal. If I apply the concept 'barn' to something, then I lay down not only certain conditions of satisfaction that must be met if the content is satisfied, but a certain open-ended and difficult to articulate, possibly very indeterminate, but nonetheless usable, rule for the manner in which it must appear if my thought that it is a barn is to be perceptually verified. Briefly, it must look the way barns do. (The fact that you do know what barns look like, but would have trouble articulating it linguistically, is itself a good indication that we are dealing with something that is not conceptual in content.) It is not verified if upon investigation it looks the way façades do. Nor is the thought that something is a barn façade verified if, upon closer investigation, it turns out to look like a closed three-dimensional structure full of tools and hay and animals. To put it another way, corresponding to an empirical concept like 'barn' is a certain intentional *horizon* or sensorimotor profile, the grasping or enacting of which prescribes how the thing will appear from various points of view.[5]

In the case of virtually all experiences of physical objects, the thing we intend in any given act of perceiving is something that is *more*, and experienced *as* more, than what is intuited or strictly perceived by means of that specific act of perceiving. Anything that can be observed from more than a single point of view, as material objects can, also has more parts and properties than can be presented in a single perceptual act. Perception is always inadequate to its object, and this inadequacy is itself a phenomeno-logically discoverable feature of such an experience; in the face of an external

---

4 Kelly (2004b, §1) provides a similar example contrasting the same objects when they are perceived as buildings in an Old West town (saloons, banks) and when they are perceived as fixtures on a movie set.
5 Though I do not think that having the concept of a barn, or any other empirical object, requires that one be able to carry out acts with such a horizon, or that one possess any recognitional capacities.

object we "know" that there is more to it than what is strictly revealed (*PP* §34: 136). This stems, not from any peculiar deficiency on our part, but from the essence of spatial objects. "Inadequate modes of givenness belong essentially to the spatial structure of things; any other way of givenness is simply absurd" (*APS*: 58). If we did not, if we treated the momentary experience as a complete presentation of its object, then we would construe any other experience to be of a different thing. Let us suppose that it is possible to have the sense experience characteristic of seeing the front of a house, but to regard what is strictly perceived as an adequately given thing unto itself rather than an essentially incomplete part of a greater spatially extended whole. In that case, one would not be perceiving a house at all:

> It is clear that a non-intuitive pointing beyond or indicating is what characterizes the side actually seen as a mere side, and what provides for the fact that the side is not taken for the thing, but rather, that something transcending the side is intended in consciousness as perceived, by which precisely that is actually seen. (*APS*: 41)

For this reason, Husserl characterizes each "individual percept [*Wahrnehmung*]" as "a mixture of fulfilled and unfulfilled intentions" (*LI* 6, §14b: 714).

In his more mature works Husserl explains this by saying that every perceptual experience has an *inner horizon*. This point needs to be handled with some care, because Husserl and his commentators refer to many intimately related but quite different things as "horizons," including:

(1)  the unperceived and further-determinable sides, parts, and properties of a perceived object;[6]

(2)  the set of *possible* experiences in which those sides, parts, and properties would be perceptually exhibited in the flesh – what I will refer to as an act's "manifold";

(3)  the *actual* empty or partly empty intentions by whose means at least some of the entities in (1) and (2) are intended or anticipated.

According to Smith and McIntyre, the horizon of an act consists of "those possible perceptions that would present the object of the given act as further characterized."[7] I don't dispute that Husserl does sometimes use the term 'horizon' to mean that. But more often, he uses it to refer to something else entirely. "The 'horizons' of perceptions are another name for

---

[6]  Husserl often speaks as though the horizon belongs to the object, rather than the act, of consciousness. See, for instance, *PP* §35: 139.

[7]  Smith and McIntyre (1982: 240). See also Christensen (1993: 760): "A horizon of an ordinary thing is ... in the first instance a set of possible perceptions with an ordering relation on it." Sometimes Husserl does mean this. See, for instance, *Crisis* §47: 162.

empty intentions ... that are integrally cohesive and that are actualized in the progression of perception in and through different orientations."[8] In what follows, I will understand the horizon of an act, not as a set of *possible intuitively filled* intentions, but as a living body of *actual empty* ones. The table I currently see looks, right now, as though it has more to it than I see. And it does so in virtue of some actual features of the actual act I am actually carrying out right now, and not (just) in virtue of bearing (possible) relations to a set of possibilia. The bare existence of a (potentially infinite) set of possible experiences (or types of experiences) cannot account for my *present* consciousness of the object as *more* than what I perceive, and the corresponding consciousness of my own perception as incomplete or inadequate.

Horizons are essential for perceiving objects that transcend our intuitive consciousness of them. The strictly intuitive contents of perceptual acts, Husserl claims, "are nothing for themselves; they are appearances-of only through the intentional horizons that are inseparable from them."[9] As I perceive the table from here, I can see some of its parts and sides, while others are hidden from view. I am conscious, not just of the seen parts of the table, but of the unseen parts as well, but emptily and indeterminately. The table gives itself as something that there is more of, that could be explored more fully, that would manifest itself differently from different points of view. The parts I do see, moreover, can be determined more closely, and they give themselves as such. I see the surface, but if I were to look more closely, I could see more of its details, the grain of the wood, the discolorations, and so forth. Were I to feel it, I would discover, in a more authentic way, its texture, its hardness, and so forth. My perception is not an adequate perception of something indeterminate, but an inadequate perception of something determinate. The table is an object of indefinitely many possible explorations and further determinations, and it is in some measure my practical purposes, rather than the table itself, which makes certain preeminent presentations of it count for me as maximally disclosive (*TS* §36).

Husserl frequently makes this point with respect to three-dimensional objects. But, as he recognizes (*Ideas 1* §41: 87), it pertains to two-dimensional

---

[8] *APS*: 144. Husserl also claims that the horizon is an "original 'induction' or anticipation" which is a "mode of 'intentionality'" which anticipatively aims beyond a core of givenness" (*EJ* §8: 33), that it "changes with the alteration of the nexus of consciousness to which the process belongs and with the process itself from phase to phase of its flow" (*CM* §19: 44), and that it is a "*horizon of reference* to potentialities of consciousness" (*CM* §19: 44). All of those sound like properties of actual empty intentions, not sets of possible filled ones.

[9] *APS*: 43. Also see *APS*: 137, *TS* §16, and *Ideas 1* §138.

objects like shadows and surfaces, and properties like color, shape, and sound as well. The color of a basketball does not manifest itself in just one way, but itself has its "profiles" by whose means it manifests itself. Its color looks differently in the light from in a shadow, or against a bright versus a dim background. And yet it is often recognizably the same color that appears. Its color is seen to be uniform even when various portions of its surface look the way white things would in other contexts. Its shadow, which is two-dimensional, also manifests itself through profiles. It appears differently when it is seen from up close than from afar, but it need not look *to be* different. The sound of a clap of thunder also manifests itself inadequately – it is the same sound that is heard by many people in the vicinity of a lightning strike, though their experiences of it are not identical. Perception's pretensions to adequacy, then, are not even realized in the case of the simple sensible qualities like color and sound. No single perception of red could, to borrow Russell's phrase, grasp it "perfectly and completely" (Russell 1999: 32). As Noë puts it, perception is *"virtual all the way in"* (Noë 2004: 193).

Horizons don't merely account for the felt inadequacy and incompleteness of perception; they don't merely specify that there is *more* to the object. They also anticipate further experiences and prescribe which further properties and courses of experience are compatible with what is perceived now. As Husserl puts it, "the process taking place in an original intuition is always already saturated with anticipation; there is always more cointended apperceptively than actually is given by intuition – precisely because every object is not a thing isolated in itself but is always already an object in its horizon of typical familiarity and precognizance" (*EJ* §25: 122). The horizon "is not a nothingness, but an emptiness to be filled-out: it is a determinable indeterminacy. For the intentional horizon cannot be filled out in just any manner" (*APS*: 42; also *LI* 6, §10: 700). Virtually no horizon will anticipate an object's non-intuited properties as determinately as subsequent experience would reveal them, but there are always restrictions on how a thing could appear if an experience were to qualify as a perception of *that* object, restrictions which, if transgressed, will render my present experiences frustrated, incoherent, illusory, or even hallucinatory, and if not, will render it harmonious. If I anticipate that something is a spotted ball, and will have spots on its unseen side, and it does not, my expectation is merely *frustrated*. If in a very short period of time I see the side that is spotted, then view the other side while merely intending the already seen side, and then move back to find the originally seen side to be unspotted, my experience is puzzling at best and incoherent at worst; either the ball has somehow lost its spots, or at least one of the experiences of the side seen twice was nonveridical. If I move closer to the object and it reveals itself to be part of a two-dimensional mural, my initial experience is exposed as illusory. And if, when I try to move closer to the object it simply disappears, then my initial experience might prove to have been hallucinatory at worst, or, at best, of something that has very few of the properties I perceived it as having, such as a hologram. Obviously anticipations of future experience can be very complex. Perceiving a house as stationary differs from perceiving a deer as stationary, since in the latter case one will anticipate that it will get farther, rather than closer, to you as you attempt to approach it. More generally, horizonal contents anticipate not only changes in experience brought about by your own movement, but changes in experience brought about by changes in the object itself – including those changes in the object that would come about through your own activity.

Horizonal contents can vary massively in how determinately they prescribe the nonintuited properties and parts of an object and, correspondingly, the experiences in which they would be perceptually given. A more determinate horizon attaches itself to my experiences of my house than would to your experiences of my house. The more specific the content of the horizon, the more possibilities there are for frustration and surprise. I anticipate a great deal about the behavior of the ball I am about to kick, and would be surprised if, after kicking it, it did not budge, exploded, or split open to reveal a baby dragon. But no matter how determinately the horizon anticipates future experience and the features of an object, it does so in the "mode of uncertainty."[10] It leaves possibilities open. After all, perception is a process of finding out about the world by determining how things are more closely, not prophesying. The horizon leaves things open because it belongs to the very sense of perception to be a process of consulting the things themselves and allowing them, so far as possible, to have the final word on what and how they are. "While the empty horizon ... fashions its next fulfillment in the march of perception, this fulfillment does not merely consist in tracing over in intuition the prefigured sense of which one is emptily conscious" (*APS*: 45).

Finally, objects are, and are perceived as, objects in a surrounding environment, thanks to the work of the *outer* horizon Apart from the fact that, say, my desk *belongs* with the objects co-given with it – a felt belongingness that can, plausibly, be chalked up to a rich background of previously

---

[10] *APS*: 81. See also Merleau-Ponty (1962: 80). "Thus the synthesis of horizons is no more than a presumptive synthesis, operating with certainty and precision only in the immediate vicinity of the object."

acquired knowledge – it has the more basic feature of appearing alongside
and in the midst of other appearing things. There is a floor that supports it,
and a window above it, and a lamp on top of it. It is illuminated by a certain
kind of light. These surrounding objects and conditions are there for me
even when I don't attend to them. And the surrounding environment itself
is both intuited and emptily intended. The door at the end of my kitchen
opens into another room, which is emptily intended but also present as a
possible object of immediate perception. So is the space behind my head.
The world does not end there; the field of possible further perceptual
experiences is unlimited, and at least some of this sense of the limitlessness
of the world is provided by actual empty intentions. The outer horizon
provides, then, not (just) an objective context in which perception uncon-
troversially takes place, but a *consciousness of* the context in which it takes
place. Both inner and outer horizons perform remarkable functions: the
inner horizon is what accounts for the fact that too little of the object is
present; the external horizon is responsible for the fact that too much is
co-given with it. But oddly enough, in doing that, they are also responsible
for the fact that the object is given at all, since a material object is essentially
such that too little of it is given, and too much is co-given along with it.

Returning to our example, part of what explains the fact that applying the
concept 'barn façade' to a seen object changes the way it perceptually
appears is that in conceiving of it in that way, a new intentional horizon,
an array of empty intentions pointing beyond the perceived sides and
aspects of the object, is awakened. My experience now prescribes a new
manner in which the object would perceptually appear were I to engage
with it further. It motivates a different set of potential experiences, as it must
in virtue of emptily intending different parts and features. And it is the
awakening of such a horizon in the living context of perception, not the bare
application of a concept to what is perceived or the joining up of mere
sensations with that concept, which is responsible for the change in the way
it appears. So, while the application of the concept 'barn façade' might cause
the object to appear differently, it does not follow that the concept itself is
part of the intentional content of the experience. Rather, it awakens a
perceptual horizon, which *is* part of the perceptual experience's intentional
content (see Noë 2004: 77).

This would go some way towards explaining why a teacup that has been
thoroughly investigated does not change its perceptual appearance once one
applies the concept 'teacup' to it. Given our hypothetical descendants'
interest in it, they would presumably have already explored the teacup
and, in virtue of that, would have already acquired the appropriate horizonal

intentionalities corresponding to different points of view on it – they would, that is, have acquired the ability and disposition to entertain appropriate horizonal contents when perceiving the cup. Similarly, if someone were to walk around the barn façade and acquire the appropriate horizonal intentionalities – the ones that would actually get fulfilled in the course of actual perception – it would not perceptually appear differently when, facing it head on again, he were to apply the concept 'barn façade' rather than 'barn' to it. It would also go some way towards explaining why the application of certain concepts to an object, namely those which designate properties that are not sense-perceptible, does not change the way something perceptually appears. If I learn that something is composed of atoms, for instance, it does not thereby appear differently, since there is no perceptual experience – or at least none that I have ever had – which corresponds to something's being composed of atoms.

It might, however, be objected that having the ability to entertain the appropriate horizonal intentional contents in the course of perceiving an object just is possessing a concept of that object. If one possesses the concept 'barn', for instance, one will have some knowledge of what barns look like. And if one knows what barns look like, then one will possess the concept 'barn'. But first, that can't be quite right, since the blind can have the concept of a barn – and even of the colors – without knowing what they look like. At best, knowing what a barn looks like is a sufficient condition for possessing the concept 'barn'. That might appear to be a threat to my account. It is not, however. Even if being able to exercise the appropriate horizonal contents were necessary and sufficient for having a concept of an object, that comes nowhere close to showing that the two things possessed are identical. Possessing a content is a dispositional state, and is quite different from actually exercising one. And the difference between horizonal contents and ordinary concepts becomes clear when we see that one can exercise a horizonal content only in the context of intuiting or perceiving an object, but one can exercise an ordinary concept completely emptily. When you merely think that a certain teacup is blue, you exercise the concept 'teacup' but do not exercise any horizon that is pertinent to a teacup. The concept cannot *be* the horizonal content if one can exercise one without exercising the other.

Furthermore, the relationship between the specific horizonal contents involved in perception and concepts is many-to-one. With each change in the properly intuitive contents in an act of perception, there is a change in the intentional horizon as well. As I walk around a barn, what was previously intuited falls away into horizonal emptiness, and what was emptily anticipated comes to proper perception. But concepts are not individuated that finely. When I walk around a barn and simultaneously think that it is a barn, my thought that it is a barn does not change as I walk around it. The concept 'barn' retains an identical sense across a multiplicity of experiences with different perceptual and horizonal contents. So, while possessing a concept might entail and be entailed by the ability to enact an object's sensorimotor profile or horizon, what are possessed here are two things, not one.

Finally, in those cases in which we acquire concepts of empirical objects by perceiving them, there is an asymmetrical dependence between possessing a concept and having the capacity to carry out perceptual acts with the appropriate horizonal intentions. It is my capacity to carry out perceptual acts with barn-directed intuitive and horizonal contents which explains my possession of the concept 'barn' and not vice versa. I do not know what barns look like because I have the concept of them; I have the concept of a barn because I know what barns look like. And so, while possessing a concept might affect the way something appears, that doesn't entail that perceptual states have conceptual content. The content in virtue of which something appears differently is horizonal content.

The phenomenon of perceiving-as, and the fact that our perceptual experiences of objects can change, and become more nuanced, sophisticated, and even prejudiced, is undeniable. My experience of a basketball differs from those of infants or dogs. In seeing it, I anticipate its weight. In handling it, I know how much force to exert to dribble it, to shoot it from various distances, and so forth. I can correctly anticipate what it will feel like to catch a pass and carry out the appropriate bodily movements to do so. My first experience of a symphony differs from subsequent ones. As I become more attuned to the piece, I anticipate its phrases, its crescendos, its pauses, and its repetitions. But this isn't because I am applying concepts or making judgments. It's because a rich, dense, interweaving nexus of intuitive and horizonal contents are at play, and because those horizons become richer and denser as we acquire experience and knowledge.

## 2.4 THE ARGUMENT FROM THE PERCEPTION OF CATEGORIALLY STRUCTURED OBJECTS

Another argument for EC begins with the claim that we are perceptually aware of a *categorially structured* world. Among the possible objects of perception are: collections (a row of trees, a legion of soldiers), specific quantities of things (four trees), complex wholes (melodies, houses), independent parts (notes, branches), dependent or nonseparable parts (timbres, surfaces), individual property-instances (the redness of this apple), properties themselves (the redness this and that apple share), events (the throwing of a ball), processes (something's grower larger), kinds (cows), relations (this apple being *on top of* the table, one light's being *brighter than* another, one event's happening *before* another), facts or states of affairs (that the car is black), and even causation (the hammer *driving* the nail, the rock *shattering* the window). I think it is fair to include most concrete particulars (Joe, the sun) among the class of categorially structured objects as well. They are, in the first place, often extraordinarily complex, both in terms of their part/whole structures and in terms of their properties. Moreover, not only are they the entities on which things like properties, relations, and states of affairs are founded, but they are in turn founded upon them. Individuals must have properties, for instance, and once an individual has a property, a state of affairs thereby exists.

There is no doubt that the world that we perceive is not a world of bare *thises*, sensible qualities, a blooming, buzzing confusion, or an unarticulated field of sensory contents. But the critical premise of this argument is that concepts are required to be aware of categorially structured objects, and this is by no means evident. Much of its plausibility derives from the familiar thought that such things could not be given in mere feeling or sensation, and that whatever kinds of contents allow experiences to reach out beyond what is given in mere sensation – in short, to become *perceptual* – is conceptual. Perception, the thought goes, occurs only when the understanding "works up" the "raw material of sensible impressions" into "that knowledge of objects which is entitled experience" (Kant 1965: B1). Concepts convert the raw sensory contents that comprise "the thin given of immediacy" into the "thick experience of the world of things" (Lewis 1929: 54). Among those who endorse some version of empiricism's "third dogma" (Davidson 1984: 189), there seems to be no consensus on just what we would be aware of without concepts. For traditional empiricists, it is sensible qualities like colors, sounds, and so forth, or perhaps sense data like colored and shaped particulars. According to William James, depending on the period, we would only be conscious of "one great blooming, buzzing confusion" (James 1952: 318) or "a *that* which is not yet any definite *what*" (James 1922: 93). According to Carnap, we would be aware of an "undivided unity" (Carnap 1967: 108). On any such view, awareness without concepts would bear no resemblance to what we all experience.

There is a good reason why it is so difficult, on accounts like this, to say what would be present to consciousness without concepts or "categories" – apart, that is, from the fact that we are never aware of any such things or the alleged process of minting the given(s) into representations of objects. It is that any conceivable thing whatsoever belongs to some onto-logical category, including raw materials of sensation and undivided unities, and the awareness of anything like that is never just an awareness of it, but an awareness of it as propertied in various ways and as standing in various relations. Consider sensations. Sensations are, paradigmatically, bodily feel-ings. The class of sensations might also include things like "sensations of red" and "sensations of sound," but that all of these comprise a natural kind is a bold hypothesis (Bennett and Hacker 2003: §4.2.1). And when that hypoth-esis became widely accepted, it was not because bodily sensations were assimilated to things like colors and sounds, which we do not pre-theoretically take to inhere in our bodies in the manner of bodily feelings, but because colors, sounds, and other sense-perceptible properties were assimilated to the paradigmatic class of (bodily) sensations.[11] However, unlike even the simplest colors and sounds, paradigmatic sensations are given as having no more to them than what is manifest in our awareness of them. A headache does not have hidden profiles from which I could get a different "view" of it. If I can, through medication or meditation, change the way my headache feels, then I have changed the headache itself. If I make my *awareness of* it go away, then I make *it* go away. That is why it would be so odd to say "I'm suffering horribly from this pain, but thankfully I'm not conscious of it." The awareness of sensations is *adequate* insofar as two experiences of sensing differ if, and only if, they have different sensations as their objects. This is why, while one can be more or less adept at procuring, prolonging, avoiding, or eliminating sensations, one cannot become more skilled at having them when they come. Acts of sensing sensations do not have intentional objects that they can present more or less adequately, such that one could become more skilled at manipulating one's body or environment in order to bring those objects into better view.

Because of this, it might seem that sensations are identical with the awareness of them. This, however, is a mistake. First, sensations are given as *objects* of consciousness. I am not aware *with* or *via* pain. I am aware *of* pain, in just the same way that I am aware of any other object of conscious-ness. Hurting is not an act of introspection. The fact that sensations such as pain are, in some sense, themselves *of* things does not support the idea that they are acts of awareness or features thereof. Pain plays an indicating role,

---

[11] See, for instance, Locke's remarks (1975, ii.viii.18: 108) in which he assimilates the sweetness and whiteness of manna to the pain and sickness that it causes.

insofar as its presence motivates a belief in the existence of something else, typically damage to some part of one's body. But like other indicators – sirens, tree rings, gas gauges, storm clouds – and *unlike* experiences and thoughts, it must first be an object before consciousness in order for it to indicate something to someone. I do not become aware of objects in the world by consulting my experiences and taking them to be reliable indicators of a world beyond themselves. I can only reflect on an experience when that experience already exists, and if it exists, then I am already conscious of *its* object. But that is how I become aware of bodily damage through the signal of pain. Pains, and sensations generally, are not *experiences*, and they do not have content in the way an experience does. They are objects of experience.[12]

Second, paradigmatic sensations have a felt bodily location (Bennett and Hacker 2003: 122). If I hurt or itch, there is always some region on or in my body, perhaps poorly defined, in which I seem to hurt or itch. But the awareness of a sensation does not have a felt bodily location. The question "Where is your pain?" makes perfect sense. The question "Where is your awareness of the pain?" does not, and if and when we do manage to make some sense of it, the most plausible candidates for answers are not the bodily locations where the pain is felt to be. Your mind, or your brain, is not what hurts, nor is it where most hurting is felt to be. Phantom limbs and rubber hand illusions do not constitute evidence that sensations do not have a felt bodily location. They reveal that they do. What makes phantom limb syndrome so remarkable is precisely the fact that the pain feels as if it is in a bodily location that does not exist, and what makes the rubber hand illusion remarkable is that the pain is felt to belong to an object which is not in fact part of one's body. But these would not be remarkable illusions if the pains were felt to be nowhere or in the mind or brain.

Sensations can be more or less intense, and they can be more or less pleasurable or painful. A pain can be "burning, stinging, gnawing, piercing, dull or throbbing" (Bennett and Hacker 2003: 124). They can last for longer or shorter periods of time, and are given as enduring through time. But if all of this is right, then even having sensations involves an awareness of more than just the sensations; it also involves an awareness of their relations to other things and their properties. To be aware of a sensation is to be aware of something occupying a location, something that has a duration, and

---

[12] Here I disagree with, among others, Tye (1995), Thau (2002), and Klein (2007). However, on my view acts of sensing sensations have content, and any difference in their phenomenal character is a difference in their content, so it is not incompatible with an intentionalist account.

something that has various properties. To be aware of a sensation, that is, is to be aware of how some part of the world – one's own body – is. But how plausible is it that one needs concepts in order to feel a pain in one's leg or an itch on one's back? And precisely which concepts would one need? The concept of a leg or a back? Does one need the concept 'burning' in order to experience a burning sensation? Does one need the concept 'enduring' in order to have an enduring awareness of an enduring sensation? If so, then sensations cannot be the stuff left over when concepts leave the scene. And if not, then the consciousness of what is categorially structured cannot, in all cases, depend on concepts.

The same points hold for another class of entities, misleadingly also called "sensations," such as colors and sounds. Like pains and itches, colors and sounds are objects rather than acts, or features of acts, of awareness. But unlike sensations, they are not given adequately. What I am aware of when I have a "sensation of red" or a "sensation of C-sharp" is given as having more to it than what I am presently aware of. And colors and sounds are not given as having a bodily location – unless I am looking at the color or listening to the sound of some part of my body. I may and do feel sensations when I see, but those are sensations of the movement of my eyes, and such oculomotor sensations are not colored, colors, or of colors. The "sensation" of red is not a sensation; it is a *perception*, complete with an act-object structure and the felt inadequacy that belongs to all "external" perception. And the perception of red is virtually always the perception of something more than that. The redness one sees is given as occupying a region of space, and is virtually always given as inhering in a surface or filling a volume. But, again, one does not need the concept 'surface' or 'volume' in order to see a color inhering in a surface or occupying a volume. Any seen color also has properties, such as hue and saturation, and any sound has properties, such as a timbre and a volume, which are perceived but rarely conceptualized.

It might seem that the advocate of EC can bite some bullets and insist that even the having of ordinary sensations requires concepts, and account for the phenomenal character of experience in terms of something even more raw or unstructured. But this introduces further difficulties. The closer the advocates of the third dogma come to realizing that even what is sensory is categorially structured, the more empty or incoherent their depictions of what is left over when concepts leave the scene are. C. I. Lewis's *Mind and the World Order* provides an excellent example of what happens when a very capable phenomenological description of what is *actually* given in ordinary experience (compromised, at times, by confusing experiences and their objects) meets the third dogma, which informs a rival discussion of what *must* be given. On the one hand, Lewis insists that our experience is always "thick": "We do not perceive patches of color, but trees and houses" (Lewis 1929: 54). Nevertheless, we must recognize a *given* element as an abstract component of thick experience, which Lewis also, in various passages, refers to as 'experience':

The world of experience is not given in experience: it is constructed by thought from the data of sense. This reality which everybody knows reflects the structure of human intelligence as much as it does the nature of the independently given sensory content. (Lewis 1929: 29–30)

Naturally concepts are the means whereby this construction occurs.

So what about the given? On the one hand, Lewis insists that it is a "specious present" containing "no genuine boundaries" that gets broken up by the "activity of an interested mind" (Lewis 1929: 58). On the other hand, Lewis insists that it *does* have boundaries. In a passage which clearly refers to something less than "thick" experiences (and the following remark would be utterly trivial if it concerned them), Lewis writes: "Experience, when it comes, contains within it just those disjunctions which, when they are made explicit by our attention, mark the boundaries of events, 'experiences' and things" (Lewis 1929: 59). The reader hoping for some way of reconciling Lewis's remarks is in no way assisted by what follows:

The interruptions and differences which form the boundaries of events and things are both given *and* constituted by interpretation. That the rug is on the floor or the thunder follows the flash, is as much given as the color of the rug or the loudness of the crash. (Lewis 1929: 59)

But if the given already contains those features which only a moment ago were declared to be "constructed by thought," then such constitution is superfluous. If the given is *already* a rug's being on a floor or a thundering's following a flash, then we do not require any further activity to become aware of them. Perhaps, in the passage above, Lewis is merely drawing our attention to the fact that we encounter rugs being on floors and thunderings following flashes in the same effortless, noninferential fashion that we encounter blobs of color and sound. But according to his own doctrine of the given, even to become aware of such sense qualities as color and loudness requires conceptual interpretation. "There is interpretation involved in calling the *sensum* '*elliptical*' as much as in calling the penny '*round*'" (Lewis 1929: 62). While sense data and ordinary objects, on Lewis's view, fall on the same side of the given/constructed divide, they do not, as the passage above suggests, fall on the given side of it.

Again, on the one hand Lewis assures us that "the given is presentation [*sic*] of something real, in the normal case at least; what is given . . . is this real object" (Lewis 1929: 58). Setting aside Lewis's indecision concerning whether what is given is a presentation of a real thing or the real thing itself, he also holds that the whatness of an object is our construction: "the whatness of this object involves its categorial interpretation; the real object, as known, is a construction put upon this experience of it" (Lewis 1929: 58). Two points are worth noticing here. First, concepts are again invoked to perform work that is already achieved without their assistance, namely getting us to the "real object." If the experience was initially of *it*, then *it* would not require any constructing at all, and neither would the experience of it. Second, if the whatness of a particular object "involves" its categorial interpretation, in the sense in which Lewis evidently means it, then the object simply would not be *what it is* apart from that categorial interpretation. So *that* could not be the object which is given. The idea that the given is identical with any real object rests on the coherence of the following thought: we don't create the objects that are given to us, we are merely responsible for *what they are*. And that is not coherent. If we are responsible for what something is, then we are responsible for *it*; "objects cannot depend on us for their *Sosein* unless they also depend on us for their *Sein*" (Van Cleve 1999: 37).

Perhaps this is why Lewis later denies the identity of the real and the given: "The real . . . is not the given as such, but the given categorially interpreted" (Lewis 1929: 197). The given as such, unlike the real, is "ineffable, always" (Lewis 1929: 53). "[W]e cannot describe any particular given as such, because in describing it, in whatever fashion, we qualify it by bringing it under some category or other, select from it, emphasize aspects of it, and relate it in particular and unavoidable ways" (Lewis 1929: 52). It should come as no surprise that we can't say what the given as such is, because for it to *be* something would amount to it's being thus-and-so. But if it is thus-and-so, then any possible consciousness of it would, on this view, require concepts, which would disqualify it from being given. If, however, nothing can be said about it, even in principle, then nothing true can be said of it. And if nothing true can be said of it, then nothing is true of it. And if nothing is true of it, then it is nothing. The difference between something with no whatness and nothing is exactly nothing.

This is not meant to be a purely internal criticism of Lewis's position. Rather, his position is founded on two genuine insights. The first is that in "thick" experience we confront a world of physical objects and states of affairs. The second is that this achievement is no less basic than becoming aware of sensations or sense data. If, therefore, we have reasons to think that concepts are necessary for the former, we have reasons to think they are necessary for the latter. That the given is a fiction, then, should lead us to conclude either that (1) since concepts are not necessary for having sensations, they are not necessary for perception either, or that (2) there is no "given," and concepts characterize consciousness all the way down.

Pursuing the latter option – rejecting the scheme/content distinction, and particularly the (non-categorial) "content" side of it – might seem to help the defender of experiential conceptualism. If nothing could be present to consciousness without concepts, then surely EC is correct. But this move is also a strike against EC. First, the claim that perceiving *just is* a matter of conceiving, judging, or anything along those lines, if not developed properly, deprives us of the distinction between merely thinking or conceiving and perception. Feeling a pain is not judging or thinking about a pain, and the experience of a color is not a thought about a color. Second, many versions of EC borrow whatever plausibility they have from whatever plausibility the myth of the *bare* given lacks. The more we exaggerate the rawness of experience without concepts, the more compelling is the idea that concepts *must* be at work in producing the sorts of experiences we actually enjoy. On the other hand, the more we exaggerate the rawness of experience without concepts, the more implausible it becomes to think that there is anything like the bare given. And that undermines the initial reason for endorsing EC. The myth of the bare given and experiential conceptualism are two sides of the same dialectical coin. Rejecting the former should not lead us into the arms of the latter; rather, it should force us to reconsider the whole battery of assumptions upon which this way of thinking about perception depends.

Merleau-Ponty memorably said that for intellectualism "judgement is everywhere where pure sensation is not – that is, absolutely everywhere" (Merleau-Ponty 1962: 39). If one's thinking starts with a theory-driven and never satisfactorily clarified distinction between raw givens and the activity of cooking them with concepts, EC is liable to appear inevitable. But why should our thinking start there? If, instead, our thinking about perception starts from the phenomenologically discoverable distinction between merely thinking about an object emptily and having it present in the flesh, we will discover no good evidence that concepts are necessary or sufficient to perceive all categorially structured objects. They certainly aren't sufficient. Thinking that my car is gray is not sufficient for perceiving that it is. Even if we take the perception of such founded entities as relations and states of affairs to consist in adding certain thought-components to the perceptual experience of more basic objects, it is not sufficient to perceive those founded entities. I can see a floor, and I can see the property brown, but synthesizing the contents directed towards the two in thought will not add up to a perception that the floor is brown. I might see a white floor and a brown table and perform just the same judgmental synthesis. Adding the conceptual component 'is to the left of' to my perceptual experience will not add up to a perception that A is to the left of B, even when I perceive both A and B, since, after all, A might be to the right of, or on top of, B, and appear like that. A's being to the left of B is something that *itself* appears perceptually, and cannot be reduced to seeing A, seeing B, and thinking of the relation between them.

Adding concepts to perception doesn't seem necessary for such entities to perceptually appear either. When I think that the floor is brown, when in fact it perceptually appears white, the reason that the content of my thought is inconsistent with that of my experience is that the experience presents, not just a floor and the color white, but the *floor's being white*. And the reason I come to judge that the floor is white is because I have already perceived the floor's being white. I do not see the floor and see its color and then glue them together in thought. In seeing its color, I see it as belonging to the floor. And in seeing the floor, I see it, in part, in virtue of seeing its color. The experience *already* presents it as white, and its doing so is what *explains* the fact that I think it to be white. The massive phenomenological differences between empty thought and intuition are apparent not only when we contrast merely thinking of the floor and seeing it, or merely thinking of the color white and seeing it. They are equally dramatic when we contrast thinking that the floor is white and seeing the whiteness *of the floor*. The intimate unity between the two is already there in experience itself – if anything, the unity is more intimate than it is in conceptual representation. When, moreover, I articulate this unity in thought while looking at the white floor, nothing appears different perceptually. I don't *then* become conscious of the floor's being white, but become thoughtfully conscious of what I was already perceptually conscious.

These points are immediately relevant to another argument for the premise that categorially structured objects can only be perceived with the assistance of concepts, this time coming from Husserl's theory of categorial intuition. This theory is spelled out in the context of Husserl's presentation of his theory of fulfillment, which will be the subject of Chapter 7. Briefly, fulfillment occurs when the object one means, thinks about, or conceives is intuitively given as it is meant. I can merely think about my desk. When my desk is given as I think about it, my thought, initially empty, is fulfilled.

Husserl's theory of categorial intuition begins with the following problem: are there parts and forms of perception corresponding to all of the parts and forms of meanings that they fulfill? What, for instance, corresponds in perception to the word 'is' when the proposition expressed by the sentence "This paper is white" is fulfilled? Let us suppose that there is a parallelism between the contents of fulfilling and fulfilled acts, as "talk of 'expression' suggests" (*LI* 6, §40: 774). In that case, the statement does not express "a mere act of seeing" (*LI* 6, §40: 776). As Husserl puts it, "I can see colour, but not *being*-coloured. I can feel smoothness, but not *being*-smooth. I can hear a sound, but not that something *is* sounding" (*LI* 6, §43: 780). And yet, Husserl insists, things like states of affairs *can* be intuitively given, and when this happens, "The object with these categorial forms is not merely referred to, as in the case where meanings function purely symbolically, but it is set before our very eyes in just these forms" (*LI* 6, §45: 785). There must, then, be "an act which renders identical services to the categorial elements of meaning that merely sensuous perception renders to the material elements" (*LI* 6, §45: 785).

Husserl's solution is to claim that objects such as states of affairs can be given, and that the parallelism between the contents of the fulfilling and fulfilled acts can be maintained, provided we distinguish between straight-forward and founded acts of intuition. Sensuous perception is capable of reaching its objects in a "straightforward [*schlichter*] manner" or "at a single act-level" (*LI* 6, §46: 787). In such acts, the object "appears 'in one blow', as soon as our glance falls upon it" (*LI* 6, §47: 788). Categorially complex objects like states of affairs, on the other hand, can only be given in *founded* acts. An act A is founded if, and only if, three conditions are met:

(1) A contains other acts $a_1$, $a_2$, ... $a_n$ as parts;
(2) A could not exist if those part-acts did not;

and, most importantly,

(3) A is intentionally directed upon an object O which is not the object of any of $a_1$, $a_2$, ... $a_n$.

So, for instance, an act directed towards the state of affairs that the apple is red is founded because it contains other acts as parts, specifically those directed towards the apple and its redness; it could not exist if those acts did not exist, and it is intentionally directed upon an object intended by none of the founding acts. Finally – and this is the crucial point – when objects come into view via founded acts, "the sphere of 'sensibility' has been left, and that of 'understanding' entered" (*LI* 6, §47: 792).

Straightforward acts of perception, it bears stressing, are not necessarily simple in structure, nor do they necessarily have ontologically simple objects.[13] Their objects are often physical objects and properties, and even things like melodies and swarms of geese can be straightforwardly perceived. A house, for instance, is a possible object of straightforward perception, even though it has a complex part/whole structure and can, and usually is, perceived in a complex, temporally extended, continuous series of partial perceptions of it. The continuous perception of a house is not, however, a *founded* act, Husserl argues, because no new object comes into view. "We find, instead, that absolutely nothing new is objectively meant in the extended act, but that the same object is continuously meant in it, the very object that the part-percepts, *taken singly*, were already meaning" (*LI* 6, §47: 790).

States of affairs, on the other hand, cannot be given in one blow, but are instead perceived via a process of "explication."[14] First, I perceive the object, W, straightforwardly by means of a perceptual act $A$. Again, both W and $A$ might be complex. My gaze might "move from one part to another ... through the manifolds of sides, aspects, and profiles" (Sokolowski 2000: 89). Nevertheless, these parts and properties are only present "implicitly." Suddenly, in the second stage, one of the properties P catches my attention, and I now perceive it straightforwardly and explicitly – without, however, losing sight of W. How is this possible? Because an intention towards P was already implicitly contained within $A$ itself. Now, however, P is intended by a new, independent act, $a_1$, that sets it in relief. The acts $A$ and $a_1$ enter into a peculiar "synthesis of coincidence" (*EJ* §24b), and it is in virtue of this experienced synthesis *between the acts* that the categorial relation *between their objects* is perceived. I apprehend the state of affairs that *W is P* when, after this second stage, I turn my attention back to W and, retaining the intentions towards P in my intentional grasp, perceive it as belonging to W. The "is" in the proposition 'W is P' is fulfilled by the "mental bond" (*LI* 6, §58: 809) between the two acts, which is interpreted or apperceived as a categorial relation between W and P.

There are several problems with this account. In the first place, objects like houses and books can be perceived in one blow – I open my eyes and thereby see a house – but it is not at all clear that they can be perceived in

---

[13] Compare with Dretske, for whom "simple seeing" is directed towards things like "tables, houses, cats, people, games, sunsets, signals, tracks, shadows, movements, flashes, and specks" (2000b: 98). Sokolowski (2000: 88) writes: "A house is a simple object, but the fact that the house is white is a categorial object." Obviously Sokolowski means by 'simple' something noncategorial, not something that is simple in its part/whole structure.

[14] For discussions, see *LI* 6, §48; *EJ* §24; Sokolowski (1981) and (2000, Ch. 7); Lohmar (2002) and (2006).

categorially unstructured acts. In perceiving a house, I necessarily perceive it as located somewhere relative to my perceiving body. Moreover, I necessarily see some of its parts and properties, and see the house in virtue of seeing those parts and properties. As I move around the house, my perceptual experience of the house changes in virtue of the fact that different parts and properties come into view. Let us suppose, with Husserl, that in a continuous series of perceptions of the house, "absolutely nothing new" is intended in the total act beyond what is intended in each of the partial acts that make it up. This entails that a continuous act $A$, whose partial acts are $a_1$–$a_{20}$, will have precisely the same object(s) as another act $A^*$, whose partial acts are $a_1$–$a_{10}$. But that doesn't seem right. Even though both $A$ and $A^*$ are of the same house, $A$ will reveal *more* of the house than $A^*$. But if it reveals more of the house, that is in virtue of revealing more of its parts and features. Furthermore, it will reveal those parts and features as parts and features of the house, otherwise perceiving them would not count as perceiving more of the house.

That the "straightforward" perception of a physical object reveals more than just the object, but the object as a constituent of various states of affairs and relations, also becomes clear when we realize that any continuous series of perceptual experiences of an object can be harmonious or disharmonious. Suppose I perceive Timmy. His face looks gray and wrinkled. I walk behind him, and when I see his face again, it appears tan and smooth. I blink, and it looks gray and wrinkled again. Whether I realize it or not, this is a disharmonious perceptual series. But if the object of the perception were, simply, Timmy, then it would not be. If each of the partial acts making up my perception of Timmy has, as its content, 'Timmy', then no conflict would be possible. A series of 'Timmy' contents ('Timmy$_1$', 'Timmy$_2$', ... 'Timmy$_n$'), each of whose members means exactly what the others do, cannot be disharmonious.[15] Conflict, and the consciousness of conflict, can only emerge when states of affairs, and the consciousness of them, emerge. A perception of Timmy cannot conflict with another unless the two present Timmy as having incompatible properties. And a perception of smoothness cannot conflict with a perception of wrinkledness unless the properties are perceived as inhering in the same thing – as Husserl himself acknowledges (*LI* 6, §11: 702).

As for the theory of explication, I think it is clear that this isn't how states of affairs always make their appearance. Rather, they too are given in a single glance. An eight-foot-tall man walking by attracts my attention instantly.

---

[15] Also see Tugendhat (1967: 59–63).

But he doesn't attract my attention in virtue of being him. He attracts my attention in virtue of being eight feet tall. And it is not just the property of being eight feet tall that attracts me. It is the fact that *that man* is eight feet tall. States of affairs are given in one blow all the time, and it's a good thing that they are, since perception needs to provide us with reasons for acting, and mere objects like tigers and Timmy are not reasons. You do not run away because *that tiger*, but because that tiger is over there, looking at you, stalking you, leaping at you. You do not hold out your hand because *Timmy*, but because Timmy is facing you from a close distance, smiling, greeting you, moving his hand to meet yours. This all happens, and often must happen, very quickly – "in one blow," to the extent that one can make plain phenomenological sense of that notion.

Finally, Husserl's demand for a parallelism between the fulfilling and fulfilled acts stems from his occasional contention that in fulfillment, the two acts must have the same matters or contents. The full evaluation of that point must wait until later when, in Chapter 4, I argue that no perceptual act could possibly have the same content as a conceptual act. But to appreciate how misplaced is the demand that there be a mirror-like correspondence between the contents of a thought and those of an intuition, consider the following case. A picture or painting, while quite different, obviously, from a perceptual experience, can also fulfill a proposition insofar as it can *illustrate* or *show* the state of affairs that the proposition represents. You can paint a picture – many, in fact – that illustrates the fact that an apple is red.

"But how," you might ask, "could I do that? I can paint an apple. And I can paint the color red. But I cannot paint the 'is'."[16] This plainly rests on a misconception. If you paint an apple, and you put the color red in the right place on the canvas, you will *thereby* have produced a painting that illustrates that the apple is red. No further work is necessary. (And you will not have illustrated it if you draw a grayscale apple, a red patch beside it, and the word 'is' in between them.) The same point holds for perception. If I perceive a red apple, if the redness is seen to be where the apple is, to move when the apple moves, to disappear and reappear when the apple does, then I see that it is the *apple*, not some other thing, that is red, and that it is *red* as opposed to blue, gray, or transparent. A very rudimentary experience of a red apple already furnishes the intuitive material necessary to fulfill the thought that the apple is red (and many other thoughts). What

---

[16] Compare Husserl: "I can paint A and I can paint B, and I can paint them both on the same canvas: I cannot, however, paint the both, nor paint the A and the B" (*LI* 6, §51: 798).

will prevent the thought from being fulfilled is if one does not possess the relevant conceptual abilities. But the intuitive experience is not, despite Husserl's lack of clarity on this point, an act of *fulfillment*, and the conditions for the possibility of the latter are much more demanding than those of the former (see section 7.1). And what about the claim that you can paint (or see) a color, but not being-colored? The response is that painting or seeing a color just is, already, painting or seeing something as colored. The "being red" of the apple *just is* the distinctive way that redness and the apple belong together, a way that is made manifest in perception. Absolutely nothing at the level of perception needs to change when we thoughtfully articulate propositions that are fulfilled by it.

Finally, even if Husserl's entire account of the distinction between straightforward and founded acts were correct, nothing in that account entails that founded acts have any *conceptual* content. This certainly isn't entailed by the fact that explication is an active process taking place under the coordinating watch of the "ego," since perception can be that. The (vague) distinction between active and passive processes has, as far as I can see, precisely nothing to do with the distinction between perception and conception. Even if a given activity, such as perceptual explication, is performed in the service of some conceptually represented goal – such as the acquisition of knowledge – it does not follow that it itself is conceptual in nature. Walking across a room is also often performed in the service of a conceptually represented goal, but walking isn't itself a conceptual activity. Furthermore, as Husserl himself is fully aware, we can distinguish between the mere thought of a state of affairs and the intuition of that state of affairs, and we cannot explain the intuition of a state of affairs in terms of the perception of some of its objects and the mere thought of their predicative and relational connections (see Willard 1984: 235). Even the "is" in the state of affairs that the house is blue is intuitively presented, according to Husserl, and not merely thought of. So, while Husserl is right that we can perceive categorially structured objects such as states of affairs, this does not entail that such acts have conceptual content.

## 2.5 THE ARGUMENT FROM PERCEPTUAL IDENTIFICATION

Another reason to endorse EC, closely related to those already discussed, is the fact that there is both too much and too little that is strictly perceived, at any time, to present ordinary objects to us: too much because every individual appears in a field of co-given objects, and too little because any physical object always has more to it than what is strictly presented perceptually. Without exercising some sortal concepts, concepts that classify objects into kinds and specify their identity conditions, or at least specify properties that distinguish them from everything else, a perceptual experience would not home in on any particular object.

One reason for thinking so stems from certain plausible claims about what is required for an utterance involving a demonstrative to refer to or single out a determinate object. Suppose someone points in the direction of a river and says "That is beautiful." What makes it the case that he is pointing and referring to the *river*, something that remains identical over time despite never consisting of the same constituents over time, rather than a momentary object like a river-stage or the water molecules then before him? What makes it the case that he is referring to the river rather than some spatial segment of the river? Merely pointing, as Quine points out, is ambiguous with respect to the temporal and spatial extent of the demonstrated object. And this sort of ambiguity "is commonly resolved by accompanying the pointing with such words as 'this river'" (Quine 1961: 67). But, Quine reminds us, "here we have moved beyond pure ostension and have assumed conceptualization." Going beyond Quine, we can then argue that there is a tight connection between perception and demonstrative reference: if you perceive an object, then you should be able to refer to it demonstratively.[17] But in order to refer to it demonstratively, one must apply some concept to it. Otherwise, one would not distinguish it from the other candidate items occupying the same region of space–time. It follows, therefore, that in order to perceive an object, one must apply some sortal concept to it.

The argument above, if sound, establishes what Campbell calls the "Delineation Thesis," according to which "Conscious attention to an object has to be focused by the use of a sortal concept which delineates the boundaries of the object to which you are attending" (Campbell 2002: 69). The considerations presented against the view that possessing sortal concepts is necessary for perceiving an object in the previous sections strongly suggest that there must be something wrong with this argument, and there is. While it is true that the use of a bare demonstrative is often ambiguous to a speaker's interlocutors, it does not follow that it is ambiguous to the speaker using it. Just because I cannot figure out which object

---

[17] Campbell (2002: 69) writes that "According to Quine, the involvement of a sortal concept is needed for there to be a determinate answer to the question: 'To which object is the subject consciously attending?'" Quine, however, merely says that such ambiguity is "commonly resolved" by the aid of a sortal predicate (Quine 1961: 68).

someone has in mind in pointing and uttering 'this', it doesn't follow that he himself doesn't know. For instance, someone might have forgotten the name of the kind of thing to which he is referring. This would render his remarks ambiguous to me. But in a bid to enlighten me, he might also try to recall the name of the thing in question, and trying to figure out the name of the thing one perceives and refers to can only occur when one already perceives and refers to it.

This response to the argument is only aimed at dispelling whatever behavioristic assumptions might underlie it. The problem with the argument, however, is that it relies heavily on those behavioristic assumptions. It requires that we assimilate demonstratively referring to something in thought and unambiguously expressing those demonstrative thoughts to others. In order to establish that the subject is not thinking of something definite without the assistance of a sortal, we must suppose that his own pointing gestures are ambiguous *to him*. Otherwise we would not have a non-behavioristic argument based on the ambiguity of bare demonstratives and pointings. And this might, at first blush, appear intelligible, but only if we adopt a third-person point of view and read back our own puzzlement into the mind of the speaker himself. We suppose, first, that *we* perceive a whole lot of things, that the subject attempts to refer to one of those things by means of a pointing gesture and a bare demonstrative, and that he fails to communicate his thoughts because it is unclear to us what kind of thing he is referring to. Then, from our inability to tell what he has in mind, we conclude that he doesn't have anything in mind; his inability to "refer" (linguistically) to the object via unambiguous language is taken to indicate that he himself is unable to "refer" (intentionally or mentally) to the object. But our inability to discern which of a number of co-given candidates the person means does not entail that there is a corresponding inability on his part.

When, furthermore, we try to correct the argument by taking up the first-person point of view, we find ourselves presupposing what the argument aims to refute. Let us take seriously the idea that S could not refer to some object O by means of the demonstrative 'this' without a sortal concept because there are too many objects that S co-perceives with O. This is incoherent; it amounts to the claim that S can't perceive O without classifying O because he perceives too many other things in addition to O. But if a whole lot of objects are perceived along with O, then O, along with all of those other objects, is perceived, which is just what the argument alleges cannot be the case. We cannot coherently suppose that the subject perceives a whole lot of things, attempts to refer to one of them demonstratively, but, for want of a sortal concept, does not perceive it or refer to it. And if we suppose that S is constituted in such a way that he is not conscious of more than one of the objective candidates for ostension, then we abandon our grounds for saying that his ostensive reference is ambiguous to him. It doesn't matter how many other objective candidates there are if the subject himself is utterly oblivious to all but one of them.

Finally, we are certainly owed some explanation of how, exactly, a concept helps you see something that is not already perceptually differentiated from its surrounding environment. I have the concepts of chameleons, ninjas, and fan blades. But that doesn't in any way help me see a chameleon or a ninja that is camouflaged against a background or a fan blade that is moving rapidly. If an object is not already perceptually differentiated from its environment, the addition of concepts will not enable one to perceive it. But if it is already differentiated, then it is perceived.

## 2.6 THE ARGUMENT FROM HORIZONS

In section 2.3 I suggested that the reason why possession of a concept can affect the way something perceptually appears is that anyone who has mastered a concept is also in a position to carry out intentional acts with horizonal contents, which anticipate how an object will perceptually appear from various perspectives. But there is good reason to think that, far from constituting an alternative, anti-conceptualist explanation for this and other phenomena, it is a concession to EC.[18] The argument is that one's perception of any physical object must, for reasons already discussed, be inadequate, and must in some way be experienced as such. It must have a sort of content that is not strictly intuitive – a horizon of empty intentional contents that point to unperceived sides and features of the object and prescribe what would and would not be compatible with the experience now. And, finally, such empty contents must be conceptual contents.

It might be thought that this argument suffers from the same defect as the previous one, namely that in setting up the problem of how some object O could be seen without the use of concepts, it presupposes that O can be seen

---

[18] Noë (2004, Ch. 6) argues that sensorimotor knowledge, which is roughly what is involved in carrying out acts with certain intentional horizons, is conceptual. And Sean Kelly (2004b: 80) has argued that "On Husserl's account, these [hidden] features are completely absent from the sensuous aspects of my experience. Rather, I *know* or *believe* or *hypothesize* or *expect* that the object has hidden features, but I do not, properly speaking, *see* it as such." For two excellent rebuttals of this way of understanding Husserl's position, see Dahlstrom (2007) and Yoshimi (2009). This issue is pursued further in section 5.3.

without the use of concepts. But this is a mistake. The most it presupposes is that certain of O's features, parts, sides, or profiles can be perceived. And while this does mean that the argument cannot establish that concepts are necessary for all forms of perceptual awareness, it might establish that they are required for perceiving objects of certain types, including ordinary objects like trees and houses, shapes, colors, sounds, and so forth. Perceiving some of O's parts and features is necessary for perceiving O, but it is not sufficient. One does not perceive a city by perceiving a square foot of one of its sidewalks. Nor does one perceive a cat if one takes its facing side to be an entity in itself, and every other side of the cat as some new object.

To see why the argument from horizons does not presuppose that we can see ordinary objects without the use of concepts, consider, for instance, Hume's description of what happens when we walk towards a table, or Russell's description of what we see as we walk around one.[19] We see, according to them, a number of different objects, with different shapes and sizes. In other words, they provide a description of experience that would be true if perceptual consciousness did not harbor empty intentions to unseen parts and sides of the object. But to see a number of different objects, with different properties, is precisely not to see the table. In order to perceive the table, one must not only strictly see some of its sides, features or parts, much less some sense-data that bear causal and/or representational relations to it, but one must be prepared to treat different perceptual states as perceptions of the same thing. If I perceive a table, then in moving around it I will see, and take myself to be seeing, more of the same object, not a bunch of different objects. But if a subject cannot be conscious of a single thing as he walks towards a table, we could not credit him with even possibly making such a discovery. For one could never learn, of something that changes or goes out of existence with the slightest discernable alteration of one's experience, that it is a table – or even a shape or a color – because such a thing could not possibly *be* a table, shape, or color. If that is all one is conscious of, one is not conscious of any physical object – not even the side of one or a property of one.

Of course, one response to the argument from horizons is that we never perceive physical objects. G. E. Moore, for instance, finds it obvious that when we make demonstrative judgments concerning the objects of perception, we are never talking about material objects:

Nobody will suppose, for a moment, that when he judges such things as "This is a sofa," or "This is a tree," he is judging, with regard to the presented object, about

---

[19] See Hume (1955: 161); Russell (1999: 3–4).

which his judgment plainly is, that it is a whole sofa or a whole tree: he can, at most, suppose that he is judging it to be a part of the surface of a sofa or a part of the surface of a tree. (Moore 1965: 10)

Moore's official doctrine is that the only objects that are ever "presented" to us are sense data. But what could be more obvious than the fact that when you say something like "This is a sofa" your judgment is about a sofa and not part of the surface of a sofa or, worse yet, a sense datum corresponding to it? What could be more obvious than that some utterances of "This is a sofa" are *literally* true? Someone can, for instance, also wish to sit on or sell the very same thing that the judgment was about. The judgment "I want to sit on that" does not normally, if ever, indicate a desire to sit on a surface or a sense datum. Evidently Moore finds it obvious that if a thing is to be perceived or "directly apprehended," then every part and property of it must be presented. This, if true, would certainly undermine the argument from horizons, since that argument does not work against a view like this. But do we really want to say that no one has ever seen or touched us, or seen or touched us directly, simply because no one has ever (simultaneously!) seen and touched every part of us? (And would we ever want to be seen or touched if it amounted to that?) And since we generally apprehend fewer properties of an object, at a time, by touch than by sight, the claim that we can touch an object directly without touching every part of it makes it all the more plausible that we could see an object directly without seeing every part of it.

This point, moreover, does not depend upon any claims concerning the metaphysical status of the objects of perception – perhaps they are mind-dependent. But if they are, then they are three-dimensional mind-dependent objects that manifest themselves through profiles, and in that sense transcend any single perceptual act directed upon them. Some can be purchased, sat in, burned down, driven, and dwelt in. Some can move, some can jump, some can spin. The question is not: "Do we only perceive ideas rather than trees, rocks, cats, and so forth?" Rather, it is: "Are trees, rocks, cats, and the other things we do perceive ideas?" To adopt a sort of argument Moore himself made famous, take any argument that you can think of for the proposition that we cannot perceive things like chairs and cats, compare the plausibility of the conjunction of its premises with the plausibility of the proposition that someone, somewhere – possibly you? – has perceived something like a chair or a cat, and see which is greater.

The advocates of sense data and their philosophical predecessors seem to think that direct or immediate perception is always *adequate* to its object, and for that reason mistake the inadequate perception of an ordinary material thing with the adequate perception of something totally different. This claim is rather clearly exploited in arguments from perceptual relativity, which invariably, with its help, move from the premise that two experiences differ to the claim that they have different objects – something which does not follow if perception is inadequate. Consider, for instance, Russell's argument that we do not see the real or intrinsic shape of a rectangular table. We think we can see real shapes because we judge them so easily:

> But, in fact, as we all have to learn if we try to draw, a given thing looks different in shape from every different point of view. If our table is 'really' rectangular, it will look, from almost all points of view, as if it had two acute angles and two obtuse angles. If opposite sides are parallel, they will look as if they converged to a point away from the spectator; if they are of equal length, they will look as if the nearer side were longer . . . But the 'real' shape is not what we see; it is something inferred from what we see. And what we see is constantly changing in shape as we, move about the room; so that here again the senses seem not to give us the truth about the table itself, but only about the appearance of the table. (Russell 1999: 3–4)

But it is Russell – who does not bother telling us why learning to draw is so hard – not the ordinary person, who is mistaken here. The table will *not* look "different in shape" – or size – from different points of view. What changes are the ways it looks, but not the way it looks *to be*. It looks differently, without looking different, and there is no straightforward entailment from the claim that an object looks differently under two conditions to the claim that it looks to be different under those conditions. Russell's view has the additional odd consequence that having things appear to you in one of several possible ways way *prevents* you from (directly) perceiving them. So, if a thing doesn't appear to you, you can't *perceive* it, and if it does, you can't perceive *it*. It is rather like claiming that we can never directly grasp anything, because we have to use our hands, and there are many different ways in which things can be grasped, or that we never directly say anything, because we must use a definite language and express ourselves using one of many possible sentences.

There is a perfectly good explanation as to why the table looks differently without looking intrinsically different that is compatible with our directly perceiving it, namely that (1) we perceive it inadequately, (2) we directly perceive *more* than it (there is no such thing as a perception that is *just* of a table) and (3) we can perceive certain of its relational properties, such as its distance-in-depth. If a table is really rectangular, its opposite sides *won't* appear to be closer together than the near sides. Rather, they will appear to be equally far apart and farther away from me. Railroad tracks don't appear to converge; they appear to be parallel lines receding away from me (see Merleau-Ponty 1962: 304). A tilted coin doesn't appear oblique; it appears round and tilted away from me. The Empire State Building doesn't appear to change size as I approach it; it appears to be increasingly nearer to me. The color of a uniformly colored wall doesn't appear to change as I dim the lights; it appears to be the same color illuminated by increasingly dim lights.

So much, then, for the response that we don't perceive physical objects. It might establish that we can perceive certain sorts of objects without empty intentional horizons, but it does not establish that, without them, we can see the sorts of objects we do in fact see. But from the fact that perceptual acts directed upon physical objects and properties must have empty contents pointing beyond the range of the strictly intuitive contents, must we conclude that those contents are conceptual? This is a very difficult question, and unfortunately the answer will have to await further investigations. In its favor is the fact that they are empty; they have no phenomenal or sensuous character. On the other hand, horizonal contents are phenomenologically nothing like judgments or sortal concepts, as I have already argued. Whatever version of EC is supported by this argument, then it is not the "high conceptualism" (A. D. Smith 2002: 101) that is often defended – at best, we would have a sort of low conceptualism defended by Noë (2004, Chapter 6). And because horizonal contents are always shifting with changes in points of view on an object in a way that general concepts do not, horizonal contents lack a certain kind of independence from the specific intuitive character of an experience to qualify as obviously conceptual. In section 5.3 I will argue that they are not.


## 2.7 CONCLUSION

Of the arguments considered for experiential conceptualism, none succeeds in establishing the strong version, and only the argument from horizons comes close to establishing the weak version. However, while at least some of the considerations in this chapter cast doubt on experiential conceptualism, we are still a long way off from a refutation of the view, and nowhere near establishing that experiences have a distinctive, nonconceptual sort of content. In the next chapter I will examine some of the epistemological reasons for endorsing experiential conceptualism.

CHAPTER 3

# Conceptualism and knowledge

In the previous chapter I examined several phenomenological arguments for experiential conceptualism. This chapter is devoted to evaluating what I take to be the most influential and widely endorsed argument for EC, the epistemological argument. According to the epistemological argument, experiences must have conceptual content, because it is only in virtue of possessing such content that they can justify empirical beliefs. My strategy is to examine two of the most thorough and widely known presentations of the argument, those of John McDowell and Bill Brewer, and conclude that the arguments they present are unsuccessful.[1] In the following chapter, I will present an argument that no conceptualist position such as theirs can adequately explain the epistemological role of perceptual experience in terms of conceptual content.

Donald Davidson argues that since "sensations" are not propositional attitudes, the "relation between a sensation and a belief cannot be logical" (Davidson 2001: 143). Rather, Davidson somehow finds it "obvious" that the relation between sensations and belief must be *causal* – apparently causal and logical relations exhaust the sorts of relations available to us. In this sense, and only in this sense, can sensations be considered the ground of our beliefs. "But," Davidson points out, "a causal explanation of a belief does not show how or why the belief is justified" (*ibid.*). It is not clear whether Davidson identifies perceptual experiences with these sensations which, allegedly, are epistemically worthless, but he does assure us that "nothing

---

[1] Before doing so, however, it is important to note that both Brewer and McDowell have since modified their positions. Brewer (2008) no longer thinks experiences have content at all, and McDowell is now prepared to say that the content of experience is not propositional, but "intuitional." McDowell still thinks perceptual-intuitional content is conceptual, but only in the extremely watered down sense that "every aspect of the content of an intuition is present in a form in which it is already suitable to be the content associated with a discursive capacity" (McDowell 2009: 264). Nevertheless, it is worthwhile spending some time considering their previous positions, since McDowell and Brewer have, respectively, the most influential and the clearest presentations of the view – which is, in many ways, an attractive one.

81

can count as a reason for holding a belief except another belief" (141). And whatever else a perceptual experience is, it is not a belief. In what follows, I will treat this argument as concluding that perceptual experiences merely cause, but do not justify, beliefs.

Every time one encounters an argument whose conclusion so patently defies the obvious, it is wise to ask whether the conjunction of its premises is more plausible than the negation of its conclusion. In this case, I think it is beyond question that the answer is negative. The claims that (1) perceptual states ("sensations") do not have propositional content and (2) if a mental state does not have propositional content, then it cannot justify a belief, are *each* significantly less plausible than the claim that perceptual states justify beliefs – despite (2)'s present status as a framework proposition in many philosophical circles. But if one needs an argument against the view that experiences merely cause, but do not justify, our beliefs, just consider what such a position entails. If it were true, then each of us would have exactly the same *justification* for believing what we do no matter what our experiences were like. If the course of our experience were different, we would of course be caused to have beliefs that differ from the ones we currently have. But as far as the justification of our beliefs is concerned, experience is simply idle – only beliefs matter. So, for instance, if I am currently justified in believing that there is a messy desk in front of me, the fact that I *see* it has no rational bearing on that fact. I would have just the same justification for believing what I now do even if my experience seemed to present me with a saguaro cactus or a firing squad. That doesn't seem quite right.

There are two broad ways of avoiding Davidson's coal pit. The first, anti-conceptualist option is to deny the claim that if a mental state provides epistemic support for a belief, then it must have propositional content. This is the option I will pursue. The second, conceptualist option, pursued by John McDowell and Bill Brewer, is to insist that perceptual states do have conceptual contents after all.

### 3.1 MCDOWELL'S POSITION

I begin with a consideration of McDowell's position as set out originally in his influential *Mind and World*. On his view, in trying to make sense of the possibility of empirical knowledge, we are prone to oscillate between two very unattractive conceptions of the relationship between our thought and the objective world. One view, the myth of the given, attempts to explain our knowledge of the world in terms of nonconceptual sensations. The other, Davidson's coherentism, only recognizes beliefs as givers of reasons.

While coherentism acknowledges that only mental states with propositional content can be reasons, it threatens to depict our thinking as "rationally unconstrained, a frictionless spinning in a void" (McDowell 1994: 42). And while the myth of the given responds to our need for some "external constraint" (9) on our thinking, its shortcoming is that the sorts of "contents" that are supposed to ground our knowledge of the world cannot serve as reasons. "We cannot," McDowell assures us, "really understand the relations in virtue of which a judgement is warranted except as relations within the space of concepts: relations such as implication or probabilification, which hold between potential exercises of conceptual capacities" (7). The myth of the given defies our understanding; according to it, "the space of reasons is made out to be more extensive than the space of concepts" (6). If experiences justify beliefs – and they do – they too must lie within the "space of concepts."

McDowell's position, I will argue, depends on, first, neglecting the distinction between contents and objects and, secondly, a strongly normative conception of epistemic justification according to which a person is justified or unjustified in believing a proposition in much the same way that a person is justified or unjustified in performing a voluntary action. I will discuss each of these in turn.

### 3.1.1. *The space of concepts*

The first reason for rejecting the myth of the given stems from a certain standard conception of what sorts of things could possibly be outside the space of concepts. The thinkers with whom McDowell is engaging – Kant, Sellars, and Davidson being the chief among them – all conceive of perceptual intentionality as involving concepts because the only other possible sorts of experiential contents are blind, raw, or "neutral" sensory contents or stuff.

Once one adopts this conception of the given as a sort of categorially bare "content" awaiting synthesis, interpretation, or articulation by a conceptual scheme, McDowell's philosophical anxieties are unavoidable. This is perhaps why McDowell suggests that the alternative to his view is that the justification of a belief can terminate in "pointing to a bare presence" (McDowell 1994: 39). The myth of the given, then, presents us with the following picture of epistemic justification:

once we have exhausted all the available moves within the space of concepts, all the available moves from one conceptually organized item to another, there is still one more step we can take: namely, pointing to something that is simply received in experience. It can only be pointing, because *ex hypothesi* this last move in a justification comes after we have exhausted the possibilities of tracing grounds from one conceptually organized, and so articulable, item to another. (McDowell 1994: 6)

And that, clearly, will not do.

McDowell presents us with a much more attractive picture: the very same kinds of contents involved in judgment are already present in experience. "*That things are thus and so* is the content of the experience, and it can also be the content of a judgement . . . So it is conceptual content" (McDowell 1994: 26). So we have eliminated bare presences, and abolished any trace of mysteriousness surrounding the relation between experiences and judgments. Not only that, but these *very same items* can be parts of the world: "But *that things are thus and so* is also, if one is not misled, an aspect of that layout of the world: it is how things are" (26). With this picture in place, there is simply no need for anything beyond the "conceptual sphere"; "the conceptual is unbounded; there is nothing outside it" (McDowell 1994: 44).

Despite my strong sympathies with many elements of McDowell's account, it is deeply flawed. It requires that we obscure the distinction between contents and objects of mental acts. As I have already argued in Chapter 1, the proposition that *things are thus and so* cannot be a layout of the (mind-independent) empirical world; it is *about* the world. And the state of affairs, the fact, that *things are thus and so* consists of the things and properties that the proposition refers to, and cannot be a content. They are categorially different things, and McDowell's account requires that they be identical.

This failure to distinguish contents and objects wreaks havoc elsewhere as well. What does not seem to occur to McDowell, and could not occur to someone who has failed to clearly distinguish contents and objects, is that we are directly aware of "conceptually organized" *objects* by means of non-conceptual *contents*. When we characterize something as "conceptually organized," we could mean any of the following:

(1) the item is itself a concept or a whole composed of concepts;
(2) the item (i.e. a mental state) instantiates ("grasps") a concept or a whole composed of concepts;
(3) the item is a conceptualized object, and is therefore the object of a mental state whose contents are conceptually organized in sense (1) or (2); or
(4) the item is an object of the ideal contents of category (1) or possible mental states of category (2).

In what way is, say, falling rain or a cat on a mat "conceptually organized?" Not in senses (1) or (2), and only periodically and accidentally in sense (3). A cat on a mat does not cease to exist, or turn into something else, when it ceases to be conceptualized by someone – which is another way of saying that conceptualizing a cat on a mat does not create, alter, distort, or organize it. To go from being conceptualized to not is a Cambridge change, and absolutely nothing more. The only sense in which it is essentially and always conceptually organized is in sense (4). Everything is conceptually organized in that sense. But this does not entail that everything is conceptually organized in senses (1), (2), or (3). And so, first, there is nothing at all unintelligible about the claim that there are items which are "conceptually organized" which no person has ever conceived of and never will. And, provided that it is intelligible that different sorts of contents could lay hold of the same objects, there is nothing immediately unintelligible about the claim that one could be aware of an item which is conceptually organized, in sense (4), by means of a content or a mental state that is not conceptual in senses (1) or (2).

Unless we can establish a link between the claim that every object of consciousness falls under concepts and the claim that every content of consciousness is conceptual, the alternative to McDowell's conceptualism is not the absurd position that we are perceptually aware of categorially unstructured "bare presences" of empiricist and Kantian mythology. The problem with the myth of the given in *that* form is that *everything* falls under concepts in the broadest sense, since everything is the subject of a possible true affirmative predicative judgment. The problem with such givens, that is, is not just that it is inconceivable how they could be in or about the empirical world, but how they could *be* at all. But a rejection of *this* myth should not be confused with a rejection of the idea that reasons can be things besides conceptual contents, including worldly states of affairs, nor with the idea that such states of affairs are given to us via contents that are not conceptual. Because McDowell does not make the necessary distinctions, he does not offer any argument for the claim that things that *fall under* concepts can only be consciously presented or represented by means of mental states whose contents *are* concepts. And that is not obvious. Things that are visible can be represented without being seen. Why would anyone think it obvious that things that are conceivable can only be represented by being conceived?

### 3.1.2. *Spontaneity and the space of reasons*

Another problem with the myth of the given, according to McDowell, is that instead of showing how we are justified in believing what we do, it merely shows us that we are exculpated. It depicts experience as the upshot of an alien force for whose effects we are not responsible. "But," he writes, "it is one thing to be exempt from blame, on the ground that the position we find ourselves in can be traced ultimately to brute force; it is quite another thing to have a justification" (McDowell 1994: 8). Brute forces do not justify. Experiences are, it is true, passive. But the "capacities at play" in them – their contents – can also be exercised in "active thinking."

McDowell is forthright in claiming that his thinking starts from a broadly Sellarsian view that nothing "given in experience independently of acquired conceptual capacities . . . could stand in a justificatory relation to beliefs or a world view" (McDowell 1998b: 365). As it stands, that is not much of a view, and certainly does not entail any form of experiential conceptualism. *Of course* a subject who lacks concepts will lack the capacity to form beliefs, and *of course* the experiences of such a subject cannot justify anything for him. But that is simply because concepts are necessary ingredients for justified beliefs, a truism that entails nothing about the role of concepts in perceptual experiences. Nevertheless, the idea that all justificatory relations are normative is something that McDowell, in self-conscious agreement with Sellars, endorses.

Sellars, for his part, writes:

In characterizing an episode or state as that of *knowing*, we are not giving an empirical description of that episode or state; we are placing it in the logical space of reasons, of justifying and being able to justify what one says. (Sellars 1997: 76)

Now the idea that epistemic facts can be analyzed without remainder – even "in principle" – into non-epistemic facts . . . is a radical mistake – a mistake of a piece with the so-called "naturalistic fallacy" in ethics. (Sellars 1997: 19)

The "logical space of reasons," in Sellars's view, consists of acts and capacities to justify what one says. And all episodes and states of knowing are "in" that space. So, to characterize S's belief as an instance of knowledge is, minimally, to credit S with certain abilities, namely the ability to convey his reasons for believing it to others. *Being justified* essentially depends on the ability to engage in the *activity of justifying*. Robert Brandom even goes so far as to claim that one is justified *because* one can engage in the activity. As he puts it, a claim

cannot have the status [of being justified] except when it is possible to redeem that claim to authority and epistemic privilege by engaging in the activity of justifying it. This claim of the priority of practice over status is a specific variety of pragmatism, to which Sellars adheres. (in Sellars 1997: 157)

The Sellarsian view, then, entails that whatever justifies a belief must itself be something that could be expressed in the activity of justifying one's beliefs to others. Since all reasons must be expressible in language, and since whatever is expressible in language must be a conceptual content, whatever is a reason must be a conceptual content.

One serious difficulty with this view is that, if it is right, pre- and nonlinguistic creatures cannot know anything. A further difficulty with this view is that it gets things entirely the wrong way round. When one goes about the activity of justifying anything to others – an action, a belief, or what have you – it is part of the very sense of that activity that one's status of being justified or not is an accomplished fact. Just as the judicial practice of determining guilt and innocence presupposes, for its very sense, that the accused has this status independently of the verdict of the court, so the practice of justifying our beliefs, assertions, and actions depends, for its very sense, on the assumption that a person's action, belief, or what have you has its status independently of the verdict of his peers (see Pryor 2000: 535–6).

Another reason McDowell opposes the myth of the given, as one might expect from his and Sellars's normative conception of epistemic justification, stems from his conception of the "space of reasons" as a realm of spontaneity or freedom, whose paradigmatic actualization is judging. Judging, he writes, is that activity "in terms of which we should understand the very idea of conceptual capacities." Furthermore, "judging, making up our minds what to think, is something for which we are, in principle, responsible, something we freely do, as opposed to something that merely happens in our lives" (McDowell 1998a: 434). While not all experiences, and not even all beliefs, are freely chosen, they are all "actualization(s) of a kind, the conceptual, whose paradigmatic mode of actualization is the exercise of freedom that judging is" (*ibid.*).

I confess I am not clear what work the distinction between spontaneity and receptivity is supposed to do in an account of knowledge. But the idea seems to be that being epistemically justified in believing something is a matter of being praiseworthy, or at least not blameworthy, in believing it. Being justified is a matter of having performed one's epistemic duties. And presumably being praiseworthy or blameworthy requires one to have some control over what one believes; one cannot be blamed or praised for what simply happens to one. "[I]t is one thing to be exempt from blame, on the ground that the position we find ourselves in can be traced ultimately to brute force; it is quite another thing to have a justification" (McDowell 1994: 8).

Whether or not this is the actual argument McDowell has in mind, I am quite sure that spontaneity, either actual or potential, is not necessary for a belief or any other mental state to qualify as warranted, justified, or rational, as McDowell clearly believes. I know that the color red is not middle C, and I know this with complete certainty. And this is a rational achievement: having apprehended both the color red and middle C, I can determine that they are not identical. But I was not free to judge that this was so. The moment it occurred to me, I endorsed it. Nor do I have any freedom, or at least none that I can detect, to believe otherwise. Nor do I have such freedom with respect to the majority of empirical beliefs that I form on the basis of perception. McDowell disagrees: "How one's experience represents things to be is not under one's control, but it is up to one whether one accepts the appearance or rejects it" (McDowell 1994: 11). Well, look at your hand in front of your face and ask how free you are to accept or reject "the appearance." You might, it is true, be free to *say* or *assert*, to others or yourself, that you do or do not believe that there is a hand there. But that does not amount to your accepting or believing that it is not there. If you do manage to believe that it is not there, that will be because you have considered evidence that it is not there, not because, keeping your evidence constant, you were able spontaneously to shift from belief to disbelief. Alston expresses the point powerfully:

Can you, at this moment, start to believe that the U.S. is still a colony of Great Britain, just by deciding to do so. (*sic*) If you find it too incredible that you should be sufficiently motivated to try to believe this, suppose that someone offers you $500,000,000 to believe it, and you were much more interested in the money than in believing the truth. Could you do what it takes to get the reward? (Alston 1988: 263)

No, I cannot. I am not *responsible* for the fact that I believe the US is not a colony of Great Britain. Neither, I wager, are you.

Furthermore, it does not even matter whether you have that sort of freedom or not, since this question has absolutely no bearing on whether or not your belief is rational or warranted. I know that the color red is not middle C on the basis of very good evidence, and my belief is a response to my apprehension of that evidence. The demand that I must also have the freedom to believe something that contradicts that evidence, or have the freedom to fail to believe what is evident, is simply incredible. How, exactly, would freedom of that sort – or freedom of *any* sort – have any bearing whatsoever on whether or not my belief is grounded in an apprehension of evidence? It would be rather odd to say: "Yes, I admit that your belief is grounded in your fully conscious apprehension of conclusive evidence in its favor. I also admit that it's true. But since you don't have the freedom to reject the proposition that red is not middle C or withhold your assent to it, you don't *know* it. All you have is an exculpation, not a justification." On the contrary, if I could make up my mind to believe or not believe that the color red is not middle C, the proper conclusion to draw would be that I in all likelihood do not have very strong evidence for it. Davidson's claim that a causal explanation does not show why a belief is justified does not entail that if a belief is caused, it is not justified. It means that a *merely* causal explanation of a certain type – one that, for instance, does not make any reference to the conscious apprehension of evidence – does not show why a belief is justified. But the alternative to being free is not being a piece of clockwork or a thermometer; one might also be conscious of things.

The fact that we can positively evaluate my belief, or the holder of it, does not mean that it was the upshot of anything I did voluntarily. Much of what we evaluate is not free or the result of anything freely done. Nor does the fact that I believe as I ought to believe entail that I have any direct voluntary control over my beliefs in the same way I do over my actions, since the 'ought' in question here might, to borrow Feldman's phrase, be a role-ought, an ought "that result[s] from one's playing a certain role or having a certain position" (Feldman 2004b: 175). Parents ought to take care of their children, scientists ought to make correct predictions, and financial planners ought to make money for their clients. In virtue of playing these roles, they ought to do them well. But this is true even if a given parent, scientist, or financial planner does not have direct voluntary control to do or refrain from doing what they ought to do. And we, who are fated to be believers, ought to do that properly as well. But this does not entail that we *can*.

Furthermore, the fact that my belief is the subject of a true normative proposition does not entail that there is anything normative about the concept or the property of being epistemically justified. Anything whatsoever can be the subject matter of a true normative proposition, provided that it is efficacious in bringing about some end. Good keys open the locks they are designed to open; good carving knives are sharp, well balanced, and durable; good airbags deploy when anything above a threshold acceleration is detected; a good rock is the one that will help me open this coconut. But none of these things do what they do in virtue of being good. They are, rather, good in virtue of doing what they do, and there is nothing normative about their doing what they do. That the notches on a key are able to turn the tumblers in a lock is a matter of physics, not ethics.

Similarly, my belief that red is not middle C is a *good* one, epistemically speaking, and I am epistemically *entitled* to hold it, in virtue of its having some non-normative properties upon which those normative properties supervene. Just what those non-normative properties are is, of course, a matter of much debate, but I think it is plausible that something like *being based upon a clear and distinct perception in a non-demon world* – call this a 'CD' – of the sort I have when I consider that red is not middle C is a sufficient condition for epistemic justification. That my belief is a good one, then, is the consequence of three propositions: (1) it is based on a CD, (2) if a belief is based on a CD, that belief is justified, and (3) if a belief is justified, it is a good one. And there is precisely nothing normative about the conjunction of (1) and (2), and it is in virtue of that, *and that alone*, that my belief has the epistemic status that it does. It is a good belief *because* it has certain epistemic properties; it does not have those properties, even in part, because it is good. To think otherwise is to situate oneself on the wrong side of a Euthyphro dilemma. Even a nihilist about values of all sorts could admit that there is such a thing as knowledge, and that whether someone knows or not is a perfectly objective fact, and yet deny that there is anything good (or bad) about being in such a condition. This makes knowledge completely unlike arguably irreducibly normative conditions and properties like being a virtuous person or acting rightly. A nihilist about values cannot consistently believe that Jones is a good person or that he acted rightly, but he can believe that Jones's belief is justified, and that having justified beliefs is instrumentally efficacious in bringing about knowledge.

Moreover, even if we were free to believe what we wanted, and even if being justified were a matter of being praiseworthy for something that was in one's control, this doesn't come close to entailing that experiences have conceptual content. Any traditional advocate of the given could easily agree with McDowell that though we are not in control over how things appear to us in experience, we are free to accept or reject those appearances. Admitting that doesn't force anyone to admit that experiences and thoughts have the same kinds of contents.

Finally, the connection McDowell draws between the space of concepts, the space of reasons, and our spontaneity requires him to make exactly those distinctions that he was required to neglect when explaining how facts, via experiences, can justify beliefs. As we have seen, McDowell writes that the "relations in virtue of which a judgement is warranted" must "hold between potential exercises of conceptual faculties" (McDowell 1994: 7). He also holds that worldly facts themselves can be reasons. But not all worldly facts are "potential exercise[s] of conceptual capacities." A cat's being on a mat is not a potential exercise of anything. And so the space of concepts, thus construed, seems quite definitely to be bounded – it does not include just anything, but includes actual and potential exercises of conceptual capacities, namely acts of thinking and perceiving, and excludes, among other things, cats on mats.

Again, according to McDowell's account of empirical knowledge discussed in the previous section, a thing's being thus and so belong in the space of reasons. Elsewhere, however, McDowell rejects one conception of the space of reasons, "rampant Platonism," according to which it is an autonomous structure, "autonomous in the sense that it is constituted independently of anything specifically human" (McDowell 1994: 77). And so, if McDowell is right, the space of reasons is *not* constituted independently of anything human. This certainly sounds like a thesis about the nature of concepts and propositions. For whatever else rampant Platonism is, it is not a thesis about the ontological status of empirical objects or states of affairs. Moreover, insofar as McDowell does not want to endorse a version of idealism according to which the empirical world is constituted by us, the space of reasons cannot, in this context, be understood to encompass that world. However, when McDowell insists that something like the fact that things are thus and so can be both a content of a judgment and a layout of the world, we are obligated to understand the space of reasons as encompassing a world that is autonomous of anything specifically human or, in opposition to what I take to be the plain realist intentions of McDowell's theory, to think of the layout of the world as constituted by us.

McDowell's attempt to navigate between the myth of the given and a frictionless coherentism, then, is unsuccessful. The claim that worldly, nonintentional states of affairs can be reasons – which is absolutely critical for his account[2] – requires that McDowell understand the "space of concepts" to be boundless. On the one hand, however, the only interpretation on which it is boundless is that according to which everything falls under concepts, and that claim does not entail that experiences have conceptual *content*, but only that they have conceptualizable *objects*. On the other hand, his conception of the space of reasons as a realm of freedom constituted, at least in part, by us, requires us to understand the "space of concepts" narrowly to include actual and possible mental states or bearers of intentionality. But in that case it is false that the conceptual is unbounded, since

---

[2] As Brandom (2002: 93) points out, "it is essential to McDowell's concept of perceptual experience that the fact that things are thus and so can be the content of a perceptual experience."

not everything is an actual or possible bearer of intentionality. The entrenched ambiguity of the term 'content' helps mask this sleight of hand: depending on the context, it can be taken to mean either a bearer of intentionality or just anything which happens to relate to thought and thinking in any way whatsoever.

The conclusion we ought to draw from this is that what we are supposed to find unintelligible, namely the idea that a judgment could be justified by something other than standing in relations to denizens of the space of reasons in the narrow sense – potential exercises of conceptual capacities – is something that McDowell does find intelligible, and rightly so. He finds it intelligible that a state of affairs, a layout of the world itself, can stand in a reason-giving relation to an act of judgment, in which case he does, after all, endorse the view that the space of reasons extends more widely than the space of concepts. And that, recall, is *exactly* how he characterizes the myth of the given. What obscures the fact that even McDowell subscribes to the myth, thus characterized, is his failure to distinguish the claim that perception has the same kind of objects as thoughts and the claim that perception has the same kind of contents as thoughts.

## 3.2 BREWER'S ACCOUNT

Bill Brewer, whose account of perception is blessedly free of any serious ambiguities surrounding the term 'content', presents the epistemological argument in its clearest form:

(1)  Sense experiential states provide reasons for empirical beliefs.
(2)  Sense experiential states provide reasons for empirical beliefs only if they have conceptual content.
(CC)  Therefore, sense experiential states have conceptual content. (Brewer 2005: 218)

I think it is clear that (1) should be construed as the claim that *some* experiential states provide reasons for beliefs. That *all* do is a much more ambitious claim. In any case, I will assume the more modest reading. Brewer defines a conceptual content as one that "is characterizable only in terms of concepts which the subject himself possesses, and which is of a form which enables it to serve as a premise or the conclusion of a deductive argument, or of an inference of some other kind (e.g. inductive or abductive)" (Brewer 2005: 218; see also Brewer 1999: 149). As it stands, I think this is inadequate. The proposition that Jim is tired and the proposition that Bill is tired share some conceptual content in common. But there is nothing that could serve as a premise or conclusion of an argument that they share in common. Perhaps, then, we should take this as a characterization of all truth-evaluable conceptual contents. Brewer also claims that reasons "must be the subject's *own* reasons, which figure as such *from his point of view*" (Brewer 1999: 151). A proposition that a subject cannot even think, for lack of the appropriate conceptual skills, might be *a* reason for him to believe what he does, but it cannot be *his reason for* believing what he does.

It is the second premise, of course, that I will ultimately reject. Before doing so, however, it should be noted that all that the argument establishes is that sense experiential states have conceptual content, not that they do not have nonconceptual content. That is, at best it establishes WEC. In order to get from (CC) to SEC, we would require the additional premise that if an experience has conceptual content, then it does not also have any other sort of content. But, given the distinction between contents and objects, that is far from evident, and the view that experiences can possess both kinds of content has notable adherents (Peacocke 1992: 90–1).

Returning, then, to the second premise, what reasons are there for supposing it is true? According to Brewer, to give a subject's reason for her believing what she does is "to identify some feature of her situation which makes the relevant judgment or belief appropriate, or intelligible, from the point of view of rationality" (Brewer 2005: 218). And to make her belief rationally intelligible involves "identifying a valid deductive argument, or inference of some other kind, which articulates the source of the rational obligation (or permission) in question" (218). And because we must identify an argument, we must identify premises and conclusion, and therefore must identify the kinds of things that can serve as premises and conclusions, namely propositions. Finally, in order to make someone's beliefs rationally intelligible, the reasons we identify must be the subject's own reasons, which "figure as such *from her point of view*" (Brewer 2005: 219). Merely identifying some reasons or other which *could* be used to support her belief, or to claim that although she does not have reasons, an epistemologist could provide some on her behalf, does not make it rationally intelligible why *she* believes what she does. And so the argument for (2) appears to go something like this:

(i) If S is justified in believing that p, then S's believing that p must be rationally intelligible.

(ii) If S's believing that p is rationally intelligible, then there is some argument we can identify that makes it rationally obligatory or permissible for S to believe that p.

(iii) The premises of any argument must be propositions.

(iv) If S's believing that p is rationally intelligible, then whatever reasons make her believing that p rationally intelligible must be available to her: they must be the *contents* of her mental states.

(v) Therefore, if S is justified in believing that p, then her believing that p must be explained in terms of her being or having been in mental states (possibly background beliefs) whose contents are propositions that logically support p.

And (2) above is just a specification of the general principle enunciated in the conclusion of this argument. Experiences, if they justify beliefs, must have the sort of content that could serve as a premise in an argument for those beliefs.

This argument is flawed for two reasons. The first is that it arguably commits Brewer to an implausibly strong version of epistemic internalism. The second is that the conception of rational intelligibility to which Brewer is committed is far less evident than he supposes it to be, and far less evident than the proposition that perceptual experiences justify beliefs *no matter what kind of content they turn out to have.* What is pre-theoretically obvious is just that perceptual experiences justify beliefs, and that were we to discover that they did not have conceptual content, the rational thing to do would be to abandon Brewer's conception of rational intelligibility rather than the claim that perceptual states justify beliefs.

Beginning with the first point, let me distinguish between two types of internalism about epistemic justification: reasons internalism and state internalism.[3] According to reasons internalism, in order for S's belief to be warranted, S must have some sort of epistemic access to the evidence that supports the *content of her belief* or *what she believes.* According to state internalism, in order for S's belief to be justified, S must have cognitive access to all of the reasons in virtue of which *her belief* – which, as a psychological state belonging uniquely to her, is distinct from what she believes – is justified. These are hugely different views, with hugely different conceptions of what is involved in showing a belief to be rationally intelligible.

Suppose, for instance, that I believe that it has recently rained because I believe that (1) the streets are wet and that (2) if they are wet, then it has recently rained. According to reasons internalism, I must have cognitive access to the propositions on whose basis I justify what I believe, namely (1)

---

[3] The distinctions I draw below are similar to and inspired by those made by Van Cleve (1985). They are also similar to Jack Lyons's distinction between evidential and nonevidential justifiers. See Lyons (2008, §I and 2009, Ch. 2, §I). Also see Hopp (2008b).

and (2). *Those* are the justifying reasons I would cite if called upon to defend the content of my belief, and the reasons that make my belief rationally intelligible. But this is not the *only* way of making my belief rationally intelligible. Another, which it is the task of the epistemologist to discover, is to deduce that my belief B (my state of believing) is justified because (3) B has property φ and (4) if a belief has property φ, it is justified (see Bonjour 1985: 31). Propositions (1) and (2) are not propositions belonging to either psychology or epistemology. Propositions (3) and (4), on the other hand, are: (4) is an epistemic principle, that is, a principle that specifies a sufficient condition for justification, and (3) is a proposition about my mental state of believing, namely that it satisfies the antecedent of (4). State internalism requires me to have access to (3) and (4) as well, since satisfying the antecedent of some true epistemic principle is, trivially, part of what makes my belief justified and rationally intelligible.

Reasons internalism strikes me as an entirely plausible theory, and I will not dispute it. State internalism, however, is false. In the first place, propositions concerning one's own mental states and the epistemic principles under which they fall are not typically among the justifying reasons that support the contents of those mental states – except, obviously, when those mental states' contents are about mental states or epistemic principles. There are a number of reasons why my belief that I have a toothache, when I in fact have one, is justified. Among those reasons are that it exists, that it is the consciousness of something, that it has the precise content it has, that it is brought about by the intuitive consciousness of the very thing that it is about (the toothache), and that it satisfies the antecedent of some true epistemic principle. But none of these is among the justifying reasons that support what I believe. I believe I have a toothache because I am sensuously aware of the toothache – not, to be clear, because I *believe* the proposition that I am sensuously aware of a toothache, but because that proposition is *true*.

I am, furthermore, far more certain that I have a toothache, when I have one, than I am of any epistemic principles. As Alvin Goldman points out, "Even many career-long epistemologists have failed to articulate and appreciate correct epistemic principles" (Goldman 2001: 221), which is evidenced by the fact that epistemologists articulate and appreciate incompatible epistemic principles. But if my belief that I have a toothache essentially depended for its justification on my beliefs concerning epistemic principles, then this would be impossible; the epistemic status of a belief cannot exceed that of some other belief on which it essentially depends. If state internalism is right, however, a person's justification for believing anything essentially depends on his having "cognitive access" to epistemic principles, in which case no belief could have a greater epistemic status than one's beliefs concerning the truth of some epistemic principle. But that is simply false. There are a whole lot of things each of us knows with far greater certainty than any epistemic principle, including, I suspect, a vast array of ordinary, commonsense empirical propositions.

It might be argued that state internalism must be true, since there are many contexts, especially philosophical ones, in which the question "How do you know?" requires that one appeal, not just to the evidence that justifies *what* you believe, but to various epistemically relevant features of one's belief itself. Michael Williams, for instance, acknowledges that a look at how "everyday justification" works makes internalism – the view that "to be justified in holding a belief, we must have 'cognitive access' to its 'justification-makers'" (Williams 2005: 207) – seem implausible. "We do not," he writes, "always require people to have reflected systematically on their abilities at large, or even on their performance in the situation at hand" (207). He continues, however, by saying that "*in the peculiar context of the skeptical challenge*, it is easy to persuade oneself that externalism is not an option" (207). But there is an easy reasons internalist explanation for this, namely that when we answer a skeptic, we are not providing justifying reasons supporting *what we believe*, but providing justifying reasons supporting various epistemic appraisals of our *beliefs* themselves. The skeptic isn't primarily interested in what our evidence is that we have hands; he is interested in why we think we know we have hands, and to answer that, we need to appeal to more than our hands. Answering the skeptic requires that epistemic facts be accessible to us for the simple reason that he shifts the subject matter from ordinary facts to epistemic facts. But it is a mistake to suppose that we do not know those ordinary facts until we can satisfy the skeptic. Appealing to one's hands ("Here is a hand") *is* a perfectly good way of justifying one's belief that one has hands. That it doesn't also justify one's belief that one is justified in believing one has hands makes perfect sense, since the latter has a different subject matter. "What makes you justified in believing *p* is one thing; what makes you justified in believing *you have justification* for believing *p* is something else" (Pryor 2000: 535).

Furthermore, when we try to answer the skeptic, we are not trying to *make it the case* that we know that we have hands, but determine *whether we know* that we have hands, and that sort of inquiry presupposes that there is a fact of the matter concerning whether we know that is prior to and independent of our ability to produce the sort of answer that would satisfy a skeptic. Suppose, for instance, that while looking for my keys, I discover that they are on the table. I now know where they are. Suppose that a skeptic challenges me with the question "How do you know that the keys are on the table?" If this skeptic is anything like those that haunt epistemology books, it will quickly become apparent that he does not care about where my keys are. What he really wants is for me to justify the claim that I *know* where they are. If I did manage to produce an answer, an answer in which I successfully defend some epistemic principle and argue that my belief falls under it as an instance, I would not only *then* know where my keys are, as state internalism predicts. The discussion would not end with me exclaiming "Oh, there are my keys!" I would, rather, discover that I knew, all along, where they were.

While Brewer does not make the distinction between reasons and state internalism, there is some evidence that he endorses the latter. He defines internalism as follows: "Crudely, this is the idea that everything which is involved in a belief's being justified for a person should be cognitively accessible to her" (Brewer 1999: 120). Since one of the factors involved in a belief's being justified is that it satisfies the antecedent of some true epistemic principle, internalism would require a subject to have cognitive access to that fact. We might chalk this consequence up to the crudity of Brewer's formulation of internalism. But in his discussion of what a subject must have access to in order for his perceptual beliefs to be rationally intelligible, there are troubling indications that he endorses some version of state internalism. On his account, the conceptual content of perceptual experience is a distinctive sort of object- and instantiation-dependent demonstrative content, expressible, initially at least, as "That thing (there) is thus" (Brewer 1999: 186). What makes such a content as 'that is thus' distinctive is that any subject who is in a mental state with such a content will understand that his being in that mental state is, in part, due to the fact that *that* actually is *thus*. "Entertaining such contents ... provides him with a reason to endorse them in belief" (Brewer 1999: 217).

That point is, I think, compatible with the denial of state internalism. Brewer, however, insists that just in virtue of being in a mental state whose content is 'that is thus', a subject also "recognizes the relevant content as his apprehension of the facts, his *epistemic openness* to the way things mind-independently are out there" (Brewer 1999: 204). This recognition, moreover, does not stem from some second-order reflection on the nature of those contents; it is a recognition that is available to one just in virtue of entertaining the contents. "Simply in virtue of grasping the content that that φ-thing is thus, he has a reason to believe that that thing is indeed thus; for he necessarily recognizes that his entertaining that content is a response to that thing's actually being thus" (204–5). Finally, this sort of recognition is required in order for a subject's beliefs to be rationally intelligible. Presumably this recognition is itself conceptual in character; Brewer insists, for instance, that a subject's reasons for believing something are "necessarily recognized as such" (Brewer 1999: 165).

The obvious problem is that this account places implausibly strong conditions on knowing, not to mention perceiving (see Byrne 2005: 244–5). All sorts of creatures with no epistemic concepts whatsoever can perceive and believe, and can have beliefs that are related, in rationally intelligible ways, to their perceptual states. Furthermore, Brewer's version of internalism seems phenomenologically inaccurate. When I perceive my bike leaning against the wall, I am not thinking about my mental state, its content, or its epistemic properties. What is present to my mind is my bike, over there, against the wall, not the fact that being in a mental state with the content this one possesses gives me a reason to endorse that content in belief. And yet if I believe that my bike is against the wall as a result of perceiving it there, I have a justified belief, and not (just) in virtue of the fact that experiences of this sort reliably lead to true beliefs about bikes, but because *I am directly conscious of my bike*. It is reason-giving in virtue of being the kind of state it is and in virtue of having the kind of content that it does, not in virtue of my recognition, whether first-order or reflective, that it is and does.

Like most versions of state internalism, then, Brewer's view implausibly entails that only creatures with sophisticated concepts like 'content', 'reason', and so forth can have reasons to believe anything, and that this is what those creatures whose beliefs are justified on the basis of experience – this means us – do when they form rationally intelligible beliefs on the basis of perception. The implausibility of this view is in no way mitigated by insisting that our recognition of the epistemically relevant properties of our mental states is built into the states themselves rather than, as on the second-order accounts Brewer rejects, disclosed by reflective acts trained on them. In either case – and even more obviously on the first-order account that Brewer endorses – it requires that a subject possess a degree of conceptual sophistication that not all knowers, and certainly not all perceivers, do in fact possess. While it is true that there must be some argument that we can identify that makes S's belief that p rationally intelligible, for any S and for any p, it does not follow that this argument must in all cases be accessible to the subject whose belief is in question. In particular, for any belief B, there is some argument we can give whose conclusion is that B is justified, and whose premises include epistemic principles and various claims about B's epistemically relevant properties. But the holder of B need not have any access to any premise of such an argument in order for his belief to be a rational achievement, as premise (iv) maintains. He doesn't need to *recognize* that he is epistemically open to the world; he only has to *be* epistemically open to the world (Van Cleve 1979; Plantinga 1993b). Such a view is compatible with reasons internalism. The state externalist can still insist that justification requires that a subject have some cognitive access to the justifying reasons or evidence that support his belief's content.

We can recast Brewer's argument in such a way that he is only committed to reasons internalism rather than state internalism. That saves premise (iv) from the previous objection. But it generates a new problem. On this reading, premise (ii) asserts that for any belief B, there is some argument consisting of *justifying* reasons or premises in support of B's content. But that seems to rule out the possibility of rationally intelligible epistemically basic beliefs, where a belief is epistemically basic if its justification does not derive from the fact that its content is justified on the basis of the contents of other mental states. And yet Brewer, despite rejecting both classical foundationalism and classical coherentism, maintains that his account has foundationalist elements in it. Entertaining perceptual-demonstrative contents provides a subject with a reason to endorse them in belief, and "In this sense, they constitute basic, non-inferential knowledge" (Brewer 1999: 217). If they are noninferential, however, then there cannot be any justifying reasons from which they are inferred. So, either premise (ii) is false, or Brewer must relinquish his commitment to basic knowledge.

Brewer's account has the resources to avoid this objection. While it is, on this view, true that every belief is rationally intelligible only if it is inferred from the contents of other mental states suitably related to its own, in the case of perceptually based beliefs these epistemically anterior mental states will be perceptual states. And presumably the question of rational intelligibility does not even arise for perceptual states themselves – there is nothing rational or irrational about perceiving what you do. And so, while there are no beliefs that are basic insofar as they do not depend on being related to other *mental states* for their justification, there are beliefs that are basic insofar as they do not depend on being related to other *beliefs* for their justification. What makes it rationally intelligible that I believe that *that is thus* is that I *perceive* that *that is thus*.

This, however, opens up a different, and ultimately deeper, problem for Brewer's account. Suppose that S's believing that p is rationally intelligible because S perceives, or has perceived, that p. Brewer is happy to claim that beliefs and perceptual states can have the very same contents. As he puts it, "Perceptual experiences enable a person to grasp certain perceptual demonstrative contents concerning the empirical world around him; and in doing so they provide reasons for empirical beliefs with those very contents" (Brewer 1999: 205). So, to explain S's *believing* that p in terms of S's *perceiving* that p qualifies as a rationally intelligible explanation. However, to explain why S believes that p in terms of S's *believing* that p is not to make S's belief rationally intelligible; thinking the same proposition twice, for instance, is not a way of justifying it. When we contrast these two cases, what makes the first a rationally intelligible explanation is that *perception* is involved. It is the fact that the justifying mental state is perceptual, rather than that its content is conceptual, that seems to make the critical difference between a rationally intelligible explanation and a complete failure of an explanation.

While this fact alone by no means shows that any of Brewer's premises is false, it does put some pressure on the second premise, according to which making someone's belief rationally intelligible involves identifying premises that logically support its content. It seems to me a much more natural starting point, when considering what makes certain beliefs rationally intelligible, is to cite the fact that the subject holding them has been perceptually conscious of the objects, properties, relations, or states of affairs that make those beliefs true. What is obvious is simply that perception can justify beliefs, *whatever kinds of contents perceptual states turn out to have.* Indeed, given the nature of perception, how fundamentally different it is from belief or judgment, and what a distinctive role it plays in knowledge, I would expect that perceptual states have quite unique intentional contents, and bear correspondingly unique relations to beliefs. And perception does play a special role: in perception, I am able to confirm a belief by consulting the portion of the world that it is about. And many other methods of justification presuppose the epistemic authority of perception. I cannot, for instance, even enter Sellars's space of reasons by engaging in the activity of justifying what I say to others if I cannot discover what my peers think and say, and I can only do that if I have *perceptual* access to the sense-perceptible signs, namely words and sentences, by whose means they express themselves. What makes perceptual experiences epistemically special is something that sets experiences *apart* from beliefs, not some feature they share with them. And this makes me suspect that any theory that attempts to explain the epistemic significance of experiences in terms of features that they have in common with beliefs will thereby fail to come to terms with what makes perceptual experience so unique. If I wonder whether there is writing on the chalkboard in the seminar room, my question is not settled by merely believing that there is. Doing that does not place me within light years of knowing. It is, however, settled, and, in normal contexts settled in a very definitive way, by seeing the chalkboard. There must, therefore, be some feature of the experience that the belief lacks, and this feature, far from being a mere epistemically worthless quale or sensation that attaches to a propositional content the experience shares with the belief, is what distinguishes experience *epistemically*.

I will pursue this thought throughout the following chapters. For now, I am content to point out that Brewer's claims concerning rational intelligibility just do not constitute an obvious starting point for an epistemological investigation into the relationship between perception and belief. It is not as though, upon learning that someone believes that her keys are on the table because she saw them there, we are unsatisfied with the rational intelligibility of her belief until we can rest assured that her perceptual state had conceptual content. Rather, explaining someone's belief in terms of her perceptual consciousness of the objects, properties, events, and states of affairs in virtue of which it is true is a paradigm of rational intelligibility, quite apart from any *further* theory about the precise nature of the contents of perception – apart, even, from any commitments to their having content at all. People find such explanations intelligible, and rightly so, long before they have the dimmest inklings of what philosophers have to say about conceptual contents.

## 3.3 CONCLUSION

None of the arguments considered above comes close to establishing any version of experiential conceptualism. McDowell's account rests largely on a conflation between the "space of concepts" as something that encompasses just everything, and the "space of concepts" as including only concepts. Brewer's argument is far superior, but it rests on a conception of epistemic justification that is not nearly as compelling as Brewer supposes. Nothing I have said establishes that it is false. It is, however, very interesting to note that Brewer and McDowell adopt conceptions of rational intelligibility that are very far from evident. It is, I think, no accident that Davidson's own views concerning the nature of justification, which McDowell and Brewer largely share, go hand in hand with his insistence that any theory according to which we can confront reality so as to compare it with our beliefs about it is "absurd" (Davidson 2001: 137). But what Davidson assures us is absurd just is not so; it happens all the time, as both Brewer and McDowell themselves insist, and when it does happen, we are in one of the best epistemic positions conceivable. I can compare my belief that an apple is red with the apple that is red, and when I do, I know something I would not have known merely by believing that that apple is red. If, moreover, we were to discover that perceptual experiences have a distinctive sort of content that is not *logically* related to the contents of beliefs, we should abandon the Davidsonian model of rational intelligibility without batting an eye. The proposition that experiences justify beliefs is more evident, *by far*, than anything Davidson, or Brewer and McDowell, say about the essential role of conceptual content in rationality and justification.

# CHAPTER 4

# *Against experiential conceptualism*

In the last two chapters I have examined phenomenological and epistemo-logical arguments for experiential conceptualism, and have argued that none of them is decisive, and have also presented a number of consider-ations that strongly speak against the theory. The task of this chapter is to argue that no version of EC can adequately capture either the phenomeno-logical character of perceptual experiences or the reason-giving role that they perform. Perception, I argue, differs in phenomenologically obvious and epistemically relevant ways from the entertaining of any conceptual con-tents, including purely demonstrative ones.

## 4.1 DETACHABLE CONTENTS

Arguably the most fundamental distinction among intentional acts or experiences is the distinction between intuitive and empty or "signitive" acts. It is possible to merely think that there is milk in the refrigerator. One can think that thought while tying one's shoes, shooting hoops, or driving home. It is also possible to perceive that the milk is in the refrigerator. In this case, the object is not merely meant or represented, but presented. Perceptual acts are the paradigmatic sort of intuitive act. In them, the object intended is not thought about or represented. It is present "in person" (*Ideas I* §43: 93) or "in the flesh" (*APS*: 140). "[P]erception is characterized by the fact that in it, as we are wont to express the matter, the object 'itself' appears, and does not merely appear 'in a likeness'" (*LI* 6, §14a: 712). Every other sort of intuitive act that is directed upon a physical object or state of affairs, such as acts of imagination, imagistic memory, and what Husserl calls "presentifications," is quasi-perceptual or quasi-presentative in character. Imaginings aspire to resemble presentations that would occur were the world a certain way; imagistic memories purport to be reenactments of perceptual experiences that in fact have occurred; presentifications or "memories of the present" (*APS*: 112) purport to resemble perceptual experiences that would occur, given the way the world in fact is, were one to situation oneself differently. These modes are secondary or reproductive kinds of intuition (D. W. Smith 1989: 6). They are not "originarily presentative" (*Ideas 1* §136: 327).

Besides having a distinctive phenomenal feel or character, intuitive acts present their objects from a point of view. When I imagine a horse, I do not simply carry out an empty intention with the content 'horse'. Rather, I mentally *picture* a horse. When I do so, the imagined horse must be oriented in some determinate way relative to, and at some distance from, my imagined "body." It will, for instance be facing some direction. It can be imaginatively presented as nearer or closer. The act of imagining, like an act of perceiving, has both strictly intuitive and empty, horizonal intentions directed towards hidden parts and sides of the object. The sensing of sensations might seem like a counterexample, since it is a form of intuitive consciousness that does not present its object from one among a number of possible points of view. But this doesn't mean that sensations are presented from no point of view; they are, rather, presented from the only possible point of view, and therein consists their radical "subjectivity."

What is remarkable about our intentional abilities, however, is that our consciousness is not confined to whatever objects and properties we are perceiving or otherwise intuiting. Thinking about my desk does not require that I perceive it or otherwise imagine it. Nor does empty thought represent its object from a perspective. If someone is just thinking about or conceiving of a horse, it does not follow that he is thinking about it from some perspective or quasi-perspective. He does not need to perceive a horse, nor does he need to form a mental image of one. If someone is merely conceiving of a horse, there is no answer to the question "Which way is it facing?" Furthermore, even if he were imagining or perceiving one, that would have no bearing on the conceptual content of the act he has carried out. His thought that the horse is white does not change its sense if the horse is imagined to be prancing, sleeping, eating oats, flying, or anything else, including changing its color from white to something else. "A comparison of a few casually observed imaginative accompaniments will soon show how vastly they vary while the meanings of words stay constant" (*LI* 1, §17: 299–300). At least some thinking is, as Gareth Evans points out, genuinely *objective* – it doesn't even involve taking up a "God's eye" point of view (Evans 1982: 152).

Husserl's distinction between intuitive and empty acts, and the corresponding ideal contents which they instantiate, is a very helpful way to get a grip on the nature of conceptual content. That Husserl has something like this distinction in mind is clear from the fact that Husserl characterizes the main task of his sixth *Logical Investigation* as clarifying "the relation between 'concept' or 'thought' on the one hand, understood as mere meaning without intuitive fulfillment, and 'corresponding intuition', on the other" (*LI* 6, Introduction: 668). Call all such contents that can be the contents of empty acts "detachable" contents – detachable, that is, from any perceptual or intuitive experience that presents the objects that such contents are about. Our initial question about conceptual content is whether the detachability thesis is true.[1] According to the detachability thesis (DT):

DT: C is a conceptual content only if it is a detachable content, that is, it is possible for C to serve as the content of a mental state M in which the relevant objects, properties, and/or states of affairs that C is about are not perceptually or intuitively present to the subject of M.

It is important to note that DT does not say that it is possible to acquire any conceptual content independently of some experience of it. It might be a necessity, for instance, that all concepts are acquired, directly or indirectly, on the basis of some perceptual or intuitive experience. The important point is that at least some acts can be carried out in which the objects are not perceptually or intuitively present. Furthermore, DT does not make any empirical claims concerning the capacities of any creatures to do this. I think it is obvious that we, in a wide variety of cases, can think without supporting intuitions. Nevertheless, all that DT claims is that conceptual contents have *possible* instances – namely mental states – that are not also perceptual or otherwise intuitive presentations of the objects that they are about.

That a wide range of conceptual contents are detachable is beyond doubt. Obviously a great deal of our thinking is empty; most of what we read and hear about, for instance, is not perceptually or even quasi-perceptually present to us. And that we can entertain contents that are detachable from present experience is a necessary condition for the dissemination and preservation of knowledge. It helps explain, for instance, the fact that one can proceed fairly far in a modern science having consulted, almost exclusively, the words of others rather than the things those words are about. It also helps explain why we are able to establish conclusions about subject matters that have not and perhaps could not be perceived. Both

---

[1] Not to be confused with Alan Millar's very different principle of the same name, according to which experiences with different contents can share the same phenomenal character. See Millar (1991b: 496).

Brewer and McDowell, moreover, seem sometimes to endorse DT. McDowell suggests that a sort of distance from immediate experience is at least a sufficient condition for something's counting as a conceptual capacity. "We can ensure that what we have in view is genuinely recognizable as a conceptual capacity if we insist that the very same capacity to embrace a colour in mind can in principle persist beyond the duration of the experience itself."[2] McDowell and Brewer both suggest that this sort of distance from perceptual experience is a necessary condition of something's counting as a conceptual content as well. Speaking of demonstrative concepts like 'that shade', McDowell writes,

We need to be careful about what sort of conceptual capacity this is. We had better not think it can be exercised only when the instance that it is supposed to enable its possessor to embrace in thought is available for use as a sample in giving linguistic expression to it. That would cast doubt on its being recognizable as a conceptual capacity at all. (McDowell 1994: 57)

On McDowell's view, then, a conceptual capacity must be such that, even if it must be acquired by means of experience, it can be exercised in the perceptual absence of the object that it bears upon. Brewer seems to endorse something similar when, speaking of a demonstrative content 'that$_A$ shade', he writes that "this must be a concept which can be employed to some extent, and however briefly, in the absence of the sample A itself" (Brewer 1999:175). Unfortunately, the conjunction of DT and EC is false.

## 4.2 THE ARGUMENT FROM KNOWLEDGE

Any adequate account of knowledge ought to be able to explain, for any given mental state with an asserting or positing quality – one, that is, which purports to represent how the world is – why it possesses its epistemically relevant properties. In the case of beliefs, we can distinguish two epistemically relevant properties: their epistemic status and their reason-giving force. The epistemic status of a belief is the degree to which it is justified. The reason-giving force of a belief is what explains its ability to confer justification of a given degree on other mental states. Presumably there is a close relation between these two features of a belief. The shakier a given belief is, the less justification it is capable of conferring on others, while knowledge tends to beget knowledge. However, both the

---

[2] McDowell (1994: 57). For a good discussion of this claim, see Kelly (2001a, especially §2).

epistemic status and reason-giving force of a belief depend, quite often, on the epistemic status of other beliefs on which it is based. My belief that the lasagna is about to burn, for instance, is based on my belief that it has been in the oven for about an hour, and that if it is in for over an hour it will burn. It is only in conjunction that those beliefs are able to confer justification on my belief that the lasagna is about to burn. Perceptual states do not have an epistemic status. They are, for reasons having precisely nothing to do with the fact that they are involuntary or receptive, not epistemically justified. But they do have reason-giving force – they make, or can make, an epistemically relevant contribution to the epistemic status of beliefs. Finally, and obviously, the reason-giving force of a mental state is relative to contents. Relative to the proposition "Snow is white," my present experience of my computer has no reason-giving force. Relative to the proposition "There is a computer in front of me," its force is considerable.

What I want to consider is a version of a view according to which the mental states comprising a noetic structure have whatever epistemically relevant properties they have in virtue of, and only in virtue of, their own intentional content, together with the intentional contents of the states to which they bear reason-giving relations. The specific variety of the view I wish to consider holds that the only kinds of reason-giving relations are *inferential* ones. On this view, the only way that one mental state's content can contribute to the epistemic status or reason-giving force of another's is by standing in inferential relations with it. And the only contents that can stand in such relations are conceptual ones. In short, on this view, once we fix all of the conceptual contents of the mental states comprising a noetic structure, together with the relations of epistemic dependence among them, we will have fixed the egocentric or internal epistemic status and reason-giving force of all of those mental states.[3] From this follows the conceptualist principle (CP):

CP: The (egocentric or internal) epistemic status of a subject S's belief B is determined by (i) B's conceptual content and (ii) the conceptual contents of those mental states M', M'', *et al.*, if any, to which its content is inferentially related.

I suspect that this is very close to the doxastic assumption of Pollock and Cruz, the chief difference consisting in the fact that CP allows for the

---

[3] Plantinga (1993a: 72) defines S's noetic structure as "the set of propositions he believes, together with certain epistemic relations that hold among him and them." That is too restricted for our purposes. We need to include (1) the contents of his perceptual states and (2) *all* of the epistemic relations that hold among all of those contents.

epistemic status of a belief to be determined by its relations to mental states other than beliefs.[4]

A few remarks about CP are in order. First, it is perhaps helpful to consider CP in terms of what it rules out. Not only does it rule out the claim that mental states with no propositional content could have any bearing on the epistemic status of a person's beliefs, but it also rules out the claim that mental states with propositional content could affect the epistemic status of beliefs in virtue of whatever other features they might possess, such as nonpropositional or nonconceptual content. "If reasons for belief must themselves be wholly conceptual, then no non-conceptual element there might be in perceptual experience can contribute to one's reasons for one's beliefs" (Heck 2007: 118). In denying that perceptual states have nonconceptual content, Brewer and McDowell both seem committed to this claim. And even if they did admit that perceptual states had nonconceptual content, it would seem to fly in the face of the spirit of their position to maintain, for instance, that while all perceptual states have conceptual content, they play the reason-giving role that they do in virtue of some nonconceptual sort of content. Brewer, for instance, writes, "sense experiential states provide reasons for empirical beliefs *only in virtue of* their appropriate relations with propositions suitably inferentially related to the contents of the belief in question."[5] The "appropriate relations" in question are broadly logical relations. And it is *only* in virtue of a mental state's propositional content that it stands in such relations. "Giving reasons," he writes, "involves identifying certain relevant propositions – those contents which figure as premise and conclusions of inferences explicitly articulating the reasoning involved" (Brewer 2005: 219). And presumably *being* a reason consists in being something that could be a premise or conclusion of an

---

[4] See Pollock and Cruz (1999: 22–3) and Pollock and Oved (2005). The doxastic assumption is "the assumption that justifiability of a cognizer's belief is a function of what beliefs she holds. Nothing but beliefs can enter into the determination of justification" (Pollock and Oved 2005: 310–11). Several near relatives of CP can be found in the literature. Compare E. Sosa's (1995: 344–5) "intellectualist model of justification," according to which "the justification of belief (and psychological states generally) is parasitical on certain logical relations among propositions," Kornblith's (1980: 599) "arguments-on-paper thesis," which states that one is justified in believing that p iff p "appears on the list of propositions that person believes, and either it requires no argument, or a good argument can be given for it which takes as premises certain other propositions on the list," and Pryor's (2005: 189) "premise principle," according to which "The only things that can justify a belief that P are other states that assertively represent propositions, and those propositions have to be ones that *could be used as premises* in an argument for P." None of these thinkers endorses the respective principles.

[5] Brewer (2005: 219), my emphasis. See also Brewer (1999: 167): "a person has a reason to believe that p, say, only in virtue of his being in some mental state suitably related to a proposition which serves as a premise in a valid inference to some other proposition suitably related to p, most likely the proposition that p itself."

inference – at least, that is how Byrne (2005: 238), rightly in my opinion, reads him. McDowell appears to share this commitment. It is a hopeless, albeit seductive, mistake to "extend the scope of justificatory relations outside the conceptual sphere" (McDowell 1994: 7). If this is right, then whatever further properties an experience might have, above and beyond its possession of its conceptual content, must be irrelevant from an epistemic point of view.

Second, I have cast CP in terms of a belief's internal or egocentric epistemic status. If internalism about epistemic warrant is right, then the internal epistemic status of a belief will be identical with its epistemic status. If a certain kind of externalism about warrant is right, namely a form of externalism according to which there is such a thing as believing rationally or with justification, and doing that is not sufficient for justification, then whatever other factors are necessary for warrant cannot be necessary conditions of believing rationally. In this case, we can factor the overall epistemic status of a belief into internal and external factors. CP, on such a view, only measures the former. Finally, if a version of externalism is true according to which we cannot draw such a distinction, CP will be objectionable for reasons other than those I present. In any case, the opponents I have in mind, namely McDowell and Brewer, are internalists about justification. And I agree with them that perception does not confer justification on beliefs just in virtue of reliably producing true ones; it also makes it rational for a subject to hold them.

Third, CP is compatible with both foundationalism and coherentism. Despite the fact that, according to the latter, the epistemic status of a belief is determined by its coherence with other beliefs, and coherence is not a mental state or the content of one, it seems clear on one very natural understanding of coherentism that all of the facts about a belief's coherence relations with others would supervene on its propositional content and the propositional contents of those beliefs to which it is inferentially related. That is, once conditions (i) and (ii) are fixed for every mental state comprising a noetic structure, the coherence relations among those states will thereby also be fixed. As for foundationalism, if both it and CP are true, then there must either be some basic beliefs whose epistemic status is fixed by their conceptual contents alone, or whose epistemic status is fixed by their contents plus their inferential relations to other mental states that do not include beliefs, such as perceptual states.

Now to the argument. If CP is correct, then any two beliefs with the same conceptual content, and whose epistemically prior mental states have identical conceptual contents, must have the same epistemic status.

However, if all conceptual contents are detachable, then this is obviously false. Since detachable contents could also serve as the contents of empty acts, the theory predicts that all of the epistemic work in knowledge could be carried out by empty acts. So, if these were the sorts of conceptual contents present in perception, then we should be able to take a given noetic structure, zap all of the perceptual states, and replace them with mere beliefs with the same conceptual contents that the perceptual states are alleged to have, without thereby affecting the epistemic status of any of the subject's beliefs. But that is absurd. Suppose Jones believes that it has recently rained on the basis of (1) his perception that Beacon Street is wet and (2) his belief that if Beacon Street is wet, then it has recently rained. Now suppose we zap his perception and replace it with a mere belief with the same detachable content: Beacon Street is wet. In doing so, we also effectively annihilate his justification for believing that it has recently rained. But if CP were correct, and if the contents of perception were the same as those of possibly empty intentional states, then we would not have altered his justification in the slightest.

We can put pressure on CP another way by asking: why is basing the belief that p on the perception that p a sound epistemic policy, while basing it on itself is not? If they have the same conceptual content, then what epistemic work can the experience do that the belief cannot? How is basing a belief on a perception different from thinking the same thought twice?

One might respond that an important difference between perceiving an object and merely thinking about it is that in the former case the object is partially causally responsible for your perceiving it. But this isn't the kind of difference that could save the present position. If we suppose that the causal relationship between a perceived object and the perception of it is not part of the content of the experience, then it cannot be a reason by the epistemic conceptualist's lights. And if we suppose, as Searle (1983) does, that the content of the experience itself specifies that there is a causal relationship between its object and the experience – if the content of the experience says that there is an object which is thus and so and is causing this experience of it – then we again fall prey to the previous objection. I can just think, or merely believe, that Beacon Street is wet and that it is causing this experience (I am having a perceptual experience right now) of it. Indeed, I can just think that Beacon Street is wet, that I am *perceiving* it, and that it is causing my perception of it. That is, in fact, exactly what I (and possibly you) just thought.

As this example illustrates, adding conceptual contents that specify what sorts of experiences you are undergoing will also not help CP, provided those contents are detachable. There is a distinction between merely thinking or emptily believing that one is undergoing a perceptual experience and "seeing," whatever exactly that amounts to in this context (and it does amount to something), that one is undergoing a perceptual experience. So, if we suppose that the difference between Jones pre- and post-zap is that in the former, but not the latter, he also entertains a proposition like "I am currently perceiving that Beacon Street is wet" or "It currently perceptually appears to me as though Beacon Street is wet," we can modify the example and contrast a case in which he merely believes – because he has been hypnotized, say – that he is currently perceiving or is being appeared-to from one in which he introspectively "sees" that he is.

Another possible response to the argument comes from Jonathan Kvanvig. Kvanvig proposes that the peculiar epistemic force of perceptual experience can perhaps be accounted for by appealing to its self-representational or reflexive nature. According to this view, "intrinsic to the character of experience is an awareness of the very experience itself in addition to outward awareness of the primary focus of awareness" (Kvanvig 2007: 172). When I have a perceptual experience, I am not only aware of, say, the tree over there. I am aware of myself as the subject of *this very experience* of the tree over there. The experience contains, as Kvanvig puts it, "an essentially indexical awareness of the state itself" (*ibid.*). According to Kvanvig, we can preserve the view that experience has propositional content by claiming that each "conscious experience" is a composite entity, containing both a content R directed towards the focal object of perception, and an indexical content R* that "includes R as a component in virtue of the fact that R* involves an indexical reference to itself that includes R" (Kvanvig 2007: 172). This content R* is propositional, and "involv[es]" R, the subject of the experience, and R*, the total experience. And such a content "implies that an experience involving R is occurring in this very subject in virtue of this very R* experience" (Kvanvig 2007: 173). Undergoing R*, then, is evidence that one is undergoing experience R and that something exists that satisfies R's content.

As for R* itself, it can either serve as the content of a nonperceptual belief (i.e. it is detachable) or it cannot. If it cannot, then we have not addressed the present argument, which is targeted against the conjunction of DT and CP. In any case – and oddly, given that R* is essentially indexical – Kvanvig rejects that option. Let us suppose, then, that R* is detachable. In any case in which R* occurs as the content of a nonperceptual belief, the belief would be "utterly incoherent." "It will," Kvanvig continues, "be a belief to the effect that this very experiencing is occurring in me, and the having of such a belief is a state of utter confusion and incoherence" (Kvanvig 2007: 173) – because, of course, under the proposed conditions the experience would not be occurring. As such, the "propositionalist" is not required to treat this as of any evidential worth.

There are two problems with this account. The first, which arises from the fact that Kvanvig thinks R* can be the content of a mere belief, is that while entertaining R* when R is not in fact occurring is an "obvious absurdity" (Kvanvig 2007: 173), the advocate of CP and DT cannot explain why. We are simply faced with the same problem already encountered: somehow the actual presence of the object – R, in this case – plays an epistemically relevant role in knowledge, but conceptualism, together with DT, entails that this cannot be so. On a conceptualist account all that matters for knowledge is whatever propositions are in my head, and those can be there whether the relevant states of affairs are present or not. Thoughts about the "inner" world are every bit as vulnerable to this argument as thoughts about the "external" one.

The second problem with Kvanvig's proposal is that even if we subscribe to a self-representational theory of consciousness, not only empty thoughts and occurrent beliefs, but acts of desiring, imagining, predicting, hoping, remembering, and so forth also have a self-referential character; the reflexive character of perceptual states is just a special case of the reflexive character of conscious states generally. When I merely think that Moscow is cold, I am aware of myself as merely thinking it. I don't wonder whether I am thinking *that*, as opposed to something else, nor is it an open question whether it is really *me*, as opposed to you, who is thinking it, nor is it unclear whether I am *thinking* it rather than perceiving, imagining, or remembering it. But if self-representation characterizes *all* conscious states, then that feature cannot distinguish a perceptual state whose content is R and a belief whose content is R. Perception is not epistemically special just because it has some feature shared by all conscious states.

My argument against experiential conceptualism has a potentially major weakness, and that is that it assumes that the advocates of the epistemological argument for EC endorse something like the conceptualist principle. While I do think they are probably committed to something like it, it is difficult to anticipate the ingenuity of philosophers. I will, however, consider another suggestion. The core idea underlying CP is that reason-giving relations are *inferential* relations. This, together with the claim that only conceptual contents can stand in inferential relations, entails that only conceptual contents can stand in reason-giving relations, and therefore that only they can confer warrant on the contents of other mental states.

But one might insist that the epistemologically significant properties of mental states do not just depend on their intentional content and their inferential relations to the contents of other mental states, but on some other features as well. James Pryor has suggested that the key to understanding the role of perceptual experiences in generating warrant is their "phenomenal force." I quote him at length:

> In my view, it's not the irresistibility of our perceptual beliefs, nor the nature of our concepts, which explains why our experiences give us the immediate justification they do. Rather, it's the peculiar "phenomenal force" or way our experiences have of presenting propositions to us. Our experience represents propositions in such a way that it "feels as if" we could tell that those propositions are true – and that we're perceiving them to be true – just by virtue of having them so represented ... I think this "feeling" is part of what distinguishes the attitude of experiencing that p from other propositional attitudes, like belief and visual imagination. Beliefs and visual images might come to us irresistibly, without having that kind of "phenomenal force" ... It is difficult to explain what this "phenomenal force" amounts to, but I think that it is an important notion, and that it needs to be part of the story about why our experiences give us the justification they do. (Pryor 2000: 547, n. 37)

This, if true, has important consequences. First, if what distinguishes perception as a way of "presenting propositions" is its phenomenal force, then we can answer the argument against detachable contents above: when we zap Jones's perceptual state and replace it with a belief with the same conceptual content, we also zap its phenomenal force. Second, we can argue that different demonstrative thoughts can differ in their phenomenal force, and that this, again, explains the difference in their reason-giving force.

However, I find the proposal inadequate. First, perceptual experiences don't present us with propositions. Propositions are about things, and the objects presented to us in perception typically are not. More importantly, if this account is to meet the argument against CP, then we must conceive of phenomenal force as some additional feature of a mental state that can vary independently of its intentional content and its inferential relations to the contents of other mental states. But I cannot find any reason to suppose this is so. Let us begin with belief. Suppose the epistemic status of my belief that global warming is occurring is greater at t2 than at t1. What could explain such a change? The answer, naturally, is that the total body of evidence relevant to its truth that I possess has changed. I might have acquired new evidence for it. I might have acquired evidence against a potential defeater of it, where a defeater is any true proposition q which, if added to my evidence, would undermine my justification for believing that p. Or I might have just consciously considered some evidence that I had merely dispositionally possessed. But the idea that my total body of evidence that I have and consider remains constant, and that my belief that global warming is occurring nevertheless changes in epistemic status, sounds hopeless. Of course, it is psychologically possible that I might become more *confident* that p despite the lack of any changes in my evidence. But if so, then the conclusion to draw is that at either t1 or t2 my confidence in p was inappropriate given its epistemic status, not that the belief has acquired, as if by magic, some new epistemically relevant property.

Furthermore, in order to become aware of more evidence for p, I must be or have been in mental states whose contents made me aware of that evidence. The evidence one has for some proposition p cannot change in the interval from t1 to t2 if one is in mental states with precisely the same intentional content from t1 to t2. But if every change in the epistemic status of one's beliefs depends on a change in one's body of evidence, and if every change in one's body of evidence depends on a change in the contents of one's mental states, then every change in the epistemic status of a belief depends on a change in the contents of one's mental states. This isn't to deny that there is such a thing as a peculiar feeling of evidence that some mental states have and others do not. But this feeling of evidence will, if a subject is rational, be a consequence of the fact that there is evidence for its content; it is a response to evidence, not constitutive of it.[6]

The theory is also a failure phenomenologically. The difference between perception and belief is not that perception is accompanied by a peculiarly strong feeling that something is true while belief is not. The difference is that in perception we are confronted with the objects, properties, relations, and states of affairs that are intended by its content, while in (mere) belief we are not. In perception reality is present in the flesh, and in belief it is merely intended. And it deprives us of a perfectly good explanation as to why perceptual states do, and mere beliefs do not, have a distinctive phenomenal force, namely that their contents are so different. This explanation itself seems phenomenologically accurate, moreover. Just as we don't regard something as morally wrong because it incites certain feelings of moral disgust or disapprobation in us, but instead have those feelings because we regard it as morally wrong, so we don't regard a content as

---

[6] "Inner evidence is no accessory feeling, either casually attached, or attached by natural necessity, to certain judgements. It is not the sort of mental character that simply lets itself be attached to any and every judgement of a certain class, i.e. the so-called 'true' judgements, so that the phenomenological content of such a judgement, considered in and for itself, would be the same whether or not it had this character" (*LI*, Prolegomena: 51, 194; also see *Ideas 1* §145). For the best discussion of Husserl's rejection of the feeling theory of evidence, see Heffernan (1997).

evident because we have some peculiar feeling when we entertain it, but instead have the feeling because it is evident. Whatever else might be said against CP, that the epistemic status of a mental state is determined by its intentional content and the contents of those states to which it is related in reason-giving ways expresses a genuine insight.[7] Phenomenal force, construed as something over and above a mental state's own content and its reason-giving relations to the contents of others, seems as epistemically insignificant as the volume of an utterance: more of it might convince, but it shouldn't.

So, to sum up, if the reason-giving force of a perceptual state is explicable in terms of its content, then the content in question cannot be the detachable sort. And if that is true, then either the detachability thesis or the conceptualist principle is false.

## 4.3 THE ARGUMENT FROM INTENTIONALITY

Perhaps we should abandon CP and retain DT by insisting that it is not just the contents of mental states that explain their epistemological properties, but their quality or psychological mode as well: perceptual states differ in quality from mere beliefs. This proposal, however, has limited appeal. First, it seems to me that the most plausible development of this view is along the lines of Pryor's account, but I have already presented reasons why this account should be rejected. Furthermore, even if perception and belief differ in quality, they don't differ in quality alone. Believing differs from doubting, wondering, and desiring in readily apparent ways. The difference between perception and belief, however, seems to lie on a completely different dimension. If anything, they seem to have very similar qualities: both (re)present their objects as actual, and have mind-to-world direction of fit. But they are extremely different phenomenologically.

We don't have to rest content with this vague claim, however. Rather, detachable contents could not possibly be the intentional contents of perceptual experience. First, let us consider strong experiential conceptualism (SEC), according to which the *only* intentional content of perceptual experience is conceptual. If so, then by DT all such contents are detachable. But if perceiving the objects that some conceptual content C is about is not necessary to be in a mental state with C as its content, then being in a mental state with C as its content is not sufficient to be in mental state in which one

---

[7] Heck (2000: 505) regards the claim that "the 'space of reasons' is contained within the sphere of (representational) content" as "near trivial."

perceives those objects, in which case strong experiential conceptualism surely fails to provide an adequate assay of the contents of experience. How could one claim to have distilled the essence of perceptual experiential content by appealing to contents that may or may not be perceptual?

One way, perhaps, is to endorse what A. D. Smith (2002: Chapter 2) calls the "dual component theory" of perceptual experience, according to which perception owes its intentionality to conceptual contents that could equally well serve as the contents of beliefs and judgments, and owes everything else that makes it specifically *perceptual*, such as its qualitative and presentational characters, to intrinsically nonintentional sensations or qualia. Obviously this solution does not help the defender of CP one bit. If sensations and qualia are nonintentional, then they are nonconceptual, since conceptual contents are intrinsically intentional. So, by CP, they must be epistemically epiphenomenal.

More importantly, adopting a dual-component view does not help anyone who wishes to explain various phenomenological features of perception either. Suppose I look out the window and think "Beacon Street is wet." Unbeknownst to me, however, I am looking at Commonwealth Avenue. What is the object of my experience? Well, *one* of the objects of my experience, if we adopt a rather distended conception of 'experience' as just any occurrent mental episode, is Beacon Street; that's what I am thinking about. It is, however, something I am *merely* thinking about. If we were to suppose that the singular concept 'Beacon Street' were part of the content of the *perceptual* experience, then we would be forced to regard the perceptual experience itself as erroneous, perhaps as a hallucination. But this is wrong. It is possible to have a perfectly veridical perception of Commonwealth Avenue and its wetness while mistakenly believing, on the basis of one's perception, that Beacon Street is wet.[8] The error here is not perceptual in character; it is a misidentification. And if it is possible for me to err in identifying the thing I perceive with Beacon Street, then I must have some independent access, through a distinct mode of presentation, to the thing that I am identifying with Beacon Street (also see Smith and McIntyre 1982: 356).

The object of my *perceptual* experience, which is veridical, is Commonwealth Avenue. And that means there must be something about my perceptual state – perhaps its intentional content, perhaps something else – in virtue of which Commonwealth Avenue is present to me. But it is not the singular concept 'Commonwealth Avenue'. For one thing, we can

---

[8] See Dretske (2000b: 97–112) for more examples.

easily suppose that in this scenario I am not even exercising – indeed, do not even possess – that concept while I perceive Commonwealth Avenue. For another, if that were the concept I was exercising, then I would be committed to the proposition that Commonwealth Avenue is Beacon Street. But I would never assent to that. Furthermore, the identity of the thing I am seeing with Commonwealth Avenue is informative, since it is something that I would, in my present mistaken but perfectly coherent state, deny. Finally, nonintentional sensations or qualia cannot themselves explain why my experience is of Commonwealth Avenue, since they cannot be of anything except when they derive their intentionality from some other sort of content.

Let us consider another case. I may veridically perceive a decoy and think "that thing is a duck." We cannot suppose that either the concept 'decoy' or 'duck' is the content of my perceptual experience. It is not the former because I am not even exercising that concept, and because I would never assent to the propositions "that$_A$ is a decoy" and "that$_A$ is a duck" at the same time. And it is not the latter because to suppose so would commit us to the claim that the perceptual experience is nonveridical. But it is not nonveridical. I am not under the impression that the decoy is a duck because it fails to appear to me, nor because it fails to appear to me as it is. Rather, I am under the impression that it is a duck *because* it appears to me, *because* it appears to me as it is, and *because* it actually is, *in those respects that appear*, like a duck. I don't mean to suggest here that the properties of being a duck or a decoy cannot be perceptually presented. They can. Ducks have all kinds of sense-perceptible properties that decoys don't, and a more adequate perceptual experience would disclose them. If I *still* take the decoy to be a duck after examining it, picking it up, and so forth, and if I actually do possess the concept 'duck' and know how to exercise it, then we should conclude that I misperceived. But on the basis of a very inadequate presentation – seeing the decoy in a lake for a few seconds from a considerable distance – the error is intellectual. In the case at hand, I have mistakenly identified the perceived property of being *thus* with the property of being a duck, and entertaining an informative identification requires that one have two distinct modes of presentation of the object(s) identified. The conclusion to draw, then, is that there are no detachable contents that can explain misidentifications of the sort described. But in that case, there are at least some perceptual experiences whose phenomenological, and specifically intentional, character cannot be explained in terms of their having detachable contents alone, or their having such contents plus further characteristics, contents, or properties of a nonintentional sort. Therefore, either SEC or DT is false.

Even weak experiential conceptualism (WEC) fails if DT is true, as the arguments in section 2.3 above suggest. Suppose, to borrow Husserl's example, I see a blackbird flying through the garden. There is no conceptual content C such that, in virtue of perceiving this blackbird, either in general or in the determinate way in which I perceive it, I am entertaining C. On the basis of precisely this perceptual experience, I can entertain the contents "That is black!" or "That is a black bird!" or "There it soars!" or any other number of others (*LI* 6, §4: 680). The perceptual experience remains what it is no matter which detachable contents might accompany it or which judgments I might justify on the basis of it. Perceiving the blackbird at dawn from a distance of twelve feet does not entail that there is any detachable content C such that I entertain it. So detachable contents are not necessary for perception, and no act whose intentionality is determined solely by detachable contents is sufficient for perception, even if we outfit it with nonintentional qualia. In that case, either the conceptualist principle or the detachability thesis must be false.

## 4.4 THE DEMONSTRATIVE THEORY

In the face of the arguments presented above, the obvious move for the defender of epistemic conceptualism is to abandon the detachability thesis. And there are good candidates for nondetachable but conceptual contents, namely *demonstrative* contents. Despite Brewer's own apparent belief that detachability is a necessary condition of a content's being conceptual, he also attempts to describe perceptual experiences in terms of "essentially experiential" object- and instantiation-dependent demonstrative contents, contents that manage to pick out some unique object in a region of space that is perceptually present to the perceiver and is identified by him relative to himself (Brewer 1999: 186–7). Such perceptual demonstrative contents are only expressible, initially at least, as "That thing (there) is thus" (Brewer 1999: 186; also see McDowell, 1998c). Later, through habituation, a thinker will be able to move from such exclusively demonstrative knowledge to "increasingly detached, non-demonstrative, linguistically articulated and categorized perceptual knowledge," for instance that *a* is *F* (Brewer 1999: 244). On pain of endorsing DT, we cannot, as Brewer seems to suggest (1999: 244–5), construe the move from perceptual-demonstrative contents to detached, nondemonstrative contents as a *replacement* of the former with the latter. Rather, to avoid the argument above, we must treat the perceptual-demonstratives as not only essentially experiential, but also regard experiences as essentially containing perceptual-demonstrative contents. In a later article, Brewer makes just such a move: "On the conceptualist view, experience of a color sample, R, *just is* a matter of entertaining a content in which the demonstrative concept 'that$_R$ shade' figures as a constituent" (Brewer 2005: 222, my emphasis). Presumably that point generalizes.

I will henceforth refer to this as the 'demonstrative theory'. It is easy to see how, if this is right, Brewer's position answers both arguments above. The argument from intentionality is taken care of in one stroke: if perceiving just is entertaining a demonstrative content, then they are one rather than two, and there is no way we can independently vary them. As for the argument from knowledge, Jones's perceptual belief essentially involves identifying a publicly specified object, Beacon Street, with a perspectivally specified object, *that* (street), and a publicly specified property, being wet, with a perspectivally specified property, being *thus*.[9] Jones's act of perceptually taking in that Beacon Street is wet, then, also involves thinking that *that* Oak Street and that x *is thus* iff x is wet. Now since the demonstratives occurring in these thoughts are essentially experiential, Jones post-zap is not in a position even to entertain such thoughts. And so we have discovered a mental state whose intentional content both provides Jones with a mode of access to the world that is independent of any detachable contents, and also serves as an epistemically prior mental state in the pre-zap, but not the post-zap, scenario.

### 4.5 SOME ARGUMENTS AGAINST THE DEMONSTRATIVE THEORY

Despite its apparent ability to answer the arguments above, I am convinced that the demonstrative theory is in bad shape. What follows are some reasons why.

### *4.5.1. The argument from empty demonstrative thoughts*

First, producing and understanding a demonstrative thought about an object or property cannot be the same thing as perceiving it, since it is not even sufficient for perceiving it. As Husserl puts it, "essentially occasional expressions like 'this' can often be used and understood without an appropriate intuitive foundation" (*LI* 6, 5: 684). Suppose I perceive my desk

---

[9] For more on the distinction between public and perspectival cross-identification, see Hintikka (1975: Chs. 3–4) and (1989), and Hintikka and Symons (2007).

and think "That thing is brown." I can continue to think this thought, and mean precisely the same thing by it, if I close my eyes for five seconds or turn my back to it and point at it over my shoulder. Again, if a friend and I admire a car on the street below from my office window, I can still understand his utterance of "That thing must have cost a fortune" even after I have returned to my seat away from the window. This point is even more obvious in the case of spatial demonstratives. One can refer to 'back there' without turning around to look at the demonstrated location. "I passed the house – it's back there" is a typical sort of thing to say while driving, and does not require one to endanger one's passengers by looking at the demonstrated location. If any demonstratives are essentially experiential, then they behave unlike any of the demonstrative contents that are linguistically expressed and communicated.

### 4.5.2. *The argument from the coarseness of demonstrative content*

The second argument against the demonstrative theory is that even if it were necessary that one have an occurrent perceptual experience of an object to entertain demonstrative contents that are about it, the precise intuitive content of that experience is not determined by one's entertaining any conceptual content. That is, indexicals and demonstratives whose referents are physical objects are detachable from *specific* intuitive contents. In the case of indexicals like 'I', 'here', and 'now', their independence from any specific intuitive content is nearly as complete as those of detachable contents. One's 'here' thoughts manage to refer to the place one is at no matter what the character of the place one is at, and no matter how it manifests itself to one in perception (though it arguably does have to manifest itself somehow). Keeping my location constant and changing the way it manifests itself to me in perception – by, for instance, keeping me there as day turns into night, removing every surrounding object and replacing it with others, blinding or deafening me, etc. – my 'here' thoughts do not change their sense. Similar points hold with 'now' thoughts and 'I' thoughts. My thought that now is 3 o'clock, carried out right now, would have had just the same sense if my present perceptual experiences had been very different. As for 'I' thoughts, while I do not recommend Hume's deflationary views concerning the self, he was in one sense right: there is no "impression," nor any pale copy of one in the form of an "idea," that uniquely characterizes 'I' thoughts. 'I', used by me, refers to me no matter what else I am feeling, perceiving, imagining, remembering, or introspecting.

Demonstrative contents like 'that' are also detachable from the particular intuitive content of an experience, at least when their object is one that could be given in more than a single way. As Husserl puts it, "a pointing reference remains the same, whichever out of a multitude of mutually belonging percepts may underlie it, in all of which the same, and *recognizably* the same, object appears" (*LI* 6, §5: 684). When I perceive an orange basketball from afar and again from up close, my utterances of "That$_1$ is thus$_1$" and "That$_2$ is thus$_2$" do not differ in either reference or sense. I am predicating what manifests itself as the same property to what manifests itself as the same thing. My "reference to 'this' is fulfilled in perception, but is not perception itself" (685).

This brings us to another point, and that is that the argument from knowledge works against this view as well. My perception of the basketball from far away and the basketball from up close differ in the degree to which they justify my belief. My belief that the ball is round and orange has a greater degree of warrant when I base it upon the latter experience than the former, despite their identical conceptual contents. The latter is a more optimal experience than the former. There are many other factors that contribute to the optimality of an experience that do not seem to make any difference to the contents of demonstrative thoughts. Consider, for instance, the orientation of an object. It is easier to recognize a face or a word when it is right side up rather than upside down. The *variety* of perceptual experiences of an object affects the epistemic status of perceptually based beliefs as well. My belief that the basketball is orange and spherical receives more support when I view the ball from various angles than it would if I were merely to gawk at it from a fixed position for the same amount of time, even though the conceptual content 'that is thus and so' might characterize both experiences (if it characterizes them at all). My belief that it is spherical will be enhanced even more if, in addition to seeing it, I pick it up and feel for any bumps or lopsidedness, dribble it, or roll it down the court. Even differences in the *duration* of experiences can affect the epistemic status of beliefs based upon them. I can think that *that is thus and so* after seeing the ball for 800 ms, and I can think it after seeing the ball for ten or twenty seconds. The latter experience will typically confer more justification on my belief that the basketball is orange and spherical, despite the identity of the conceptual contents which might be taken to characterize the experiences. But if two experiences differ in their reason-giving force despite having the same conceptual content, then the conceptualist principle must be false.

Furthermore, if two experiences with different intuitive contents had different demonstrative contents, it would almost never be the case that two people will understand precisely the same demonstrative thought simultaneously. Material objects and their parts and properties are almost always given to one via intuitive contents that differ from those via which they are, at a time, given to others. David Woodruff Smith acknowledges as much. On his view, according to which the senses of demonstratives, or "acquainting senses," are as fine-grained as perceptual states, a hearer is never in a position to entertain a demonstrative thought with the same conceptual content as the speaker's. As he puts it, "the hearer cannot share that acquainting sense on the occasion of utterance, because he cannot then be precisely in the speaker's shoes and so cannot be having a perception presenting the referent (veridically) from the speaker's perspective" (D. W. Smith 1982a: 193). That seems right. It also seems like an excellent reason not to identify the senses of demonstratives with acquainting senses – which is why Smith himself acknowledges that only certain components of the acquainting sense, the generic and specific senses of a demonstrative, are properly expressed linguistically. When I say "that is orange," someone who perceives the demonstrated object and understands English is in a position to entertain the very same thought that I express by means of that sentence and, if he hears me, will almost certainly do so. He does not have to nudge me out of the position from which I uttered the sentence so that he can see the orange thing in precisely the way I did. I can think of no principled reason why the predicate demonstrative 'is thus' would behave any differently. However, the mode of presentation of the object will almost inevitably be different: as Husserl puts it, "Every chance alteration of the perceiver's relative position alters his percept, and different persons, who perceive the same object simultaneously, never have exactly the same percepts. No such differences are relevant to the meaning of a perceptual statement" (*LI* 6, §4: 680).

Given the intimate connection between linguistically expressible and communicable content and conceptual content, this argument would be even stronger if successful linguistic communication required that interlocutors share the very same thoughts. However, both McDowell and Evans have argued that it does not (McDowell 1984: 290; Evans 1982: 315–16). Successful communication and mutual understanding might not require *shared* thoughts, but merely "different thoughts that, however, stand and are mutually known to stand in a suitable relation of correspondence" (McDowell 1984: 290). I have no argument against this view. Still, when I *communicate the thought T* to you by means of some sentence S, you are thereby in a mental state whose content is T. Otherwise, I would not have communicated *the thought T* to you, but, at best, some other thought T* which you (somehow) know to stand in a "suitable relation of correspondence" to T. But communicating thoughts, in the literal sense, is a familiar phenomenon. When I say "Cows give milk," and you hear and understand me, we both think the same thing, and we think it because my utterance of that sentence, together with your perceptual and linguistic abilities, causes you to think it. The McDowell–Evans point does not establish that this doesn't happen, or that it is not what normally happens. Rather, it establishes that communication can sometimes succeed *despite* its not happening. And it seems to me that not every utterance of a demonstrative thought is a case of its not happening.

It is important to note that this argument doesn't rest on any denial that demonstratives have senses. There are, on the contrary, very good reasons to suppose that co-referring demonstratives can differ in sense. The paradigmatic cases are those in which the identity of the referent of the two expressions is not evident. For instance, it is informative to learn that *that₁ wire* is *that₂ wire* when one is coming out of the floor and the other is coming out of the wall (Campbell 2002: 84–5). But the present cases do not conform to that model. First, it is not informative to tell someone that *that is thus* when it is true, because if he is in a position to entertain the thought, he probably already knows that *that is thus*. That probably no one has, in the context of a living conversation, ever actually uttered the sentence "that is thus" is likely not due to the fact that our listeners will invariably fail to grasp the precise thought it expresses, but for exactly the opposite reason: saying so violates Grice's maxim of quantity, which bids us to say what is informative and avoid saying what is not (Grice 1975). Or rather, that *would* be the reason if such a content even occurred to one in the process of perception, and I cannot detect any reasons, beyond the needs of a theory of justification that hardly qualifies as evident, to think that it does. Nor is it informative to learn, as I rotate an upside down picture of someone in a second's time while perceptually tracking it, that *that₁* is *that₂*. Nor is it informative to learn that the basketball I saw at t1 is the same one I saw at t2, when I have been tracking that very ball continuously from t1 to t2. Elsewhere (Hopp 2009b) I have suggested that such thoughts are what Evans calls "dynamic Fregean thoughts." As Evans puts it, "the *way of thinking of an object* to which the general Fregean conception of sense directs us is, in the case of a dynamic Fregean thought, a *way of keeping track of an object*" (Evans 1982: 196). I am not thinking two thoughts when I think 'that₁ is thus₁' and 'that₂ is thus₂', but thinking the same thought at two different times. When we keep track of an object, in a continuous perception of it under favorable conditions, the object is given in each now-phase after the first as the same object that was already given.

### 4.5.3. *The argument from the explanatory primacy of perception*

Moving on, then, a third consideration against the view that perceiving just is a matter of entertaining demonstrative contents is that perceiving something causally explains how one can demonstratively refer to it (Campbell 2002). As Heck puts it, "Demonstrative concepts ... are ones I have only because I am presently enjoying (or have recently enjoyed) an experience of a certain kind" (Heck 2000: 492). O'Shaughnessy (2000: 327) writes, "the thought with indexical perceptual content – 'that thump is happening' (let us say) – must be a distinct existent from the perception of that thump, since it manages to refer to its object only through the agency of the already existing perception." And Husserl, on the basis of the previous argument, writes, "When I say 'this', I do not merely perceive, but a new act of pointing ... builds itself on my perception" (*LI* 6, §5: 683). Even McDowell and Brewer in places write as though there is an asymmetrical dependence relation between perceptual content and demonstrative content. McDowell insists that we can grasp a concept as fine-grained as the (object of) an experience by means of a demonstrative concept which "exploits the presence of the sample" (McDowell, 1994: 56–7). McDowell does not say that the demonstrative thought *is* the presence of the sample, or that it exploits itself, or that the presence of the sample exploits the demonstrative. The presence of the sample and the demonstrative reference to it seem, plainly, to be two different things. Brewer, commenting on what is required to grasp context-dependent demonstrative concepts, writes,

Of course, far more is required to grasp such concepts than simply the ability to mouth such expressions in the presence of the items in question; and part of what the additional requirements must achieve is a certain distance between the subject's conception of the relevant semantic value and the mere obtaining of her confrontation with it which makes this way of thinking of it available to her in the first place. (Brewer 1999: 171)

This seems to imply that items can be "present," and presumably present *to consciousness*, independently of whatever further abilities are necessary for demonstrative reference, and that the "confrontation" with an object is necessary but not sufficient to entertain demonstrative contents. But what could perception be if not the conscious confrontation with a present object? Again, then, the confrontation with or presence of the object seems to be something distinct from, and presupposed by, the ability to think demonstrative thoughts about it.

A second, and related, worry is that a demonstrative account cannot provide us with the materials to know which thing we are perceiving

(Campbell 2002: 125). Demonstratives and indexicals don't come with their interpretations in hand. If I see the sentence "I love you" carved into a tree, I have no idea who loves whom. And if I am blindfolded, spun around to become disoriented, taken for a walk, then say or think "That is lovely," I have no idea what thing is supposed to be lovely. As Ruth Millikan puts it, a use of 'that', accompanied by a pointing finger, "is understood only if what it points at is visible, or otherwise independently accessible" (Millikan 1990: 728). It is this independent access (or not) that *explains* why it is easy to interpret some indexicals and not others. I can appreciate my own utterances of "I" so well because I have a distinctive sort of access to myself that I don't have to someone, say, yelling "I love Susie" from behind my back in a crowd, a sort of access that already presents me and which is presupposed, not constituted, by my understanding of "I" (Millikan 1990: 728).

Brewer, in his response to Heck's statement of this argument, agrees that perceiving an object does explain our grasp of demonstratives, but the explanation here is not causal but constitutive. "On the conceptualist view, experience of a color sample, R, *just is* a matter of entertaining a content in which the demonstrative concept 'that$_R$ shade' figures as a constituent" (Brewer 2005: 222, my emphasis). But that, as we shall see, carries problems of its own.

### 4.5.4. An argument from illusion

Heck anticipates this reply, and offers another argument. On one understanding of indexical and demonstrative expressions, their reference is fixed, crudely, by (a) their character or dictionary meaning and (b) the context – that is, the actual layout of the world – in which they are uttered. Consider, then, an utterance of "*That* part of my desk is *that* color" (Heck 2000: 494). On a broadly Kaplanian understanding of demonstratives, if I have expressed any thought at all, it is bound to be true in the actual world, since the circumstance of evaluation is the context of utterance. *Whatever* color I just predicated of my desk, that's the color my desk has in the actual world, since the reference of "that color" is "fixed by the world" (Heck 2000: 494). But then the thought, which is bound to be true, does not necessarily express the content of my perception, since I might misperceive the color of the table. If it appears yellow to me when it is in fact brown, then I have still managed to *say* something true, even when my experience is nonveridical.

Brewer's way around this objection is rather curious. According to Evans's theory, which Heck appeals to in his arguments against experiential conceptualism, demonstratively referring to something requires that one have the ability to keep track of it. One must, for instance, keep track of the same shade in different viewing conditions. Brewer thinks this is a sufficient condition for veridical perception as well: provided someone can track a color in different conditions, the demonstrative thought "That is colored thus" is "bound to be true" (Brewer 2005: 222). Errors are nevertheless possible: they occur when tracking fails. In that case, the demonstrative concept 'colored thus' is not available, and one's experience consists of a "failed attempt to grasp that concept" (Brewer 2005: 223).

This response fails for several reasons. First, while the ability to keep track of an object might be necessary for entertaining demonstrative thoughts about it, it is not a necessary condition for perception. I can see raindrops even if they are too fast and too numerous for me to track any one of them for any appreciable amount of time, or two steel balls rotating around an axis too quickly to track (Kelly 2004b: 281).

Second, one might be able to track the color of the surface of the desk simply by tracking the desk itself. If it doesn't get painted, varnished, stained, spilt on, or otherwise modified in color-changing ways, then one is fairly certain to keep track of its color. One can also simply track its *illusory* color through different contexts. If it is brown but appears yellow, then there's no principled reason why I shouldn't be able to keep track of its "yellowness" across a wide variety of conditions. But that doesn't make the error go away. Instead of an isolated illusion, I will now have one that persists through time and through different circumstances. It is hard to see why that doesn't just make my illusion worse.

It might seem that the obvious response in the face of the argument from illusion is to deny the model of demonstrative reference that underlies it. While demonstrative *utterances* might refer to what is objectively present, or might be such that third parties are constrained to interpret them as doing so, demonstrative *thoughts* refer to what is *perceived to be present*. It is not sufficient for you to think demonstratively about an object that you bear some *de facto* relation to a context of utterance in which that object figures. You are not, for instance, entertaining a demonstrative thought about a stalagmite if, surrounded by utter blackness, you just happen to point in its direction and mutter "that." You've got to *see*, or have quite recently seen, the stalagmite. Nor are you demonstratively referring to a color just by pointing to a surface and saying "that shade" or "is colored thus." Nor, finally, are you referring to the objective color of the table if the color you perceive it to have is not its real color. Someone who points to the surface of an exquisitely colored brown desk and thinks "I would never get a desk that is *colored thus*" is not thinking that she would never get an exquisite brown desk if the color she perceives it to be is a putrid yellow. It would be unfair of us, for instance, to criticize her taste. Rather, she is thinking – here I adopt a referentially transparent characterization of her thought – that she would never have a putrid yellow desk, a thought which, though founded on a misperception, does not impugn her taste. On this view, moreover, we can answer the argument from illusion as follows: the thought "*That* part of my desk is *that* color (or colored *thus*)" is not guaranteed to be true after all. It is only true if the table and its color are veridically perceived. But this model of how the reference of a demonstrative is fixed makes it all too obvious that the sense and reference of a demonstrative is parasitic on how things are perceived to be. If, as Heck points out, the perceptual experience fixes the content of the demonstrative, then it must be something different from the demonstrative (Heck 2000: 496).

### 4.5.5. *The argument from impossible perceptual experiences*

The fifth argument against EC is that entertaining a demonstrative content of the form 'that is thus' is not sufficient for perception, since there are far too many demonstrative contents which are thinkable on the basis of perception, but which are not and in some cases could not possibly be the contents of a perceptual state. This follows from the thesis that conceptual contents obey Evans's generality constraint, according to which a thinker capable of thinking both $Fa$ and $Gb$ is also capable of thinking $Fb$ and $Ga$.[10] It also follows from a much weaker thesis concerning the systematicity of conceptual contents, one which makes no empirical claims about thinkers and their abilities, to the effect that if $Fa$ and $Gb$ are well-formed conceptual contents, then so are $Fb$ and $Ga$. Indeed, it follows from the following examples and countless others like them, independently of any controversial general claims about the systematicity of concepts or conceptual thought as such.[11] Suppose, for instance, that I see a brown football next to an orange basketball, and entertain the demonstrative thoughts "that$_{football}$ is thus-brown" and "that$_{basketball}$ is thus$_{orange}$." This puts me in a position to entertain the contents "that$_{basketball}$ is thus$_{brown}$" and "that$_{football}$ is thus$_{orange}$."

At least those are the kinds of contents that could be confirmed in a possible perceptual experience. But entertaining such contents also puts me in a position to entertain necessarily false propositions like "that$_{basketball}$ is

[10] For more on the generality constraint, see Evans (1982: 100–5) and Peacocke (1992: 42 ff.).
[11] On why such claims are not obvious, see K. Johnson (2004).

that$_{football}$." But none of these expresses the content of my current perception, and the latter could not express the content of any perception. Adding further contents only increases the number of thoughts I can entertain. I can think the football is over there$_{left}$ and the basketball is over there$_{right}$ even when I perceive them to be in the opposite positions. Perception, therefore, cannot just be a matter of entertaining such demonstrative contents. It puts me in a position to entertain such contents, and it is necessary that I perceive or have recently perceived everything to which those demonstratives refer in order to entertain them. But plainly perception is one thing, and entertaining such contents is something else.

Incidentally, this argument also refutes Brewer's claim that the mere entertaining of demonstrative contents like 'that is thus' provides one with a reason to endorse them.[12] On the contrary, there are very many such contents that can be entertained while enjoying a perceptual experience, only a smallish percentage of which receive any confirmation from that experience itself.

The examples above illustrate something about conceptual content that makes it critically different from the sorts of contents that could be combined to constitute a possible perceptual experience. Without making any claims about the systematicity of conceptual contents as such, it is clear that conceptual contents can be lawfully combined into propositions that designate states of affairs that could not possibly obtain or possibly be presented in a corresponding perceptual experience, even when the constituents of those propositions designate sense-perceptible features and properties. The scope of conceptual thinking, even of the sort consisting entirely of object- and instantiation-dependent demonstrative contents, massively outstrips the scope of possible perceptual experience (*LI* 6, §63: 824). The content expressed by the sentence "The Empire State Building is tall" is a conceptual content, for instance, but so are a wide variety of others in which 'The Empire State Building' is substituted by terms that belong to the same semantic and syntactic category. The contents expressed by "The War of 1812 is tall" and "The Hammerklavier Sonata is tall" are also conceptual contents. These sentences do not express nonsense (*Unsinn*), as, for instance, the sentence "Mount Vesuvius Jim the" does, otherwise they would not have a truth value and their (true) negations would likewise be meaningless. Rather, they express counter-sense or absurdity (*Widersinn*)

---

[12] "Simply in virtue of grasping the content that that φ-thing is thus, he has a reason to believe that that thing is indeed thus; for he necessarily recognizes that his entertaining that content is a response to that thing's actually being thus" (Brewer 1999: 204–5).

(*LI* 4, §12). Even if we stick with mere demonstratives, we can produce contents that can be combined into patent absurdities. While hearing a concert on the lawn, I can think "that$_{song}$ is that$_{blade\ of\ grass}$." Seeing a man running towards a building, I can think "that$_{building}$ is thus$_{running}$." Such contents are "patterns of meanings assembled together into unitary meanings, to which, however, no possible unitary correlate of fulfillment can correspond" (*LI* 6, §63: 824, emphasis omitted). If the laws governing how conceptual contents can be concatenated to produce meaningful wholes are completely different from those governing the way in which intuitive contents can produce possible intuitive wholes, then there is every reason to believe that the two kinds of contents are different in kind.

## 4.6 CONCLUSION

Experiential conceptualism is not a viable view. Even the demonstrative theory, which is so watered down that it preserves only the letter of every historically prominent version of EC, cannot explain the intentional character or epistemic properties of perceptual experiences. The task of the following two chapters is, first, to provide a phenomenologically grounded conception of conceptual and nonconceptual content, and then to argue, against the relational view, that perceptual experiences have two kinds of nonconceptual content.

# CHAPTER 5

# Conceptual and nonconceptual content

In the previous three chapters, I have considered and rejected several arguments for experiential conceptualism, and provided several arguments that the intentional and epistemic properties of perceptual experiences cannot be explained in terms of whatever conceptual contents they might reasonably be thought to possess. It might be thought that this straightforwardly entails that perceptual experiences have nonconceptual content, and my own use of the term 'intuitive content' might reinforce that conviction. However, it does not. It might turn out that perceptual experiences have no kind of content at all. In this chapter and the next I will argue against that view. It is my contention that perceptual experiences not only have nonconceptual content, but that they have two distinct but necessarily related kinds of nonconceptual content: intuitive contents and horizonal contents.

## 5.1 NONCONCEPTUAL CONTENT

The current literature on nonconceptual content is a mess. Some of this can be chalked up to the already discussed ambiguities surrounding the notion of mental content. Some of it can be chalked up to the fact that the term 'nonconceptual content' tells you what this type of content is not, and there are perhaps many sorts of contents that conceptual content is not. Some of it can be chalked up to the inexplicable fact that almost no one provides a definition that is based on independent definitions of the terms 'content', 'concept', and the prefix 'non'. And some of it is due to the fact that many characterizations of nonconceptual content are ambiguous between defining a special kind of state and a special kind of content. All of these conspire to make the current literature on nonconceptual content especially frustrating.

To get an initial handle on just what nonconceptual content is supposed to be, we ought to take a look at the work it is supposed to do. Let us consider, briefly, two standard arguments for nonconceptual content. The first is the richness argument, which runs, roughly, as follows: my perception of the color of this tablecloth represents a very fine-grained shade of green. I don't just perceive it as green, but as a determinate shade of green. But I have no concept of that shade. I do not, for instance, possess the vocabulary required to characterize it. Nor could I reliably re-identify that color if confronted with an array of green color samples. But I perceive it. And so I am somehow conscious of the color in question, without having any concept of it. My mental state, then, must have a sort of nonconceptual content. And the same holds for perceptual states generally: they, for the most part, represent the world in a more fine-grained way than do any of the concepts that I possess.

A second prevalent argument for nonconceptual content is that animals and pre-linguistic humans are capable of being in intentional states, such as perceptual states, even though they do not possess concepts of the objects of which they are aware. Both my neighbor's cat and my infant son can perceive a door, but this does not mean that they have the concept 'door'. And so, once again, they are capable of standing in intentional relations to objects without having concepts of those arguments, and this is only possible if their mental states possess nonconceptual content.

These are not my favorite arguments for nonconceptual content, and a discussion of their merits would only retrace a fairly well-worn path. However, it seems pretty clear what nonconceptual content is supposed to do. Simply put, it enables its possessor to be conscious of, or intentionally directed upon, an object without possessing (and therefore not exercising) a concept of that object. Given the Husserlian understanding of contents as bearers of intentionality, rather than objects intended, we can then say that nonconceptual *contents* are contents that are not composed of concepts of O, and a nonconceptual *state* or *experience* is one whose content or intentional matter is nonconceptual. That will be my understanding throughout. A few words, however, are in order about contemporary treatments of nonconceptual content, partly so I can situate my own position within the broader nexus of debates, and partly to shed some light on what I regard as an unconscionably obscure area of contemporary philosophy. According to what is probably the most prominent definition, a mental state has nonconceptual content if and only if the subject of that state does not need to possess concepts which "characterize" or "specify" that state's content. Bermudez writes, "A nonconceptual content can be attributed to a creature without thereby attributing to that creature mastery of the concepts required to specify that content" (Bermudez 2003: 184). Crane tells us that "X is in a state with nonconceptual content iff X does not have to possess the concepts that characterize its content in order to be in that state" (Crane 1992: 149). And Byrne writes, "Mental state S with content P is nonconceptual iff someone who is in S need not possess any of the concepts that characterize P" (Byrne 2003: 265).

I have never been able to understand these definitions. First, it's unclear what it means to "specify" or "characterize" a content. Do concepts "characterize" a content when they are about it? Or when they are constituents of it? Or something else? Second, many have found it unclear whether the definitions define a special kind of content or a special kind of state (or both). According to the content view, a content is intrinsically or absolutely conceptual (or nonconceptual), independently of when and by whom it is entertained or grasped. As Speaks puts it, a content is *absolutely nonconceptual* iff it has a different kind of content from beliefs, thoughts, and other propositional attitudes (Speaks 2005: 360). The state view, on the other hand, holds that conceptuality and nonconceptuality are not intrinsic properties of the contents of mental states. They are, rather, features of the *states* in which those contents figure, and only relative properties of the contents of those states (Huemer 2001: 74). According to Speaks, whose definition of relative nonconceptual content expresses the state view, "A mental state of an agent A (at a time t) has *relatively nonconceptual content* iff the content of that mental state includes contents not grasped (possessed) by A at t" (Speaks 2005: 360).

Worse yet, because of the ambiguity of the term 'content', it is unclear whether the definitions are about the contents or the objects of mental states. Accordingly, I shall discuss these definitions under the object interpretation and the content interpretation, and discuss relative nonconceptualism (the state view) and absolute nonconceptualism (the content view) under each heading. That is, I will be discussing four distinct views: relative and absolute nonconceptualism under the object interpretation (henceforth 'RNO' and 'ANO'), and relative and absolute nonconceptualism under the content interpretation (henceforth 'RNC' and 'ANC').

### 5.1.1. *The object interpretation*

A natural understanding of the definitions would be as follows: by 'content' the above authors mean the *object* of a mental state, and by 'characterizing' or 'specifying' a content they mean *being about* that content, in which case a mental state has "nonconceptual content" just in case its subject need not possess the concepts (if any) which "characterize," or are about, its object in order to be conscious of that object. Under this interpretation, the distinction between ANO and RNO comes down to the following question: if the arguments for nonconceptual content are successful, do they establish that perceptual states have different kinds of *objects* from states like belief and judgment (ANO), or merely that they are different kinds of *states* directed at the same kinds of objects (RNO)?

Jeff Speaks often seems to have the object interpretation in mind, a fact that partly explains the ease with which he dispatches the claim that RNO entails ANO. Consider, for instance, his response to Sean Kelly's argument that perceptual states have nonconceptual content because, unlike states with conceptual content, no account of such states could specify their content without specifying the context in which a property is perceived and the particular individual whose property, or rather "dependent aspect," it is (Kelly 2001b: 607). According to Kelly, "Concepts, even demonstrative ones, pick out situation independent features, but the perceptual experience of a property is always dependent upon the two aspects of the situation I mentioned above – context and object" (Kelly 2001b: 608). While Speaks concedes that "Kelly's examples do seem to indicate that the properties perceived in experience sometimes include properties like being well lit or being a property of a wool rug," he goes on to say,

for this to be an argument that the contents of experience are absolutely nonconceptual, we would need the further claims that such properties cannot figure in thought, and that these properties are somehow different in kind from the properties that can figure in the conceptual contents of thought. (Speaks 2005: 367)

It should be clear that in this context at least, by 'content' Speaks means 'object'. He takes Kelly to be arguing that the properties presented in perception could not "figure in thought" – that is, be thought about – and, quite rightly, protests.

There are several problems with understanding the debate over nonconceptual content in this way, however. In the first place, most of the advocates of nonconceptual content do not claim that the objects of perception differ from those of thought. Kelly does, it is true, sometimes suggest that this is so. If concepts can only pick out context-independent features, and if perception presents us with context-dependent features, then, it seems, the features picked out by concepts are not those picked out by perception. But Kelly's point doesn't seem to be that the properties differ, but that the *perceptual experience* of any property is necessarily dependent on a particular context and a particular object that instantiates it. After all, it is rather obvious that the properties given in perception can be thought about. For instance, one can write an article about the woolly blue of the carpet in order to point out that its manner of perceptual givenness is totally different from the givenness of the shiny blue of a steel ball. Furthermore, in the process of arguing that the blue of the carpet is radically different from the blue of a shiny steel ball, one of Kelly's pieces of evidence is that he "can always rationally wonder whether they are in fact the same color" (Kelly 2001b: 607). But wondering is not perception. It is a conceptual activity that entails the ability to think about the things wondered about. The ability to wonder whether A = B guarantees the ability to judge that A = B or its contradictory, which of course entails that A and B can be objects of *thought*. If Kelly were arguing that the perceived colors could not be objects of thought, then his conclusion would be fatally undermined by one of the premises for it. This makes me suspect that Kelly is not defending ANO. To give another example, Christopher Peacocke should not be interpreted as claiming that such things as squares and regular diamonds, whose modes of perceptual givenness are quite different despite their identity, cannot "figure in the conceptual contents of thought," since he has written numerous books and articles in which he expresses his thoughts about them, with the full knowledge that when you read those articles, you will think about them too.

Perhaps the closest thing I have seen to an endorsement of ANO is in Adrian Cussins's work, in which he claims that conceptual content "presents the world to a subject *as* the objective, human world about which one can form true or false judgments" (Cussins 2003: 133). It presents the world as "divided up into objects, properties, and situations: the components of truth conditions" (Cussins 2003: 134). Nonconceptual content, on the other hand, exists just in case "there are ways in which the world can be presented ... which do not make the objective, human world accessible to the subject" (Cussins 2003: 134). Nonconceptual contents, that is, do not present the world as divided into objects, properties, and situations.

But this cannot be right. Consider the following sentence:

(S) The world is not divided into objects and properties.

(S) expresses a conceptual content, but it does not present the world as divided into objects and properties. Neither do the ontologies of Whitehead or the late Brentano. And a perceptual state, one in which, say, my brown desk, blue chair, and white wall are all perceived, does present the world as divided into objects and properties. This view almost sounds incoherent: conceptual content and nonconceptual content both present us with "the world," but one of them fails to make the "objective, human world" accessible. Is there another world we should know about? And if there is, doesn't an article about it make it accessible via conceptual contents? In any case, I am strongly convinced that even Cussins does not endorse ANO, but is merely impressing on us the radically different ways in which the world manifests itself in thought, on the one hand, and in engaged action and perception, on the other. In one of his most memorable examples, he discusses the difference between the way in which his speed is presented to him while riding his motorcycle and the way in which it is presented to him conceptually. But it is, after all, the very same thing being presented here; he wasn't traveling at *two* speeds, a conceptual one and a nonconceptual one. What differs are that speed's modes of givenness. Finally, Cussins is quite clear that by 'content' he does not mean the object of a mental state, but rather "the way in which some aspect of the world is presented to a subject; the way in which an object or property or state of affairs is given in, or presented to, experience or thought" (Cussins 2003: 133).

One reason why it is both easy to establish that none of the arguments for nonconceptual content establishes ANO and very hard to find any defenders of it is that it is simply hopeless. A great deal of what is thought about, though certainly not everything (not concepts), can be perceived. When I think about my house, and then see my house, there are not two objects of consciousness: what I see is the very thing I thought about. More importantly, as I have already argued, *everything* that can be perceived can be merely thought about, though perhaps not by the creature who perceives it.

A second reason for resisting the object interpretation is that it leaves another important question completely unaddressed, one that does occupy the attention of many involved in the debate over nonconceptual content. Given the hopelessness of ANO, the real debate turns on whether RNO is correct: that is, whether perceptual states differ from conceptual states despite having the same kinds of objects. If the answer is affirmative, there still remains a rather serious issue: in virtue of what can perceptual states and beliefs be of the same object, but differ? What are their respective features, parts, and properties? They cannot, after all, both be a sheer or bare awareness of their objects (though *one* of them could), since that would leave nothing to distinguish them. One answer is this: beliefs and perceptual states, though of the same kinds of objects, have different *contents*, where 'contents' here refers to contents, not objects. One kind of content is composed of concepts, and another is not. For instance, one might hold that both kinds of states have "Russellian propositions" or states of affairs as objects, but that beliefs have, while perceptual experiences do not have, Fregean thoughts as contents. And in that case, the differences between the two kinds of *states* would be parasitic on a difference in their *contents*. In short, RNO naturally leads to a discussion of the different manners of givenness or modes of presentation of identical objects, which in turn leads to a distinction between the objects of consciousness and the contents of consciousness. And whether mental states with identical objects can nevertheless have fundamentally different sorts of contents seems quite obviously what many in the debate are concerned to establish or refute. The object interpretation simply neglects this question.

### *5.1.2. The content interpretation*

One good reason to adopt the content interpretation is that there is a clear difference between being in a state whose content is conceptual and being in a state whose objects are conceptual. This is clear merely by reflecting on the term 'nonconceptual content' itself: it *expresses* a conceptual content without being *about* conceptual content. There are, however, also problems confronting us when we interpret the definitions above as holding of contents rather than objects. Let us consider Crane's definition again: "X is in a state with nonconceptual content iff X does not have to possess the concepts that characterize its content in order to be in that state" (Crane 1992: 149). Under the content interpretation, it is absolute nonconceptualism which makes perfect sense, while relative nonconceptualism is barely coherent, and is not at all motivated by the main arguments for nonconceptual content.[1] According to RNC, recall, nonconceptuality is a relational property of contents, and mental state has relatively nonconceptual content just in case "the content of that mental state includes contents not grasped (possessed) by A at t" (Speaks 2005: 360). But what could it even mean to say that (1) a mental state M "has" a content C, (2) M is S's mental state, but (3) S does not "possess" or "grasp" C? What better case could be made for S's possessing or grasping C (at t) than that S is in a mental state whose content is C (at t)? What the definition asks of us is that we make a distinction between S's *mental state's* having a content and S's grasping or

---

[1] Of the state view (or relative nonconceptualism), Heck (2000: 486, n. 6) writes: "I suspect that the view is indefensible – even incoherent, if coupled with the view that the contents of beliefs are conceptual." Speaks, on the other hand, writes, "Every author who defends nonconceptual content appears to hold the view that the contents of perceptions are relatively nonconceptual, in this sense" (Speaks 2005: 392, n. 3). I'm not sure why Speaks is so confident in implying that Heck holds a view that Heck suspects is indefensible, but my hypothesis is that it is because under the object interpretation, which appears to be the one Speaks most often has in mind, it is the state view, not the content view, that is both less ambitious and more plausible.

possessing that content. And this seems to call for a sort of alienation on S's part from his own mind.

We can, in fact, imagine various ways in which such alienation might be brought about. One way, perhaps, is if M is sub-personal, a state of S's amygdala or occipital cortex, for instance, whose comings and goings are, from S's point of view, inscrutable. Certainly positing such states is a requirement of our best empirical theories of the mind. But even so, one might reasonably object to considering such states to be states of S, as opposed to, as Gareth Evans appears to hold, S's brain or central nervous system (Evans 1982: 158). In any case, I will set this sort of case aside, because I am discussing the contents of personal, conscious mental states.

Another sort of case might be like this: I say to a young child, "Repeat these words to Smith: 'Ontogeny recapitulates phylogeny'." Such a child may reliably take in, store, and later transmit this information to the intended recipient. And one might be tempted to suppose that the content of this sentence is the content of the child's mental states – I suspect Evans, for instance, has something like this in mind when he characterizes testimony as belonging to the "informational system." Still, the child does not grasp that content. He will not, for instance, henceforth be on the lookout for kids with vestigial tails. However, this line of thought is mistaken. The content of the sentence would not, in such a case, be the *content* of his mental state. Rather, the sentence itself would be the *object* of his mental state; his mental state, in this case, is about the sentence. The fact that the sentence, owing to the conventions of a broader linguistic community, is itself a bearer of content is immaterial. One is not automatically in a mental state with the *content* C just because the *object* of one's mental state has the content C or means C. If that were so, then, a dog, upon seeing this sentence, would be in a mental state whose content is the content of this sentence, and you would be in a state whose content is that of a Linear A sentence just in virtue of seeing an inscription of it. But that is obviously wrong. In virtue of his ability to reliably emit noises that closely resemble those he takes in, the child is capable of serving as a medium through which information is transmitted. But that information need not be among the intentional contents of any of his mental states. It is enough that the vehicles carrying the information be the objects of his mental states.

More importantly, for our purposes, the two arguments for nonconceptual content we have considered do not require any sort of alienation on the part of their subjects. When I perceive a determinate shade of blue for which I have no concept, my perceptual state has a content that is *fully mine*. I "grasp" or "possess" the content of my perceptual state, while I am having it, as fully and completely as I grasp any content of any intentional experience I have ever had. Of course I do not possess it after the experience has ceased. But if the content of the experience is essentially experiential – if the only way to be in a mental state with that content is to have that sort of experience – then of course I will no longer "grasp" or "possess" it when I am not having that experience. It is the *content* that differs from that of a thought or belief, if the argument is sound, and the perceptual *state* is nonconceptual in virtue of having that sort of content. And, while I cannot speak for infants and cats, nothing in the argument from the character of their cognitive achievements requires that they do not possess or grasp the contents of their own mental states. And so RNC, if it is coherent at all, is certainly not demanded by, or even motivated by, the arguments for nonconceptual content above.

What makes RNC perhaps appear coherent is the following idea: suppose that S is perceptually conscious that some patch is some determinate shade of color, such as $red_{24}$, but that S does not have the concept of that shade of color. Nevertheless, we can report the *content* of his perceptual state by saying "S sees that the patch is $red_{24}$." So, he bears some relation to a content, the one we express in the above report, even though he does not have or possess that content. What this means, I suggest, is this: we can report that the *object of which he is conscious* is the state of affairs of that patch's being $red_{24}$. And the only way to do that is by means of conceptual contents. But it is a mistake to suppose that the content we use to describe *what he is conscious of* is itself the *content by whose means he is conscious of it*, and almost incomprehensible to suggest that although that content figures in his conscious life, he somehow doesn't "grasp" or "possess" it. Attributing a content to a thinker that he does not possess makes no more sense than attributing a property to an object that it does not possess – that is, in fact, *exactly* what it amounts to. If someone is conscious of a $red_{24}$ patch, but does not possess the concept '$red_{24}$', then that concept cannot be among the intentional contents of his mental state, even if it is the concept we must use to report what his mental state is about. Rather, he is conscious of the color $red_{24}$ by means of some *other* intentional content, one that, if linguistic expressibility is a sufficient condition for conceptuality, and if the content in question is nonconceptual, will not be linguistically expressible.

Returning, then, to ANC, which will be our exclusive concern throughout what follows, do the definitions make any sense of it? Does it make sense to say that there is a certain sort of content which is such that a person could be in a mental state with that content, without having the concepts that "specify" or "characterize" that content? This depends on what it means to "specify" or "characterize" a content. If a concept "characterizes" a content just in case it is a *constituent* of that content, then this definition cannot be right. For, setting aside the questionable cases of alienation discussed above, one cannot be in a mental state whose content is p without possessing the content p. But in order to possess that content, one must possess whatever concepts are its constituents. One simply cannot be in a mental state whose content is that snow is white without possessing the concepts 'snow' and 'white'. If someone is somehow conscious of snow or whiteness without possessing the concepts 'snow' or 'white', then he is conscious of those objects via some *other* content, not in virtue of standing in some peculiar relation to the content 'snow is white' and its constituents.

If, on the other hand, a concept "characterizes" or "specifies" a content in virtue of *being about* that content, then virtually every content will turn out to be nonconceptual. For none of the concepts which make up the proposition that snow is white characterizes or specifies that content – that is, that proposition – or any of its constituents. The concept 'snow', for instance, is not about, and so does not "characterize," in the present sense, a concept or a proposition. It is about snow. But it seems plainly possible for a subject to be in a mental state whose content is the proposition that snow is white, and for that subject to possess that content, without having any concepts that are *about* that content. At least, it is not at all obvious that, necessarily, in order to be able to be in a mental state whose content is the proposition that snow is white, one must possess the concept of the concept of snow, or the concept of the concept of white. But if that is right – if it is possible to be in a mental state whose contents are concepts without possessing any concepts of those concepts – then almost every content will turn out to be nonconceptual, *even those all of whose constituents are concepts*. That seems plainly unacceptable.

Perhaps, then, what is meant is that a nonconceptual content is such that one need not possess the concepts *we* would use in accurately reporting what the content of the state is. That is a perfectly coherent characterization of nonconceptual content. Tye, for instance, writes, "to say that a mental content is nonconceptual is to say that its subject need not possess any of the concepts that we, as theorists, exercise when we state the correctness conditions for that content" (Tye, 2000: 62). Fortunately, there is an even clearer way of expressing this. It seems fairly clear to me that that what is being argued for is the existence of a sort of *content* (not object) that is about some object O, despite not consisting of concepts of O. And so the suggested definition would read:

NCC: S is a mental state M with nonconceptual content if and only if S can be in M without possessing any concepts of the object O that M is about.

That the distinction between contents and objects allows us to frame a definition of nonconceptual content that makes straightforward sense is yet another thing to recommend it.

Even NCC is, however, unsatisfactory. I can think of at least two objections. The first is that it rules out, by fiat, the spotlight view of perceptual intentionality. An advocate of such a theory could admit that one can be conscious of an object via acquaintance without having any concept of that object. But he would insist that it does not follow from this that the mental states in which such acquaintance is achieved have non-conceptual content, or any sort of content at all. Rather, perception is simply the bare awareness of an object; where perceptual states differ, they differ in having different objects. Moreover, while the spotlight theory is untenable as an overarching account of intentionality, its merits as an account of perception remain to be determined. In any case, its truth cannot be settled by a definition. The fact that an intentional state does not have conceptual content doesn't entail that it has nonconceptual content. It might have no content.

The second argument against such a definition is that there might be higher-order, or founded, mental states that necessarily have *both* concep-tual and nonconceptual content. I have in mind acts of fulfillment, which I will discuss at great length in Chapter 7. For instance, I might think the proposition 'my tablecloth is blue' while I perceive my blue tablecloth, and these two intentional acts might be related to one another in such a way that a new intentional experience, one of *perceptual verification*, occurs. I verify the proposition on the basis of the perception. Such an experience cannot occur without both intentional acts occurring. Just to think or judge that my tablecloth is blue is not to verify that it is on the basis of perception. Nor can I verify the thought just by perceiving the tablecloth; if I cannot, for want of the relevant concepts, even think the relevant thought, I cannot verify it. But (1) if the content of the perceptual act is nonconceptual, and (2) the content of the thought that it verifies or fulfills is conceptual, as seems plainly possible and admissible by most advocates of nonconceptual content, then the definition cannot be correct. For an act of this sort does have nonconceptual content, but could not occur unless the subject had concepts of the object or objects that the act is about. At best, then, the definition above states a sufficient condition for a mental state's having nonconceptual content.

In what follows, I will understand a nonconceptual *content* as a type of intentional content that is not a concept, or whose constituents are not concepts, and a nonconceptual *state* as one whose content is nonconceptual. Furthermore, there is no way that someone could be in a mental state with C as its content without possessing C and all of C's constituents; being in a mental state with content C *just is* to possess C. This characterization, however, is perfectly unhelpful without some understanding of what a conceptual content is.

## 5.2 CONCEPTUAL CONTENT

On this point there seems to be a bit more clarity. In Chapter 2, I articulated a few rather uncontroversial and widely shared assumptions about the nature of concepts. First, they are a species of intentional content: they are about things. Second, the contents of judgments and beliefs, namely propositions and all of their constituents, are conceptual. Third, all linguistically expressible contents are conceptual. It also seems plausible that all conceptual contents are linguistically expressible, though nothing in what follows hangs on it.

In light of the considerations from the previous chapters, however, we also have the resources to frame a phenomenological characterization of conceptual content. In particular, they support the thesis that there is no perceptual experience E such that undergoing E is either necessary or sufficient to be in a mental state with conceptual content C, in which case there is no conceptual content C the entertaining of which is necessary or sufficient to undergo E. In the case of all detachable contents, this is obviously true; I do not need to undergo any particular perceptual experience in order to think about snow, to think about anything's being white, or to think that snow is white, nor does my thinking so entail that I am undergoing any particular perceptual experience. In the case of demonstrative contents like "That is thus," we have seen that entertaining such a content does not require that either the object or the property demonstratively referred to must be experienced in any particular way, or even that one perceive the things it refers to at the time one entertains the contents. Nor is entertaining such a content sufficient for undergoing any particular perceptual experience, since one can entertain the content "That is thus" in cases in which that is not perceived to be thus, and can even think it when there is no possibility of that's being thus. One can think, for instance, that that$_{symphony}$ is thus$_{tall}$ while listening to a symphony and looking at a skyscraper. Finally, perceiving can take place without one's thinking any demonstrative thoughts at all – perceiving isn't thinking. This point, moreover, generalizes to all intuitive experiences – dreams, imaginings, rememberings, and so forth. All such experiences have, for lack of a better term, an *intuitive character* in virtue of which they present their objects in the determinate way that they do. And what distinguishes conceptual contents is their independence from the intuitive character of experience. Two experiences that have identical conceptual content do not thereby have identical intuitive characters, and two experiences that have identical intuitive characters do not thereby have identical conceptual contents. I propose, then, that *C is a conceptual content if and only if C does not determine, and is not determined by, the intuitive character of any experience E.*[2] Any type of intentional content that does determine, or is determined by, the intuitive character of an experience is a nonconceptual content.

This characterization is only true for the most part, however, and there are a couple of counterexamples. First, entertaining the demonstrative thought "*This* experience has *this* intuitive character" while undergoing some experience E is, arguably, sufficient for undergoing E. But this content is plainly not identical with E's content (if any), since experiences are not about their own intuitive characters. This content does not even have the same intentional object as the experience it is about. So, we can modify the characterization above accordingly: C is a conceptual content if and only if C does not determine, and is not determined by, the intuitive character of any experience E, all of whose intentional objects are identical with those of C.

Even this, however, is not quite right. Sensations, as I have argued (section 2.4), are intentional objects of the intuitive acts of sensing in which they are given. But entertaining the content "*This* sensation feels like *this*" is, again, sufficient for undergoing the act of sensing in question, and this thought *does* have the same intentional object as the act of sensing, namely the sensation's feeling the way it does. Obviously, however, the two acts do not have identical contents. One could have a sensation without entertaining any such proposition – I suspect that virtually every sensation I've ever had, prior to working on this topic at least, falls into that category. Moreover, in both kinds of counterexamples, the conceptual contents in question can be entertained only *in virtue of* undergoing experiences with a certain intuitive character. And despite the fact that entertaining those contents is sufficient for undergoing those experiences, those experiences

---

[2] A similar thesis – the conceptual thinking must be stimulus-independent – has been defended recently by Elisabeth Camp (2009, esp. §3).

do not exist and have their intuitive characters in virtue of your entertaining those conceptual contents. Thoughts with these sorts of contents are, in fact, radically parasitical on the intuitive characters of the experiences that make them possible, tailor-made to track them precisely. The characterization above, then, holds of conceptual contents that are not of the radically parasitical category.

Finally, one type of concept that might not satisfy my definition is the phenomenal kind. Phenomenal concepts are concepts of phenomenal experiences and their phenomenal characters. According to virtually anyone who believes in them, they can only be *acquired* by actually having been in a phenomenal state of the kind to which they refer. According to some of their advocates, they can only be *entertained* when one is currently undergoing an experience of the type to which they refer.[3] It seems obvious to me that phenomenal concepts, like nonindexical concepts of anything else, can be entertained in the absence of their referents. I can, for instance, exercise a phenomenal concept of (phenomenal) pain without hurting. When I do so, I am not thinking of pain as a brain state, or as bodily damage, or as something that indicates bodily damage, or as the occupant of some functional role, but, precisely, of pain as the painful kind of thing that pain is. It is also worth noting that making phenomenal concepts radically experience-dependent undermines one of the philosophical strategies for whose sake they are invoked. They are often summoned to explain how it is that the connection between physical states and phenomenal states appears contingent – a phenomenon that sustains many familiar arguments against materialism. The answer, briefly, is that when we entertain a psychophysical identity statement of the form "M = B," we are, in the case of the true ones, exercising a phenomenal concept and a physical concept of the very same thing. That may be. But note that the relation between, say (phenomenal) pain and a brain state B appears contingent even when one entertains thoughts about each when one is not in pain. That is, a statement like "Pain = C-fiber stimulation" seems contingent even when I think it and am not in pain. But if I can only entertain that phenomenal concept while I am in pain, then the phenomenal concept strategy cannot explain the felt contingency of empty thoughts about mental–physical relations.

This characterization of conceptual content hooks up nicely with several widespread assumptions about the nature of conceptual content. First, linguistically expressible contents or meanings are the paradigmatic sort of

[3] David Papineau writes, "there is only one property in play when a phenomenal concept refers to a phenomenal property: namely, the phenomenal property itself" (2002: 104). Also see Balog (2009).

conceptual content. And what distinguishes the vast majority of such contents is that they can be communicated and shared among persons who are not having identical perceptual or otherwise intuitive experiences. This gives linguistically expressible or conceptual content a kind of *objectivity* that perceptual and other intuitive experiences lack. We shouldn't misinterpret this claim. First, the claim is not that intuitive experiences are not about objective or experience-independent objects. They are. What I perceive right now are ordinary things like books, chairs, walls, and so forth. Second, the difference between intuitive characters and conceptual contents is not that the former, unlike the latter, are necessarily "private." The instances of conceptual contents, namely individual episodes of thinking, are also "private" in the sense that two people cannot have the same one. And the intuitive characters had by experiences are themselves instantiations of certain properties, and those properties are, at least ideally, shareable. Two people can have precisely the same *type* of experience. But the sharing of mental contents would be greatly restricted as a real possibility if, in order to do so, the individuals sharing it needed to be in mental states with the same intuitive character. Conceptual contents, on the other hand, enable me and someone on the other end of a telephone, or you and someone who lived several thousand years ago, to share the same thoughts. They are objective in the sense that they do not require those entertaining them to adopt any special perspective or have any particular sort of intuitive experience.

Second, it is because conceptual contents have this character that a body of shared content and knowledge is intersubjectively available. As Husserl puts it, after drawing a tight connection between "conceptualizing thought" and "the formation of generalities taking place in it" (*EJ* §49: 204): "Only general thought leads to determinations which create a store of cognitions available beyond the situation and intersubjectively" (*EJ* §80: 319). And again, "It is only the act of apprehension in the form of generality which makes possible that detachment from the here and now of the experiential situation, implicit in the concept of the objectivity of thought" (*ibid.*). Although it would appear, from these remarks, that only general contents are conceptual, this is only because Husserl has a rather liberal conception of generality. According to Husserl, even the contents expressed by proper names are general, a generality that consists not, as in the case of common nouns, in the fact that their extensions include numerous objects, but in the fact that each of their meanings covers "an ideally delimited manifold of possible intuitions, each of which could serve as the basis for an act of recognitive naming endowed with the same sense" (*LI* 6, §7: 692). And that is precisely to say that the meaning of a proper name is such that it can be the content of acts that differ from one another in their intuitive character. "Each and every name obviously belongs to no definite percept, nor to a definite imagination nor to any other pictorial illustration. The same person can make his appearance in countless possible intuitions" (*LI* 6, §7: 693). He makes the same point, as we have already seen, about demonstrative contents.

Third, the idea that conceptual contents are, in virtue of being inter-subjectively available, independent of the specific intuitive characters of experiences, and therefore independent of the particular perceptual situations in which experiences with those characters occur, is something that coheres well with what many others have said about conceptual content. We have already seen, in section 4.1, how both McDowell and Brewer seem to endorse the detachability thesis. And many have pointed out that non-conceptual content is, while conceptual content is not, radically context dependent (Dummett 1994: 123; Kelly 2001b). Cussins, for instance, discussing the difference between the way his speed on a motorcycle is presented in perception and action from the way it is present conceptually, writes that in the former context, "the speed was not given to me as a referent, an object, that I could present to the policeman, to myself, to the traffic courts, to other drivers, in other driving conditions, objectively, as the very same object, the very same speed in all of these different contexts or perspectives" (Cussins 2003: 150). Or, as Tyler Burge puts it:

Even those perceptual concepts that are conceptualizations of perceptual representations are more abstract than the perceptions in the sense that they are less connected to concrete sensation-presentations and can occur independently of any perceptual application. They can be consciously used in conditionals, for example, when no perceptual representation occurs, and when none can be brought to mind. (Burge 2003: 525)

Conceptual contents, that is, are contents that can be instantiated in mental states across different circumstances and situations – that is, across experiences that differ in their intuitive character.

What enables conceptual contents to come loose from the intuitive character of experience, from the ways in which objects present themselves to finite and embodied biological organisms, is, in the first place, that the sorts of wholes in which concepts are by their nature fit and destined to be parts, namely propositions, can be transformed into other propositions with a different sense via law-governed transformations. Within a wide range of cases – possibly all cases – a proposition containing a concept C will remain

meaningful (even if absurd) if we replace C with another concept C*
belonging to the same semantic category.[4] Propositions themselves, moreover, remain meaningful when they are transformed into their contradicto-
ries by negation or when they are concatenated with others via the logical
connectives. Furthermore, it is both an ideal possibility and an empirical
fact that some creatures – like us – who can understand one proposition will
be able to understand transformations of that proposition which contain
concepts that those creatures possess, a claim embodied in Evans's generality constraint. If I can understand the propositions that snow is white and
that coal is black, then I can also understand the propositions that snow is
black and coal is white. And my doing so does not depend on me perceiving
any snow, any coal, or anything that is black or white. As Hurley (1998:
137–8) puts it, "Conceptual content has a decompositional structure that is
not context-bound."

   This fact alone, however, does not explain how creatures could actually
come to grasp such contents; if we had context-bound minds, as some
creatures presumably do, then we could not entertain contents that are not
context-bound. What enables propositions and their law-governed transformations to be comprehensible to us, no matter how far they stray from
the objects and states of affairs presented to us perceptually, is that their
constituents themselves, concepts, are objective in the sense that they do not
depict their objects perspectivally or from any point of view. The price to be
paid for that kind of objectivity is radical inadequacy. They aspire to
represent the object itself, in-itself, as it itself is, and from no perspective.
And in virtue of that radical objectivity, none could characterize the content
of an experience. No single experience could "fill out" a conceptual content,
at least not one whose object is a physical one. Even demonstratives have
this sort of objectivity. Perception is the occasion on which we are able to
exercise those concepts, but is not for that reason characterized by those
contents.

## 5.3 THE ARGUMENT FROM HORIZONS REVISITED

In section 2.6 I considered an argument to the effect that because perceptual
experiences always have a surplus of *empty* intentional content over and
above whatever constitutes their intuitive character, they have *conceptual*
content. In light of the considerations of the past few chapters, we can now
evaluate that argument. If we have good reasons for thinking that the

---

[4] See *LI* 4, §10.

content of perception is not conceptual, as we do, and if horizons are necessary for perception, as they are, then we have a good reason to think that horizons are not conceptual.

That horizonal contents are not conceptual is a point that has been made before. Kenneth Williford, for instance, distinguishes empty from conceptual contents. The empty "mode of representation" involved in horizonal intentionality, which is both "nonsensory and nonpropositional," is "informationally poorer" than either of the other modes (Williford 2006: 121). This is not, it seems to me, quite sufficient to serve as the basis of an argument for the conclusion that horizonal intentionality is not conceptual. After all, some conceptual contents are incredibly poor in informational content. To generate one, simply take any proposition whose informational content is incredibly rich and negate it.

The first person, to my knowledge, to distinguish empty intentions from conceptual ones is Adolf Reinach (1982: 326–8; also see Dubois 1995: 18–20). When I see a book, he points out, the whole book is presented, but only some of it is intuited. But we should not say that the nonintuited parts of the book are *meant* or conceived of. Rather, the nonintuitional contents of perception are intimately bound up with an act of presentation, an act in which the book itself is perceptually present. We can see their difference, he argues, when we perform a judgment of the form "The rear side of the object is ..." Here, says Reinach, we can readily grasp the difference between the enduring nonintuitional or horizonal content that is bound up with the perceptual experience and the "linguistically clothed, temporally punctual, self-contained" act of judging itself (Reinach 1982: 327). The latter is not enduring and is not bound up with any particular perceptual experience. We can elaborate on Reinach's point by noting that such a judgment can be performed even when (1) the rear side comes into view and is therefore intuited and (2) the object is not perceptually present at all. Here the horizonal content varies or disappears entirely while the judgment remains constant. But if horizonal contents can vary independently of any conceptual contents, then they cannot be identical with any conceptual contents.

Reinach's argument only establishes that horizonal contents are not the kinds that figure in judgments. Daniel Dahlstrom presents what I take to be more powerful arguments that horizonal contents are not conceptual. First, he argues, the horizon is something that is "interwoven" with and "pervades" an act of perceiving. Secondly, and importantly, he argues that "there is a new horizon for every appearing-of-a-thing at every phase of perception" (Dahlstrom 2006: 209). Dahlstrom's second point is the most relevant for our considerations, and has been made more recently by Jeffrey Yoshimi as well (Yoshimi 2009: 125). Both Dahlstrom and Yoshimi are in self-conscious agreement with Husserl, who writes:

the process taking place in an original intuition is always saturated with anticipation; there is always more cointended apperceptively than actually is given by intuition – precisely because every object is not a thing isolated in itself but is always already an object in its horizon of typical familiarity and precognizance. But this horizon is constantly in motion; with every new step of intuitive apprehension, new delineations of the object result, more precise determinations and corrections of what was anticipated.[5]

If, for instance, I am looking at my couch from position P, then any change in my position will change the intuitive character of the act. It will bring into view a part that was merely intended, for instance, or hide from view a part that was previously perceived. But corresponding to every such change is a change in the horizon of the act as well. The revelation of new parts brings with it further anticipations of yet more parts, and the sinking into emptiness of previously perceived parts which are emptily retained in new, and richer, horizons. But since conceptual contents are neither determined by nor determine the intuitive content of an act – since, that is, there is no type of conceptual content which is such that every change in the character of experience brings with it a change in that type of conceptual content – horizonal contents are not conceptual. So, Dahlstrom's and Yoshimi's point, together with the present account of conceptual contents, shows that horizonal contents are nonconceptual.

## 5.4 CONCLUSION

Having distinguished conceptual and nonconceptual content, and established that there is at least one kind of content that is nonconceptual, we now turn to the question whether the intuitive character of perceptual experience is due to a peculiar kind of intentional content, or whether we should understand perceptual consciousness in some other way.

---

[5] *EJ* §25: 122. Also see *CM* §19: 44: "Every subjective process has a process 'horizon,' which changes with the alteration of the nexus of consciousness to which the process belongs and with the process itself from phase to phase of its flow – an intentional *horizon of reference* to potentialities of consciousness that belong to the process itself."

# CHAPTER 6

# *The contents of perception*

We can be sure that an experience has nonconceptual content if it has a kind of nonparasitic content that either determines or is determined by the intuitive character of an act. But why think that perception has *content* at all? Recently, a number of philosophers have endorsed the view that we can partially or even completely describe the character of a veridical perceptual experience merely by citing the objects that it is of, together with the conditions under which they are perceived. M. G. F. Martin, who favors such a view, writes: "According to naïve realism, the actual objects of perception, the external things such as trees, tables, and rainbows, which one can perceive, and the properties which they can manifest to one when perceived, partly constitute one's conscious experience" (Martin, 2009a: 93). Campbell goes further: "On a Relational View, the qualitative character of the experience is constituted by the qualitative character of the scene perceived" (Campbell 2002: 114–15). And Brewer, having abandoned his earlier commitment to experiential conceptualism, now endorses what he calls the "object view," according to which "the core subjective character of perceptual experience is to be given simply by citing its direct object" (Brewer 2008: 171). In this chapter, I will argue that the relational view is incorrect and that perceptual states have intuitive nonconceptual content.

## 6.1 THE RELATIONAL VIEW

The most obvious piece of supporting evidence for the relational view is phenomenological: in perception, mind-independent objects and their properties are directly *present* to us. They are not merely represented, emptily thought about, or presented indirectly by means of pictures, images, or appearances. Rather, they are themselves present in person: "every perception within itself is not only, in general, a consciousness of its object, but ... it gives its object to consciousness in a distinctive manner.

Perception is that mode of consciousness that sees and has its object itself in the flesh" (*APS*: 140).

Because perception is presentational in this way, it cannot possibly be "indirect" in the way that at least some theories have supposed. According to one once-popular theory, sometimes called "indirect" or "representational" realism, the only direct objects of perceptual consciousness are ideas, appearances, sense data, or something of their ilk. Physical objects are perceived "indirectly." But this is a sham. Being conscious of A through the presentational consciousness of some distinct object B is precisely not a presentational consciousness of A. It is not *perception*. Perceiving a representative of President Obama is not to perceive President Obama, even if the representative resembles him. Perceiving Air Force One, or a limo containing Obama, or Obama's jacket on a hook, is not to perceive Obama. The only remotely plausible way in which one might be said to perceive Obama indirectly is by seeing an image of him. But it would be incredibly misleading to claim that one has "seen Obama" just in virtue of seeing an image of him. There are lots of ways to see Obama – from up close or far away, from up front or in profile – but "indirectly" is not one of them. If someone told me that he saw Obama indirectly, and meant by that that he had seen, in the ordinary sense, a picture of Obama, my unequivocal response would be: "So, you didn't see Obama after all." Indirect realism – or, better, direct idealism – should be construed not as a position that we perceive the physical world indirectly, but as a position that we simply do not *perceive* any physical objects *at all*. The theory should not be allowed to present itself as preserving even *part* of the commonsense idea that we perceive the physical world.

This should be cause for alarm. Since trees are physical objects, the theory entails that no one has ever seen a tree. But I have seen a tree. You have too. And it won't help to go idealist about trees by folding them into consciousness, since all the familiar problems that motivate indirect realism in the first place – the problems of perceptual relativity, illusion, and hallucination – will still exist, and we will, if we ever trusted the argument for indirect realism in the first place, have to say that trees are mental objects that can't be directly perceived. These problems don't arise because trees are *physical* or "*external*." They arise because they are *trees*. Provided we preserve one essential feature of trees, namely that they cannot in principle be adequately perceived, "phenomenalizing" them won't change a thing epistemically. Trees cannot get any "closer to the mind" than they already actually are. And if we don't preserve that property of trees, then we will not have incorporated trees into consciousness.

There is yet another reason for phenomenological alarm, and that is that perceptual consciousness is not like sign- or image-consciousness at all. When one is conscious of a sign or image, one grasps it, however marginally, *as* a sign or image. This doesn't mean that one applies the concept 'sign' or 'image' to it. Rather, the image is "immediately felt to be an image," to point beyond itself to something else (*PICM* §12: 28). No matter how lost I am in viewing a movie, for instance, the characters, objects, and scenes depicted therein don't normally seem present in person; I don't take cover when the characters shoot guns, and I don't expect them to respond to me when I talk. But most objects of perception aren't grasped in that way at all. And if a sign or an image is not grasped as a sign or image, then it might as well not be a sign or image to the person grasping it. If, for instance, the placement of churches in a village were a kind of code or sign used by a secret society, that would mean nothing to the rest of us. It would be incorrect, for instance, to claim that in perceiving the churches we are indirectly aware of something else. "Only a presenting ego's power to use a similar as an image-representative . . . makes the image *be* an image."[1] If indirect realism is true, however, virtually everything we perceive is not only an image of something else, but, in virtue of pointing to a world beyond, functions as an image for us. But this is false. To see so, pick out any randomly perceived object and ask: what is *that thing* a sign, image, or representation of? If you have an answer (because, say, you turned to a word or a picture), just turn to something else. Eventually you'll be stumped. A tree is not of anything, nor is it apprehended as being of anything, in anything like the way an image, picture, or representation is of something (though it does, like everything whatsoever, carry *information* about other things). And when you see a tree, there is nothing *less* than the tree that is functioning as an image or sign of it – not even an "appearance." That the tree appears doesn't entail that you perceive a tree-appearance. You perceive a tree in a way, but not a tree-in-a-way. By construing perceptual experiences as, simply, the direct and immediate apprehension of physical objects and properties, the relational view provides one of the most plausible accounts of how reality itself can be present to us in the way it seems to be.

A second virtue of the relational view is that it provides a good explanation of how and why perceptual experience, unlike any other kind, is

---

[1] *LI* 5, appendix to §11 and §20: 594. He continues: "We must realize that a transcendent object is not present to consciousness merely because a content rather similar to it simply somehow is in consciousness – a supposition which, fully thought out, reduces to utter nonsense – but that all relation to an object is part and parcel of the phenomenological essence of consciousness, and can be found in nothing else."

capable of ultimately grounding our ability to think directly about individual objects. Even if Kant is right that we can know something about any possible object of experience a priori, such knowledge would be merely descriptive; we would know, at best, what properties an object must have if it is possible to experience it, just as someone might know what properties somebody must have if he or she is to be president of the United States. But we do not have the ability to think *directly* about the world and its denizens – or many of its properties, for that matter, which we do not invariably think of by description – a priori. And no other type of experience is capable of explaining it. Dreaming, imagining, and hallucinating do not give one the ability to think directly about individuals or natural kinds, for instance (Johnston 2009). Mere thinking can – we can think directly about Socrates – but only because our intentions are ultimately parasitical on someone else's, which are ultimately themselves grounded in perception. And many rival theories of perception cannot explain it. The sense datum theory only gives us the ability to think of worldly objects descriptively as just whatever is causing the things we directly experience. But we plainly do think directly about physical objects. And the best explanation is that in perception, those objects are directly present to us. As Campbell puts it, "We are not to take the intentional character of experience as a given; rather, experience of objects has to be what explains our ability to think about those objects" (Campbell 2002: 122). We don't, in all cases, first entertain contents concerning actual individuals and situations and then hunt around to determine whether they have existing objects. Rather, perception explains our ability to think of things in the first place. What better explanation could there be for both the directness of perceptual experience and the fact that it makes it possible to think of worldly objects than that those objects are literally *constituents* of our experiences of them?

## 6.2 THE RELATIONAL VIEW AND HALLUCINATION

The considerations above do not entail the relational view, since a properly developed content view – that is, one which claims that the phenomenal or intuitive character of a perceptual experience is determined by its intentional content – can account for them. Indeed, construing objects as *constituents* of our experiences, far from making our perception of them intelligible, makes perceptual experiences stand out as curious exceptions to a general rule. The general rule in question is that the constituents of a typical mental act, its contents, are almost never what the act is directed upon. When I think about the number 2, I am not thinking about any constituents of my act of thinking. And it is, I will argue in this section, at least mandatory that we attribute intentional, nonconceptual content to illusory and hallucinatory experiences.

If objects and properties (and relations and facts – in short, parts of the world) constitute the subjective character of perceptual experiences, then something else has got to constitute the subjective character of hallucinations. Accordingly, any version of the relational view is committed to some version of disjunctivism. What unites virtually every version of disjunctivism is a rejection of what J. M. Hinton calls "the doctrine of the 'experience' as the common element in a given perception and its perfect illusion" (Hinton 1973: 71). That is, every version of disjunctivism rejects what M. G. F. Martin calls the "Common Kind Assumption," namely that "whatever kind of mental . . . event occurs when one perceives, the very same kind of event could occur were one hallucinating" (Martin 2006: 357). Hallucinations might be introspectively indistinguishable from veridical perceptions, but that doesn't entail that they have the same basic nature.

Some version of disjunctivism must be correct, I will argue. No veridical experience can have precisely the same nature as a hallucination, since they could not have precisely the same intentional content. But there are a lot of ways to deny the common kind assumption, and not all of them are created equal. And many of the ways the relational view has been developed are unsatisfactory, since they do not adequately explain how and why hallucinations are errors. In what follows, I will consider two relational accounts of hallucination: weird object disjunctivism and radical disjunctivism.

Radical disjunctivism's most notable advocates include M. G. F. Martin and William Fish. On Martin's view, a hallucination has no positive nature at all. Its nature consists entirely in its being (impersonally) indiscriminable by reflection (alone) from a veridical perception.[2] William Fish goes a step further and claims that, while hallucinations can have the same cognitive effects as veridical perceptual experiences on a subject in the same doxastic setting, they do not have a phenomenal character at all.[3] This is a heroic view, and I strongly predict that one would be hard pressed to sell it to someone who is hallucinating a bear attack, or even a casual user of hallucinogens. People don't drop acid just to achieve certain cognitive

---

[2] "[W]hile there is a positive specific nature to the veridical perception, there is nothing more to the character of the (causally matching) hallucination than that it can't, through reflection, be told apart from the veridical perception" (M. G. F. Martin 2006: 370; also see 2009b: 301).

[3] "I submit, then, that a hallucination is a mental event that, while lacking phenomenal character, produces the same cognitive effects in the hallucinatory that a veridical perception of a certain kind would have produced in the same doxastic setting" (Fish 2009: 114).

effects, but for the *experience* of it. Weird object disjunctivism, according to which hallucinations and perceptual experiences have categorially different kinds of objects, has been endorsed by John McDowell (1982), who holds that in hallucination we are aware of "mere appearances." Alston's theory of appearing is also, on some possible developments, a version of it.[4]

One of the biggest objections to the views of Martin and Fish is that they cannot explain why hallucinations are *errors*. This is also true of weird object disjunctivism. I begin with the latter. McDowell endorses disjunctivism because he regards it as the way to block a familiar argument against direct realism. "In a deceptive case," writes McDowell, "what is embraced within the scope of experience is an appearance that such-and-such is the case, falling short of the fact: a mere appearance. So what is experienced in a non-deceptive case is a mere appearance too" (McDowell 1982: 386). This line of thought, according to McDowell, can be overcome by denying last step of the argument. As he puts it, "the object of experience in the deceptive cases is a mere appearance. But we are not to accept that in the non-deceptive cases too the object of experience is a mere appearance, and hence something that falls short of the fact itself" (McDowell 1982: 387). We should, in short, be disjunctivists about the objects of hallucination and veridical perception.

We can get a better grip on McDowell's argument by considering the following inconsistent set of propositions:
(1) Intrinsically identical experiences have the same (kinds of) objects.
(2) Hallucinations and perceptions are intrinsically identical.
(3) The objects of hallucination are mere appearances.
(4) The objects of perception are worldly objects (facts).
The argument from deceptive cases argues from (1)–(3) to the negation of (4). McDowell, on the other hand, endorses (3) and (4). Since (1) is practically a truism, he rejects (2). It is (3), however, which should (also) be rejected. There might be a lot of good reasons to endorse disjunctivism, but the conjunction of (1), (3), and (4) is not among them.

The problem with McDowell's argument is that he treats the conjunctivist as committed to (3). Part of the reason is that he claims that, on such a view, a hallucination must "fall short of the fact itself" because one's "experiential intake" is "consistent with there being no such fact" (McDowell 1982: 386). But this is not the case. While the conjunctivist

---

[4] Alston (1999: 191) suggests that the object of a hallucination of a dagger might be "the air occupying the region where the dagger appears to be," "the part of the brain playing a causal role in the production of that experience," or "a particularly vivid mental image."

may be committed to the claim that (1) the *occurrence* of such an experience is consistent with there being no actual fact corresponding to it, he need not be committed to the claim that (2) the *correctness of the experience's intentional content* is consistent with there being no such fact. And the former claim does not entail that the experience is not about a worldly fact. The occurrence of an act of judging can also be consistent with there being no fact corresponding to it, otherwise there would be no acts of judging falsely, but that does not mean that the satisfaction of its content is.

McDowell makes the mistake, common to most versions of the sense datum theory, of thinking that hallucinatory experiences are about something less than worldly states of affairs. But this is wrong, and does not square with McDowell's own claim that an experience is "deceptive when, if one were to believe that things are as they appear, one would be misled" (McDowell 1982: 385–6). If the intentional object of a hallucinatory experience were a mere appearance, then the hallucination would be a perfectly veridical perception of a mere appearance.[5] And in taking things to be as they appear, one would take an appearance to be as it appears, and be right. After all, if McDowell's view is right, appearances exist and have properties that manifest themselves to us under certain conditions. But merely being of such a thing as that cannot, in itself, be an error of any kind. To be aware of something that exists as that thing is the very furthest thing from error.

It would not, moreover, be a nonveridical perception of a worldly fact. If it genuinely *fell short* of a worldly fact, it could not qualify as any sort of error about any worldly fact, since in order to nonveridically or falsely represent some object or fact, one's experience or thought must minimally be *about* it. I am not entertaining a false belief about Genghis Khan when I believe that my shoe is untied, because my belief isn't even about him. But hallucinations are errors. They don't present appearances as they are. They present the world as it is not. This is why Wittgenstein, in his discussion of the truism that "When we say, and *mean*, that such-and-such is the case, we – and our meaning – do not stop anywhere short of the fact," clarifies the consequences of this by adding, "*Thought* can be of what is *not* the case" (Wittgenstein 1958: 44). He is not suggesting that meanings or thoughts, including empty and false ones, ever do stop short of the fact, but insisting that they do not. The whole point of the remark is to make it clear that false thoughts about the world aren't true thoughts about something else. And

---

[5] See Siewert 1998, §7.4 for a good discussion of how poorly the sense datum theory handles perceptual error.

exactly the same point holds of experiences. Nothing – well, almost nothing – falsifies the nature of hallucination more than treating the nonveridical awareness of the world as the veridical awareness of "appearances" or something else that falls short of it. Wittgenstein's point is to warn us against making the sort of mistake that McDowell makes.

Radical disjunctivism is in no better condition. According to it, hallucinations have no positive features at all. But if they have no positive features, then they do not have the feature of being about anything, since being about something, however construed, is a positive feature. But if they are not about anything, then, like clouds or pieces of gum, they aren't the kinds of things that can be right or wrong about anything.

Probably the most obvious response to this objection is that hallucinations are not, as I have assumed, intrinsically erroneous. Rather, what are erroneous are the beliefs they tend to produce. Brewer endorses such a view: "*Error*, strictly speaking, given how the world actually is, is never an essential feature of experience itself," but instead arises from our responses to an experience (Brewer 2006: 169). For instance, the weird object disjunctivist can argue that what makes a hallucination erroneous is that it is of something, an appearance, which is easily mistaken for something else, like a house. When we hallucinate, on this proposal, the error consists in the fact that we form beliefs, or are inclined to form beliefs, about worldly facts that do not obtain. The radical disjunctivist can also say that we are inclined to form false beliefs about our environments because hallucinatory experiences are indiscriminable from veridical experiences (Martin), or they *just are* things with such effects (Fish).

All of these responses fail. Beginning with radical disjunctivism, Fish's account effectively defines hallucinatory experiences in terms of their cognitive effects. And as he admits (Fish 2009: 114), that deprives us of an explanation of why hallucinations have those effects. Such a question is ill-posed if hallucinations *just are* things with those effects.[6] But the plausibility of that proposal is intimately bound up with the plausibility of his contention that hallucinations have no phenomenal character, a claim whose plausibility ranks alongside that of eliminativism in other spheres of mental life. Furthermore, it does seem as if there is an

---

[6] "Hallucinations *just are* those events that have the same kinds of effects as, and are therefore indiscriminable from, veridical perceptions of a certain kind" (Fish 2009: 114). Unfortunately, this claim entails that veridical perceptions are hallucinations, since they have the same effects as, and are indiscriminable from, themselves. But this, no doubt, can be repaired along Martin's lines: perceptual states differ in having a positive intrinsic nature over and above this. Their nature is not exhausted in having certain cognitive effects.

explanation of why a hallucination of a duck produces beliefs that there is a duck around: it's *of a duck*, or, at least, of something that is duck-like and physical.

Martin's account, on which the nature of a hallucination consists in its indistinguishability by reflection alone from a veridical perception, fares no better than Fish's. Martin's account offers no positive reason why that experience is indistinguishable from a perception of a duck. On his view, there are no parts, properties, or features of the hallucinatory experience in virtue of which it is indistinguishable from a perception of a duck, but perfectly distinguishable from a perception of a house or a football game or countless other things. And while Martin's defense of the view that hallucinations are exhaustively characterizable by the negative epistemic property of being indistinguishable from veridical experiences is quite sophisticated, none of that sophistication enables me to comprehend how something's nature could consist simply in that. I could understand if someone said that what we call 'hallucinations' do not comprise a natural kind, but a rag-tag collection of states whose only *common* feature is that of being indistinguishable from veridical experiences. But I cannot make heads or tails of Martin's position, according to which any possible individual hallucination is such that its *only feature* is its indistinguishability from some veridical perceptual experience. In order for something to resemble or be indiscriminable from some other thing, it has got to *be*, intrinsically, some way. So, at any rate, it seems to me.

The weird object disjunctivist response is also implausible. To see something as it is and mistake it for something else is not a hallucination. If I see Jim's twin Tim, and mistake Tim for Jim, I have not hallucinated. This response also deprives us of any way of explaining why hallucinations are bad cases across the board, rather than merely contingently bad for creatures like ourselves. If appearances exist and can be seen, there doesn't seem to be anything impossible about a race of creatures seeing them almost all the time. And if they did, they would quite conceivably form beliefs, not about worldly states of affairs, but about appearances. After all, they see appearances in the same way we see houses and trees. And if, once in a while, they caught a glimpse of the world, they would probably form a false belief about an appearance. But if we pursue the line of thinking, glimpses of the world would be the bad cases for these creatures. But that is not so. It would be a *good* case of seeing the world. And if it is a good case of seeing the world, despite generating false beliefs, then our seeing appearances shouldn't count as a bad case either. But it is a bad case, both in our world and that of the hallucinators. The theory that ascribes world-directed content to hallucinations can explain why: a race of hallucinators would be in bad shape, not because it's bad to see appearances rather than the world – I'm sure some of them are quite lovely, if they exist – but because they are not seeing appearances. They are having experiences that are intrinsically erroneous, because those experiences depict a world of physical objects that do not exist and worldly facts that do not obtain.

Furthermore, no theory that explains why hallucinations are errors in terms of the kinds of beliefs they produce can be right, since producing false beliefs is neither necessary nor sufficient for hallucination. It is not necessary since hallucinations remain nonveridical even when one is savvy to them. Suppose you take a powerful dose of *Salvia divinorum* and begin to experience everything around you flattening into a two-dimensional plane and slowly draining through a hole in the middle of space, while you, meanwhile, distinctly seem to be in several places simultaneously. (Yes, users report experiences like this.) You are savvy to the experience. You know it's nonveridical. In fact, you've got bad habits, and have become accustomed to the effects of this drug. It does not have a propensity to produce false beliefs in you or any of your unwholesome friends. (We can even imagine an entire community of savvy *Salvia* junkies.) Are we then to say that the experience you are having is not a hallucination? No. As Husserl says of "unmasked" hallucinations, "the phenomenon of the standing there of the Object in the flesh persists or can persist" (*TS* §5: 13). Your experience presents the world other than it is, and it does this whether you like it or not. Nothing you believe or fail to believe can alter that. And the only way for it to stop being erroneous is for it simply to stop. This, moreover, would be true if there were not a single creature in the world who has so much as a disposition to form false beliefs while on *Salvia*. The beliefs the experience generates do not determine its intentional content. As Mark Johnston puts it, "being susceptible to visual hallucination is a liability which just comes with having a visual system ... and does not require the operation of the ability to think or believe" (Johnston 2009: 217).

Producing false beliefs is also not sufficient for hallucination. Suppose that you, for various philosophical reasons, think the physical world does not exist, and that, through years of meditation and training, you have convinced yourself that all of your veridical experiences are in fact non-veridical. You believe the contradictory of everything that you previously would have believed on the basis of perception. For instance, when you experience rain, you believe that it's not raining. We can even imagine a whole community of people who have acquired this ability, or a race of creatures who are hard-wired in this way. The fact that your experiences produce false beliefs does not make them hallucinatory. They are veridical no matter what you happen to believe or what propensities to believe you have.

Because we can always imagine possible scenarios in which hallucinatory experiences fail to produce false beliefs, any attempt to characterize them along such lines is inadequate. A better proposal is to characterize them (in part, at least) in terms of the beliefs that they immediately *justify*, or what a rational agent *would* believe if he bracketed his background beliefs. Hallucinations are experiences that immediately and defeasibly justify, in a reasons-internalist sense of 'justify', false beliefs about one's physical environment.

The radical disjunctivist cannot hold such a view. If hallucinations are not about anything, then they cannot justify anything, at least not in any evidential way, since only the consciousness of something can be the consciousness of *evidence for* something. Weird object disjunctivism is in no better shape. If its defenders claim that having a hallucination immediately justifies beliefs about physical objects, despite presenting an appearance as it is, then they face a dilemma. If they say that hallucinatory experiences do not justify beliefs about the appearances that they are in fact about, then they are committed to the view that there are certain objects which, despite existing and having sense-perceptible properties, are such that no direct presentation of them can justify beliefs about them. But that's absurd. Seeing something exactly as it is, and believing of it that it is the way it is seen to be, is the absolute ideal of knowledge. If, on the other hand, the defenders of weird object disjunctivism say that hallucinations justify beliefs about appearances as well as physical objects, then they should also say that veridical perceptual experiences justify both beliefs about the physical world and beliefs about appearances. But that too is wrong. When I see my table, there's no appearance that I am justified in believing anything about, since my perceptual experience is not of an appearance, but a table.

Finally, one might claim that hallucinations are errors because they prevent our perceptual faculties from performing their proper function, which is to make the world directly available for action and knowledge. Hallucinations undoubtedly do that, but doing that is not sufficient to make something a hallucination. There are lots of ways in which the proper functioning of our perceptual faculties can be impeded. We can be struck blind. We can be struck unconscious. We can be struck dead. We can become delusional, so that we always form beliefs that are unsupported by our *veridical* experiences. If one thinks tumbleweeds are demons, one might believe that a field is teeming with demons when all that one's experience presents is a field teeming with tumbleweeds. We can also hallucinate, and that differs in obvious ways from all of the other cases. Moreover, whatever it is in virtue of which hallucination interferes with the proper functioning of our perceptual systems, it must be something that renders it *erroneous* as well. Being struck blind or comatose is not an error. Neither is dying. Being delusional is, but being delusional is perfectly compatible with having veridical perceptual experiences. A content view that ascribes world-directed but nonveridical intentional contents to hallucinatory experiences can say exactly why they both interfere with perception and are erroneous: they present the world other than it is, and doing that directly interferes with the function of perception. But it's difficult to see how radical disjunctivism or weird object disjunctivism can explain those phenomena.

Neither radical disjunctivism nor weird object disjunctivism (nor the sense datum theory) seems able to provide a satisfactory account of why hallucinations are errors, and why particular episodes of hallucinating constitute very particular kinds of errors. And this point generalizes: *no* theory that denies that hallucinations have world-directed intentional content can satisfactorily explain why they are errors about the world. Something that isn't even *about* the world can't be *wrong about* the world. If, therefore, disjunctivism is true – and some variety of it must be if the relational view is true – then it must be some version that at least ascribes intentional content to hallucinations, even if it retains the relational conception of veridical experience.

This has one important consequence, and that is that nonconceptual content must exist. Since the objects of hallucination do not exist, and so cannot possibly constitute a hallucination's phenomenal character, hallucinatory experiences must have intentional content. And this intentional content cannot, for virtually all of the reasons discussed over the previous three chapters, be conceptual. So, it has nonconceptual, and specifically *intuitive*, intentional content. If there are no conceptual contents the entertaining of which is necessary and sufficient to be in any perceptual state E, then there are no such contents which are necessary and sufficient to be in a state that is indiscriminable from E. But hallucinations, or at least some possible hallucinations, are indiscriminable from veridical experiences.

Another important consequence is that one of the most common complaints against the content view of perceptual experience is misguided. According to the content view, or what Campbell calls the 'representational view', "the representational content of your experience may be exactly the same in both [the veridical and hallucinatory] cases" (Campbell 2002: 117). And if that is right, the thinking goes, then "all that the experience of the object provides you with is a conscious image of the object – the image which bears the representational content" (Campbell 2002: 123). But that is just not so. The content view is not committed to the existence of any images, appearances, or sense data figuring in a hallucination at all; it is not committed to the view that a hallucination which is of something requires that there be any existing object whatsoever that it is of, much less one that actually instantiates that properties that the experience presents its object as having. Hallucinations do not have to be of anything less than the world, and they do not have to be of the world in anything less than a direct way. Again, Paul Snowdon writes, "The experience in a perceptual case reaches out to and involves the perceived external objects, not so the experience in other cases" (2005: 136–7). While hallucination cannot *involve* its object, since its object does not exist, it does *reach out* to the external world: it is erroneous *because* it reaches out but does not involve, and would not be erroneous if it reached out towards *and involved* a mere appearance. And the difference between a hallucination and a veridical perception might turn out to consist entirely in the involvement but not in the reaching – perception might just be a case in which the intentional content that it shares with a possible hallucination is satisfied. Such a view in no way entails that the intentional content falls short of the world in either case.

## 6.3 FURTHER CONSIDERATIONS AGAINST THE RELATIONAL VIEW

The relational view is similar to the sense datum theory insofar as both hold that the character of an act of perception can be characterized by citing its object.[7] In the case of sense data, knowing which sense datum someone is conscious of is simply the end of the story concerning the character of that person's experience. Russell even appears to hold that attentional modifications can be explained as differences in the object perceived, and calls objects which one attends to "emphatic particulars" (Russell 1984: 40–1). One reason is that the perception of a sense datum is often held to be adequate – that is, perfect and complete – in which case no two experiences that differ qualitatively or present their objects differently could possibly be of the same sense data. But, as the problem of the speckled hen illustrates, these pretensions to adequacy are difficult to maintain even with respect to

---

[7] See Martin 2009b: 273 for a comparison of the views. Brewer (2008: 17) writes that the object view "retains the early modern conviction that the core subjective character of perceptual experience is to be given simply by citing its direct object."

the awareness of sense data. If I perceive a sense datum corresponding to a hen with a number of speckles, the sense datum itself will have a number of speckles. But if that number is sufficiently large, and my perception sufficiently fleeting, I will neither know nor perceive how many speckles it has. This problem, as Chisholm (1942) points out, is not an isolated one.

In the case of physical objects, the fact that we cannot simply say what an experience is like by citing its object is even more obvious. Knowing that a given creature perceives a certain tree tells us nearly nothing about the subjective character of his experience: he might be viewing it at night or at noon, or from very far away or up close. He might be a "normal" human, or he might be a bat, or a superhero with microscopic vision. He might be paying attention to the tree or not. The tree might look just like a man waving to him in the distance, and he might mistake it for one. And so on.

The relational view can address many of these issues. First, the subjective character of an experience is determined not only by "the" object perceived – the focal object, that is – since almost no perceptual experience consists of seeing only one object, but by the total environment perceived. When one perceives a tree in daylight and at night, the total object of one's perceptual state is different, since one will also perceive the lighting conditions themselves; one can perceive that it is day rather than night. When one perceives the tree from up close, one also perceives it as being close to one, in which case the experience has a different total object from one in which that tree is perceived from far off. Nor does the theory have difficulty explaining why the white part of the wall basking in the light looks differently from the part of the wall in the shadow, since we are also conscious of the light and the shadow: one part of the wall looks like a white surface in a shadow, while another looks like it is illuminated.

Second, the theory can go some way towards explaining the subjective character of experiences by citing the objects in the environment together with the conditions under which they are perceived. The theory does not absurdly predict that viewing the Empire State Building from across the East River will have the same phenomenal character as viewing it from 34th St. Nor does it predict that in perceiving a tree one will perceive every leaf, every cell, and so forth, since one's own constitution partially determines the conditions under which something is perceived. So, while the view *might* entail that "two ordinary observers standing in roughly the same place, looking at the same scene, are bound to have experiences with the same phenomenal character" (Campbell 2002: 116) it does not entail that an ordinary human observer and an ordinary lamprey will. In virtue of having evolved in the way we have, and having the distinctive sensory, bodily, and cognitive abilities and skills that we do, only *some* objects and properties can constitute the subjective character of our experience. If we vary in our capacities, as we surely do, then some features of the environment will be available to some that are not to others. Bats are acquainted with properties that we are not. And if those faculties break down radically, then physical objects will no longer constitute the character of our experience.

William Fish (2009: Chapter 3) discusses a variety of conditions which, in addition to the object perceived, help determine the character of a perceptual experience. These include the distribution of objects in the environment, the subject's own position, the nature of the subject's visual and other perceptual systems, a subject's attentional state, and even the subject's conceptual resources. This is all surely right. Moreover, the fact that all of these factors, including the massive amount of cognitive processing that perception involves, are required for objects to present themselves to us in no way speaks against the claim that when our sense organs and brains are working properly, the objects of veridical perception constitute the subjective character of our experiences.[8] In particular, that a massive amount of cognitive processing is required for us to perceive things veridically does not entail that we construct a picture or model of the world in our brains or that we fail to see objects as they are in themselves. It might just take a lot of work for these objects and properties to reveal themselves as they are. Every other biological process requires fine-tuning to "process" real objects, and this doesn't entail that they don't relate directly to those objects. Hands don't grasp representations of tools, stomachs don't digest representations of food, and a properly functioning immune system doesn't attack representations of pathogens. Why, then, would a mind or brain deal directly only with representations of the objects that determine the survival of the organism it functions to sustain in being? The idea that a mind is best equipped to grasp the mind-independent world when it is as close to featurelessness as possible is just a myth, one which, unsurprisingly, has been promulgated more often by anti-realists than realists. The truth is far more likely to be that objects will only "give" themselves to minds that have, whether through exertion or luck, assumed the proper shape to receive them.

Precisely the same point, however, holds of intentional contents. That a mind must instantiate intentional contents, that it must be configured in some determinate way, in no way entails that its contact with the world is in

---

[8] "On a Relational View, we have to think of cognitive processing as 'revealing' the world to the subject; that is, making it possible for the subject to experience particular external objects" (Campbell 2002: 118).

any way indirect. That would be like supposing that because my hand must be configured in some definite way to grasp a hammer, I do not directly grasp the hammer. And, as it turns out, Fish's list of factors that influence the character of one's experience is only the tip of the iceberg. There are a wide variety of *intentional* factors that are necessary for perceptual experiences to occur. Perceptual consciousness involves larger acts consisting of founding and founded acts, acts directed upon other acts, acts directed upon different aspects of the world, both intuited and nonintuited, acts directed towards the body, and so forth. Here are some of the specifically conscious, intentional factors, over and above those discussed by Fish, that help determine the phenomenal character of experience.

### 6.3.1. Time-consciousness

Every conscious act takes place in time, and within the consciousness of time. Time-consciousness, unlike dog-consciousness or food-consciousness or even space-consciousness, is absolutely pervasive. And it is genuinely the consciousness of time, not (just) a sequence of consciousnesses in time. This is best illustrated by the fact that we can take hold of temporally extended objects, processes, events, and so forth. Listening to a melody is not a matter of the consciousness of A followed by the consciousness of B. It is the consciousness of B-following-A. But A is no longer *present* when I hear B. It is just-past. Nor do I hear a chord of B and a dim A, all there at once. Rather, I hear B as following A. Even merely gawking at a stationary object involves time-consciousness. After having stared at something for five seconds, I am not having the same experience I had when I began. Rather, after five seconds I am also aware of having perceived the object. After a few more seconds, I will become bored. This is how I can be perceptually aware that it has not changed, and how it can give itself as not having changed – something I could not discover in a point-like instant. Holding still, remaining unchanged, is also something that can only manifest itself in time-consciousness.

Husserl calls this consciousness of the just-past 'retention'. As the present experience "sinks down" into the past, I retain it, along with its own object, in my present consciousness. Let my experience at the now-moment be $P_3$, and its object C. Then in undergoing $P_3$, I also have a retention of $P_2$, the previous experience, along with $P_2$'s intentional object, B, which, we will suppose, is identical with C. The present experience, in other words, includes among its present intentional objects both C as it just-was, and

P2 itself as a just-past perception of that object. P2 will have just the same structure: it will be a present impression of B, and a retention of both P1 and P1's object A as it just-was. This "comet's tail" of retentional states eventually dies out.

In addition to all of that, each experience is characterized by protention. Each experience anticipates what is about to follow. So, not only is P3 the consciousness of C as present, the consciousness of B and P2 as just-past, and the consciousness of A and P1 as just-just-past, but it is also the empty or anticipatory consciousness of P4 and its object D. Even within time-consciousness, then, we have three distinct intentionalities: primal impression, retention, and protention. Not only that, but the *whole structure* is itself pervaded by two distinct intentionalities: the "transverse" intentionality, in virtue of which both present and non-present *intentional objects* are intended, and the "horizontal" or "longitudinal" intentionality by whose means both present and non-present *experiences of those objects* are intended (*PCIT* §39).

Because both retentional consciousness and protentional, anticipatory consciousness involved in time-consciousness are directed towards what is not actually *present*, they cannot simply be lifted off of the object perceived. It is not the tree that I see or the melody I hear that alone explains why I retain their past temporal moments or the experiences of those moments, but the peculiar intentional structure of my consciousness of them. Naturally this doesn't prevent me from perceiving those things as they are, but is a condition of my doing so. If the temporal spread of retentional consciousness were greater, even more states of affairs could appear perceptually. I could then not only see that the stars have moved, but see them move. But this would not be due to any new properties of stars.

### 6.3.2. Horizons

I have already discussed (section 2.3) the fact that perceptual experiences are always inadequate to their objects, at least when the objects in question are physical things, their intrinsic properties, and many of the relations among them. No single experience of an object is perfect and complete, and each one leaves open the possibility of there being further experiences that disclose it further.

[E]very perceptual object in the epistemic process is a flowing approximation. We always have the external object in the flesh (we see, grasp, seize it), and yet it is always at an infinite distance mentally. What we do grasp of it pretends to be its essence; and it is it too, but it remains so only in an incomplete approximation, an approximation that grasps something of it, but in doing so it also constantly grasps into an emptiness that cries out for fulfillment.[9]

The fact that physical things, including their parts and property-instances, can always be perceived from other points of view, and therefore cannot be adequately perceived from any single point of view, is something many theories can accommodate. But what needs to be explained is not merely that physical objects cannot be given adequately, but that our experience is felt to be inadequate, and that, correspondingly, the object itself is perceived to have more to it than what we perceive. As A. D. Smith puts it, the claim that objects are given inadequately is not just an "incursion into the pure phenomenology of the 'objective' knowledge that physical objects have unperceived sides." Rather, "Physical objects *appear* like that – i.e. *as* having more to them than is revealed in one glance – and we take them to be like that" (A. D. Smith 2008b: 324). It is not the bare fact of incompleteness or inadequacy, but the *consciousness of it*, that needs to be explained. And merely appealing to the object cannot explain it, since that sense of inadequacy is part of what explains why I perceive the object in question.

As in the case of time-consciousness, the horizons that help bring objects to consciousness not only aim at parts, features, and objects in the world that could be brought to perception proper, but at the experiences in which those objects could be perceived. The object is given as more precisely because, and only insofar as, my present experience of it is itself given as inadequate. This is not to deny that this consciousness of one's own experiences is marginal or apperceptive, but without some awareness of how one's own experience is related to the object, the consciousness of inadequacy could not arise. And so, as in the case of time-consciousness, the object itself cannot explain how it is that my experience instantiates precisely the empty internal and external horizons that it does. The barn façade itself cannot determine, when only its face is perceptually intuited, why my act prescribes that it has a closed interior rather than not, even though the difference between carrying out acts with barn-horizons and façade-horizons is a difference at the level of perception itself.

---

[9] *APS*: 58–9. Again: "[W]e cannot speak of an adequate perception of a thing in the sense of an appearance of it which, as absolute givenness, would leave nothing more open, no possibilities of re-determination, enrichment, or more precise determination" (*TS* §37: 108).

### 6.3.3. The body

Perceptual experience is necessarily perspectival, and having a perspective means being located in an environment of surrounding objects. Being thus located, furthermore, implies, and perhaps entails, being embodied.[10] Objects are presented as being a certain distance from where I am; they lie in various directions such as *to the right* or *below*. Not only that, but, in order for my perception to qualify as of objective things and places, it must present objects as related *to me*, to the right of *me* or below *me* and my body. "The 'far' is far from me, from my Body; the 'to the right' refers back to the right side of my Body, e.g., to my right hand" (*Ideas II* §41a: 166). To take *being to the right* as a monadic, non-relational property of an object is a kind of "idealism about space, on which there is nothing more to where things are than where they presently appear to be" (Brewer 1999: 195). In normal perception, on the other hand, objects are given relative to an egocentric frame of reference that can change without altering the perceived objective locations of things. One's body is perceived to be both a zero-point of orientation and an objective feature of the world itself, just as every other body is perceived as both occupying an objective portion of space and a possible egocentric point of space. We can and do recognize where we are, our egocentric point of orientation, as identical with an objective portion of space allocentrically specified – that is, specified in some object-centered way. I can move myself *over there*, and then *that* location, the very one that I'm tracking as I move, becomes my egocentric origin.

It is also in virtue of having a body that we do not treat all changes in the character of our experience of objects as changes in the objects of experience. Or, in Kant's terminology, it is critical in distinguishing between "the *subjective succession of apprehension* from the *objective succession of appearances*" (Kant 1965: A193/B238; also see A. D. Smith 2002: 170). When I squint in order to get a better view of the precise shape of something, my experience changes without any perceived change in the object I experience. (There is a change in both the content and object of the experience, since previously unperceived features come into view with more specificity than had been anticipated, but the object is not perceived as changing.) The same is often true when I walk towards something, turn my head, move my eyes back and forth, and so forth. When I glance from one side of a house to another, the house does not appear to move. Part of what clues me in to the

---

[10] "If something appears perspectivally, then the subject to whom it appears must be spatially related to it. To be spatially related to something requires that one be embodied" (Thompson 2007: 248).

difference between changes in experience and changes in the objects of experience is that I am conscious of my body and its movements or lack thereof. I feel myself squint, for instance. As I turn my head left, stationary objects are supposed to "move" to the right of my visual field. If I keep my head stationary, moving objects are supposed to "move" through my visual field. I can tell the difference between these experiences and the states of affairs they present, despite potentially identical "visual data," because I am proprioceptively and kinesthetically aware of my own movements or lack thereof.[11] The awareness of myself as moving spells the difference between a perception of me moving towards an object and that of an object moving towards me. Again, if I pet a stingray at the aquarium, I can tell the difference between moving my hand over a stationary animal and the animal moving under my stationary hand, even when precisely the same tactile sensations are involved.

We are normally aware of our body in two ways. For one thing, our bodies are often perceptually present as objects among objects. I see my hands and forearms as I type, for instance. I can also direct my attention towards my own body. I feel my leg as an object when I tactually explore a bug bite on it. I have, in short, a "body image," a body as intentional object that can be represented in both perceptual and empty, conceptual consciousness.[12] Gallagher distinguishes this from the "body schema," defining the latter as "a system of sensory-motor capacities that function without awareness or the necessity of perceptual monitoring" (Gallagher 2005: 24). On Gallagher's view, it would seem that the consciousness of the body is carried out solely by means of the body image. Evan Thompson, however, following Husserl and Merleau-Ponty, claims that we are also aware of the body-as-subject:

One's consciousness of one's body ... is not limited to the body image, nor is the body image the most fundamental form of bodily consciousness. On the contrary, most of the time one's body is experienced in an implicit, tacit, and prereflective way. This kind of experience is consciousness of the body-as-subject. (Thompson 2007: 249–50)

I am not unconscious of my own movements as I walk towards or around an object, nor am I *only* conscious of my body as an object among objects. I am

---

[11]  "With mere eye-movement, the visual image wanders over the visual field and undergoes a determinate series of modifications, including qualitative ones. If the eye is stationary, the exact same series of modifications can still elapse, and then movement appears" (*TS* §50: 148).

[12]  "A body image consists of a system of perceptions, attitudes, and beliefs pertaining to one's own body" (Gallagher 2005: 24).

also conscious of it as a percei*ving* body, in a way exactly analogous to the way in which I am conscious of my own mental acts when I live through them. When I run my fingers down the spine of a stingray, my fingers aren't *just*, or even primarily, perceived objects. They are parts of my perceiv*ing* body, the means whereby the stingray's skin is perceived. My hands are not just objects, but *bearers*, of intentionality.

The difference between the way the body manifests itself when it is given as an intentional object and when it is given as a bodily subject becomes apparent when we consider that in the former case, but not the latter, one's body is itself given perspectivally. If I look at my hand or feel my arm, the seen hand and the felt arm are, like any other sort of material object, only partially and inadequately given, given *from* a perspective *to* me. But, like acts of consciousness themselves, my seeing eye and feeling hand are not given perspectivally. This isn't because they are given adequately. It is because they are not given to me in the same way that objects are at all. They do not stand *over against* me; they are not *Gegenstände*. They are, rather, that to which their own objects – *my* objects – are related perspectivally. When I treat my foot and my knee as two intentional objects, the former is farther away from *me* insofar as it is farther from the hand, the bearer of bodily subjectivity, that would touch it. There is a Heideggerian, existential sense of "farther away," one which measures the accessibility of a thing for possible action and use rather than its geometric relations to me, on which my internal organs are as far from me as the floor of the sea.[13] But when I, as I usually am, am intentionally directed towards the world and not my own body, my body only shows up as an *object* in a marginal way. My foot and my knee, as parts of a body-as-subject given proprioceptively, are not such that one of them is farther from or closer to *me*.[14] Thus Gallagher writes, "Proprioception operates within a non-relative, non-perspectival, intra-corporeal spatial framework that is different from both egocentric and allocentric frameworks" (Gallagher 2005: 138).

Time-consciousness, horizonal consciousness, and bodily consciousness all involve some form of self-consciousness, and each is essential for perceptual experiences directed at what is physical. Self-consciousness, then, along with time-, horizonal, and bodily consciousness are all features of experience, and intentional features of experience, which, in addition to the

---

[13] See Heidegger (1962: 135): "Every entity that is 'to hand' has a different closeness, which is not to be ascertained by measuring distances. This closeness regulates itself in terms of circumspectively 'calculative' manipulating and using." Thanks to John McHugh for this observation.

[14] "Whereas one can say that this book is closer to me than that book over there, one cannot say that my foot is closer to me than my hand" (Gallagher 2005: 138).

perceived worldly object, help constitute the phenomenological character of experience. More importantly, however, in the case of both time-consciousness and horizonal consciousness, we are aware of both (1) objects that are not present to consciousness and (2) experiences or experience-stages that are not occurring. But our consciousness of these things cannot be lifted out of the perceived objects themselves. The immediate past and future, as well as the unperceived parts, sides, and more determinate properties of a thing, are present *intentionally* and, in some cases, completely *emptily*. But it is only in virtue of those things being present intentionally that physical objects can appear to us at all.

This points to a stark difference between the relational view and the sense datum theory that it in part emulates. In the case of sense data, there is at least some plausibility to the idea that our perception of them is adequate. Even the consciousness of one's own body can drop away in the case of sense data, since they are not constituted intentionally as identities given in different experiences – there is no question of distinguishing changes in the sense datum and changes in the experience of it – and, as a consequence, their properties would be given unambiguously even if all bodily awareness were to fall away. There is, likewise, no need for inner horizons, since to take a closer look at a sense datum is to see a numerically different sense datum. In the case of physical entities and properties, on the other hand, adequacy is out of the question. Brewer, for reasons having to do with the alleged prevalence of illusions in normal experience, criticizes the content view on the grounds that if it were true, "Full direct contact between mind and world is never actually established in human perceptual experience" (Brewer 2008: 171). Brewer is wrong that direct contact is never established on a content view. But he is right that full contact, understood as adequate contact, is never established – which is exactly the result we want. It cannot be an objection to the content view that it entails what is, and must be, the case.

The problem with the relational view is that, first, it does not do justice to the massively complex intentional acts and their contents that are required for perceptual consciousness. With the possible exception of acts of attending, which may or may not differ from others in virtue of their intentional content, even Fish's list of factors that help determine the character of an experience makes no mention of any occurrent acts with intentional content. Secondly, by construing perceived objects as constituents of the experiences of them, it cannot explain why our experiences of them and all of their parts and features are necessarily inadequate. If objects are *constituents* of our experiences, in any remotely acceptable sense of 'constituent', then every part, feature, and property of those objects must be a constituent of our experience. And if every part, feature, and property of an object is a constituent of an *experience*, then everything is present perceptually in that experience. After all, the whole point of claiming that objects are *constituents* of experience is to distinguish something's being perceptually present from its being represented in any other, more derivative way. For something to be a constituent of an experience is, one suspects, rather like being something with which one is *acquainted* in Russell's sense. Campbell, for one, explicitly compares perception to acquaintance, and Brewer compares his theory to that of the early moderns such as Berkeley (see Campbell 2002: 6; 114–15). But Russellian acquaintance is an ideal towards which perception aspires but cannot reach. In the interests of supporting naïve realism, the relational view naïvely exaggerates how much of the world we actually perceive, and how well we perceive it.[15] And in doing so, it conflicts with phenomenologically discoverable truths about our experiences themselves.

If the relational view were right, then at least some physical objects could be perceived adequately; *full* contact with worldly objects would occur. But no physical object can be perceived adequately. Therefore, the relational view is not right. The content view, on the other hand, can explain how a direct perception of something physical can nevertheless be inadequate to it. An intuitive content, one that manages to present some object, aspect, or feature in the flesh, only presents its object partially or one sidedly. Furthermore, this does not amount to it presenting some part of its object, or some appearance of it, adequately, and then emptily intending the rest. It is inadequate all the way down. Another way of putting this is that there is absolutely nothing physical – no object, nor any part or side of an object, nor even any property-instance belonging to a physical object – that could be perceived without the assistance of empty intentional horizons or horizons pointing towards more determinate features of what is perceived:

What 'properly' appears cannot be separated from the physical thing as, let us say, a physical thing for itself; in the full sense of the physical thing, the sense-correlate of what 'properly' appears fashions a non-selfsufficient part which can only have unity and self-sufficiency of sense in a whole which necessarily includes in itself empty components and indeterminate components. (*Ideas I* §138: 331)

---

[15] Commenting on Campbell's grounds for answering Molyneux's question affirmatively, Janet Levin writes: "My hypothesis is that Campbell has succumbed to the temptation to think that, unlike perceptual experiences of kinds such as skunks or states such as rottenness, perceptual experiences of shape, whether visual or tactual, display to our scrutiny the nature or essence of those properties themselves" (Levin 2008: 17). While this isn't the objection I develop, it does run along similar lines.

It would, therefore, be a mistake to suppose that in perception, parts, sides, or features of the object are literally constituents of the experience, and that all of the further work in establishing that experience's phenomenal and phenomenological character is performed by intentional contents. Rather, because experience is inadequate all the way down, it is intentional all the way down. Strip an experience of everything intentional, and specifically horizonal, in it, and one will be left without any consciousness whatsoever of anything physical.

### 6.4 A DEFENSE OF MODERATE DISJUNCTIVISM

The object of a perceptual experience is not a constituent of that experience. Rather, its constituents are the intuitive and horizonal contents in virtue of which that object is perceptually present to consciousness. Endorsing such a view does not, however, force one to hold that a perceptual state and a hallucination can have precisely the same intentional content. There are, rather, strong reasons for holding that the contents of perceptual experiences could never be identical with those of hallucinations.

Before turning to hallucinations, I intend to discuss some related issues regarding the relationship between an experience's subjective or phenomenological character, its content, and its object. First, it seems plausible that if two mental states are indistinguishable upon wakeful, sober, and attentive reflection, then they have the same phenomenological character. Phenomenological character, it might be thought, just is what is given to us in reflection. Call this thesis "introspective access":

IA: Necessarily, if two experiences are indistinguishable from one another by introspection alone, then they have the same phenomenological character.

Second, it might seem plausible that the contents of perceptual experiences are determined by their phenomenological character. Call this thesis "phenomenological sameness":

PS: Necessarily, if two experiences have the same phenomenological character, then they have the same content.[16]

PS is the converse of weak intentionalism – the claim that experiences with the same content have the same phenomenal character (Tye 2007: 608) – and faces some of the same objections. Specifically, it is false if qualia inversion is possible. Although I don't think it is possible, what follows

---

[16] Speaks (2009) calls this the "Phenomenology/Sense Principle."

doesn't hinge on that. Finally, contents are those features of mental states in virtue of which they are intentionally directed upon their objects in a determinate manner. Call this thesis "object determination":

OD: Necessarily, if two experiences have the same content, then they (re)present the same object.

This is most famously enshrined in Frege's doctrine that sense determines reference.

Let pure internalism be the conjunction of IA, PS, and OD. Since hallucinations can be indistinguishable from veridical experiences by introspection alone, it is easy to see how pure internalism entails a conjunctivist account of hallucination. On its face, however, pure internalism is not a good theory. The reason is that, although it might be a defensible account with respect to the experience of certain sorts of properties, it does not provide a compelling answer to the "problem of particularity" (Searle 1983: 62) or familiar twin earth cases. Two experiences might be of two different objects and yet be introspectively indistinguishable. If A and B are two qualitatively identical steel balls, then my perceptual experience of A might be exactly like the experience I would have had if I had seen B instead. But one experience is of A, while the other is of B. Twin earth cases are expressly designed to illustrate this possibility. By IA and PS, these two experiences have the same content. But by OD they do not. So, when it comes to the experiences of A and of B, pure internalism entails that they both do and do not have the same content.

One way to preserve pure internalism in the face of this example is to deny that the two experiences are of different objects. But this response doesn't work. Consider the available alternatives. Either we can hold that (1) both experiences are of A, (2) both experiences are of B, or (3) neither experience is of either A or B. But all of these options are unattractive. Suppose (1) is true and suppose that B is physically present and causally responsible for my perceptual experience. If the experience is of A, then it must be counted as a hallucination, since A is nowhere in sight. But that is surely the wrong answer. What we have here is a veridical experience of B, not a hallucination of A. I might wrongly identify B as A, but that's a mistake at a different level, a cognitive rather than a perceptual one. These remarks hold, *mutatis mutandis*, for option (2).

Option (3), finally, is hardly more attractive than (1) or (2). There are a couple of ways of developing it. The first is to claim that the perceptual experiences simply don't reach out to any ball at all; in no complete description of their conditions of satisfaction would any ball of any type figure, any more than, say, Ganymede figures in the conditions of satisfaction for the thought that my shoe is dirty. This view has, in my opinion, almost no plausibility. It would fit well with a sense datum view according to which we infer the existence of things like steel balls on the basis of experiences of other things, but, first, there are compelling reasons, as I have already argued, to reject sense datum theories, and, secondly, the problem of particularity applies to sense data as well. It even holds for experiences.[17]

A second way to develop (3) it is to treat the content of the experiences descriptively, so that my perceptual experience is veridical if and only if there exists a steel ball with such-and-such properties before me (see McGinn (1982) and Davies (1992) for a defense of this sort of view). To claim that such a content is "of A," on this account, is really just to say that A is the thing that happens to satisfy it. But this really isn't a matter of the content being *of A*. The content of my experience is not genuinely of A because if B were there instead, the content would still be satisfied. Consider an uncontroversial example of thinking of A descriptively. I see a certain hole in the window, and think that whatever put this hole here must have been traveling quickly. Suppose A put it there. In that case, I think of A as just whatever produced the hole. But this thought isn't really *about A*. Keeping the content of my thought constant and changing scenarios so that B caused it, my thought would now be about B – all without any change in the content of my thought. Picking things out by description is a kind of lazy intentionality. It can succeed even when we have absolutely no idea which things we're thinking about. When we do it, we exploit objects about which we can think directly and allow contingent facts about the world – facts of which we might be totally ignorant – to do the rest of the work for us.

If the relational view gets anything right, it is that this is not how perceptual intentionality works. I don't see *some ball or other* when I see A. The content of my perceptual experience is not satisfied if there is a steel ball in front of me. It is not even satisfied if, as on Searle's (1983) view, the content of my experience is that there is a steel ball causing *this very experience* and some steel ball or other is causing this very experience (Bach 2007). It is satisfied only if *this* particular ball is before me. And even if I'm not in a position to know that *this is A*, I am in a position to know that the general modal status of the proposition that *this is A* is necessary. That is, I can know that if it is true, it is necessarily true, and if it is false, it is

---

[17] See McDowell (1991: 263–4), where he criticizes Searle for never explaining how an indexical reference to "this visual experience" is possible on a "Fregean" picture of intentionality.

necessarily false (see Casullo 2003: 91). Suppose, on the other hand, that perception only affords me a descriptive way of identifying A; A is "the F," say. I might not know that *A is the F*, but I can know that the general modal status of the proposition that *A is the F* is contingent. It is possible that B, rather than A, is the F.

One way out of this mess is to abandon OD. That is David Woodruff Smith's solution. "Phenomenologically indistinguishable experiences have the same content" (D. W. Smith 1982a: 191). Nevertheless, "two perceptions may have the same structure, or content, but have different objects" (D. W. Smith 1989: 146). This is because they may "occur in *different contexts*" (145). On Smith's view, perceptual experience is characterized by its "sensuous character" (38), its "intentional character" (39), and its "demonstrative structure" (41), and it is in virtue of the latter that perceptual experiences acquaint us with objects. The demonstrative component "prescribes" or "is satisfied by" a particular object only if the experience in which that content figures "stands in an appropriate contextual relation to the object, or the object plays a proper role in the context of the experience" (D. W. Smith 1989: 158). In perception, the appropriate contextual relations are "spatiotemporal and causal" ones (140).

Although Smith is not committed to the view that a perception and a matching hallucination have the same objects, Smith's account is conjunctivist about the *content* of perception; perceptual experiences and hallucinations can have the same content. As Burge says of his own, similar view, "The very same demonstrative thought might have lacked a referent if the world beyond the thought had been different" (Burge 1991: 208). While this theory is superior to the versions of disjunctivism considered in section 6.2, since it can explain why hallucinations are errors, I don't think it works. In particular, as we have already seen (section 4.4), there are many reasons not to assimilate perceptual intentionality to that of demonstrative and indexical reference (in this connection, also see Willard 1988: 313–15). The most notable reason is that demonstrative reference is a founded mode of intentionality, and what it is founded on is the antecedent, presentational consciousness of the object that is demonstrated. I can successfully understand an utterance of the form "That is F" only *because* I perceive, or have very recently perceived, the demonstrated object. Demonstrative and indexical reference, to borrow McDowell's phrase, "exploits the presence of the sample" (McDowell, 1994: 56–7). I know which thing is being pointed to *because* I see it.

D. W. Smith himself, at times, seems close to acknowledging as much. Perception is a form of acquaintance with an object, and contains both a *sense of the object's presence* and a *demonstrative content*. The latter presupposes the former. As he puts it, "The sense of sensuous presence, normally presupposed by the demonstrative content, makes the experience a *perceptually acquainting* experience" (D. W. Smith 1989: 65). And the sense of presence seems to be even more fundamentally involved in acquaintance than the demonstrative content, since the demonstrative content must "single out or individuate that object by appeal to its sensuous presence" (65). Or again: "with no sense of presence behind it, an awareness is simply not indexical, and cannot qualify as acquaintance" (175). But if the demonstrative content singles out an object by an appeal to *its* presence, then it's difficult to see how "the demonstrative content in a perception . . . does the fundamental work of perceptual *acquaintance*" (65). The response might be that the demonstrative element is responsible for the "sense of individuality" – that is, the feature that makes perceptual awareness a singular presentation (65). But surely when I perceive an object and have a sense of *its* sensuous presence, the work of singling it out has already been accomplished. It is not as though, staring straight at a tree in good light, one could have a sense of the tree's presence without also being in a position to know which object one is in the presence of.

There are several options available to us at this point. As far as I can tell, if one abandons OD, some sort of demonstrative view is the best available option. Since that account is untenable, the solution is to retain OD and drop either PS or IA. This means that a perceptual experience of ball A has an intentional content that differs from the content of an experience of B, even if the experiences are indistinguishable and have, or seem to have, the same phenomenological character. But why should this not be the case? Why couldn't there be some constituent of the content of the experience of A in virtue of which it is about A rather than B? Husserl, for whatever it's worth, seems plainly committed to such a view.[18] As we have already seen, Husserl says that the "matter" or content of an act as that moment "which makes the act present just this object in just this manner" (*LI* 6, §25: 737). And yet the content of an act is an intrinsic property of it. By the time of *Ideas I*, Husserl holds that every "noematic sense" contains a "determinable X," which is the "the identical" something which remains constant across acts in which the same object is given as having different predicates (*Ideas I* §131: 313). I am suspicious of the noema – between the chair I see, with its properties, the act of seeing it, with its properties, and the relations among them, I cannot find anything else, especially not the chair-as-it-is-

---

[18] See A. D. Smith (2008b). I am deeply indebted to this article for much of what follows.

perceived – but we can express this by saying that part of the content of each act includes a component, a "noetic X," in virtue of which it succeeds in picking out its object and no other. And it is not, as A. D. Smith points out (2008b: 321–2), merely an abstract X, identically the same in all acts directed towards individuals. Rather, two acts have the same X only if they are directed upon the same individual. "In the essence of the mental process itself lies not only that it is consciousness but also whereof it is consciousness, and in which determinate or indeterminate sense it is that" (*Ideas 1* §36: 74).

On this view, then, each act of perception will include, as an essential aspect of it, a content that picks out its object and no other. It does not do this in virtue of having some generic sort of content that, together with a context of perceiving, yields an object. It does so just in virtue of being what it is. In other words, contents directed towards individuals work just like contents directed towards properties and other "eternal" entities; one is conscious of an individual only if one undergoes an experience which instantiates certain intentional properties or contents that are of it. The difference between an experience of A and one of B is that the former has, while the latter lacks, a singular content whose object is A.

This response will surely fail to satisfy many. D. W. Smith expressly rejects it on the grounds that it is "mysterious":

> There may well be such singular contents embodying presentations of objects themselves without further ado, but how does such a content, all by itself, succeed in prescribing an object – and the right object for each occasion of acquaintance? By magic, it seems, simply "zapping" the right object. (D. W. Smith 1989: 150)

This is another version of the Putnam charge of mysteriousness already discussed (section 1.3), except that it is confined to singular, occasional contents. The first thing to note – and something Dallas Willard (1988) repeatedly notes in a discussion of this view – is that if Smith's criticism holds at all, it should hold for a similar account of non-singular contents as well. But first – this is *ad hominem* – D. W. Smith (and Smith and McIntyre 1982) does not level this criticism at those accounts, and secondly, we have already seen that this is not a good criticism of those accounts. There is nothing mysterious about having the property of being *of* x, no matter what sort of entity x is, and we encounter those sorts of properties and their bearers all the time. What may be more or less mysterious are accounts of how those properties come to be instantiated in mental acts. But, compared with possible accounts of how concepts of abstract entities or absent particulars come to be instantiated, an account of how and why my experience instantiates the property of being of A in the context of perception is among the least mysterious of all. Part of that explanation is that I bear the right causal and spatiotemporal relations to A. How, being awake and sufficiently attentive, could my mind *fail* to acquire new intrinsic properties – intentional contents – when A rolls into view?

To be fair, part of D. W. Smith's worry is that the X apparently reaches its object "without appeal to any of its properties such as its appearance or even its contextual relation to the perceiver or the perception" (D. W. Smith 1989: 149). That, however, is not a commitment of the view I am proposing. It is perfectly consistent to claim that an X can only exist as a component of a larger intentional act or series of acts in which such things as appearances, properties, and contexts are also represented, and, at the same time, that it performs the task of singling out its particular object. As Husserl says, the X "is necessarily to be distinguished from [its predicates], although not to be placed alongside and separated from them" (*Ideas 1* §131: 313). I cannot perceive ball A without perceiving it as propertied in some way and as located in some context, but I can still distinguish the component of content that picks out A, since it is what remains constant as the contents directed towards its perceived properties vary.

The other worry, of course, is that on this account, there is a gap between the introspectable character of an act and its content; just because an experience seems to have a certain content to a mature and reflective perceiver, it doesn't follow that it does, and this seems, to many, wrong. If there's one thing I can be sure of, it is the contents of my own experiences! But why, exactly, should we think that? The idea that we are in a position to have infallible access to the contents of our own consciousness is a hangover from a period of philosophizing in which the phenomenon of intentionality, the world-directedness of perceptual experience and thought, was practically lost from view. Intentional consciousness, however, reaches out to and involves the world, a world that is often opaque to it. And this means that intentional consciousness is often opaque to itself. Insofar as some things look like other things, "why on earth should it *not* be the case that, in some few instances, perceiving one sort of thing is exactly like perceiving another?" (Austin 1964: 52).

I think there's something right about that response. However, I also think that, in a certain clear sense, we are in a position to distinguish those experiences, and their objects, when we are undergoing the relevant experiences. It's tempting to think, when faced with the problem of particularity, that we are given a third-personal, conceptual description of some perceptual experience of type E and a third-personal, conceptual designation of the object of that experience. Our task is then to determine whether the experience we are having is of the E-type and whether the thing we see is A or B. Only then do we know which thing we are seeing and which experience we are enjoying. Similarly, it might be thought that a person doesn't know how fast he is riding his motorcycle until he can state it in a standard unit of measurement like miles per hour, or that a person doesn't know how tall he is unless he can state it in a standard unit of measurement like feet and inches.

There are no doubt contexts in which we would say that. Consider Wittgenstein's joke about the person who says "But I know how tall I am" and proves it by laying his hand on top of his head (Wittgenstein 1958, §279: 96). Contrary to Wittgenstein, however, who confuses the question of whether a statement is meaningful with the question of whether there are circumstances in which someone would bother stating it, the butt of this joke does in fact know how tall he is; what he may not know is some proposition that represents his height in a different way. What makes such a speech act so absurd isn't that its content is meaningless, false, or unknown, but that it's only too well known to anyone in a position to understand it. We can appreciate this when we contrast their knowledge with the knowledge I would have by saying "He's as tall as the palm of a hand resting on his head." They are, and I am not, capable of exploiting the presence of his height itself. They can, and I cannot, determine whether he is taller or shorter than someone else. And when Adrian Cussins gets pulled over and asked whether he knows how fast he was traveling, while he may not be able to state his speed in miles per hour, he does know how fast he was traveling, since his speed was presented to him in the very experience of going that fast (Cussins 2003: 149–50).

Similarly, even if I do not know whether what I'm seeing is A or B, or whether the experience I have is of the E-type or not, I am in a position to know which thing I'm seeing and which experience I'm having precisely because the thing I'm seeing is seen and the experience I'm having is had (compare McDowell 1986: 231). This ball is before me, and this ball isn't identical with some other ball. Note, moreover, that in saying that this ball is before me, I am not exploiting the fact that the context of utterance is identical with the circumstance of evaluation, so that my utterance is guaranteed to be true provided there is a ball before me. Rather, I am appealing to the sensuous presence of the ball itself, in a way that I could not if my eyes were shut. And while I cannot tell whether this ball is A or B, that question can only arise once I already have access to the ball itself. It would be absurd to hold up the ball I'm seeing and say, "Since you can't tell whether this ball here is A or B, you cannot perceive this ball." That statement is false just in virtue of my understanding it. Similarly, if I am the victim of a switcheroo in which A is replaced by B while I'm not looking, I can not only understand, but entertain as a live possibility, that this ball I see now is not identical with the one I saw a moment ago. Not only does this require me already to have access to the respective balls, but it means that even on my own terms, introspective indiscriminability is not sufficient for sameness of intentional objects. What's "inside" consciousness is beholden to what's "external" to it – and this is just how things seem from the "inside."

What these sorts of examples all exploit is the massively inadequate givenness of the relevant objects. If we make the relevant experiences more adequate to their objects by pursuing the indications present in the acts' horizons, things look rather different. Part of what distinguishes an experience of A from an experience of B is that those experiences are parts of larger systems of possible experiences in which their respective objects would present themselves – something Husserl often refers to both as an experience's "horizon" and its "manifold." I will stick with the latter term, since I have already appropriated the term 'horizon' for different purposes. Smith and McIntyre (1982: 244) define the manifold as "the set of all possible acts of consciousness that are co-directed with the given act," and point out that the manifold, thus construed, does not only include perceptual acts. For convenience, I will limit this discussion to the *perceptual* manifold – as, Smith and McIntyre acknowledge, Husserl himself often does. A manifold, unlike a horizon, is a multiplicity of possible experiences, not an actual body of empty intentions.[19] The two bear a very intimate relation to one another, however: it is some portion of these "possible perceptual multiplicities" making up an act's manifold – along with the object's properties themselves – towards which the act's inner horizon "points ahead" (*Ideas I* §44: 94) as more or less motivated possibilities (*Ideas I* §140). The horizon is a "*horizon of reference* to potentialities of consciousness" (*CM* §19: 44) – without itself *being* those potentialities. However, manifolds exist whether any actual consciousness of the relevant object is carried out; an unexplored cave, for instance, has its perceptual manifold. For this reason, we can understand manifolds as belonging to objects themselves. And though I will speak, with Husserl, of possible experiences, we can just as readily think of the manifold as a set of

---

[19] Though, as A. D. Smith (2008b: 325) points out, Husserl routinely characterizes the infinities of possible experience as implicit within any actual experience. Also see Smith and McIntyre (1982: §3.1).

perceptual or intuitive contents that could be instantiated in possible experiences of the same object. Just as there is some set of propositions about any object, so there is a set of nonconceptual contents that are about that object.

Any sense-perceptible object has its distinctive manifold, a "multiplicity of noetic mental processes . . . all of them united by being consciousness of the same thing" (*Ideas 1* §135: 323). This manifold includes "the ideal total content of 'possible perceptions'" of the same object" (*TS* §11: 26–7). It is "infinite on all sides," and if we pursue any of its "lines" over time, we will experience a "harmonious concatenation . . . in which the X, given always as one and the same, is more precisely and never 'otherwise' continuously-harmoniously determined" (*Ideas 1* §143: 342). Starting from my present perception of the ball, the possibilities are infinite but bounded: I can move my eyes, head, neck, and body to look at it from other points of view. If it rolls away I can follow it or sit watching it recede into the distance. What all of these possible paths of experience share in common is a basic compatibility among their constituent phases: as I carry them out the relevant continuous syntheses, I experience an "identity-consciousness" (*TS* §10: 24). In each phase of the experience, the same ball presents itself to me, and presents itself as the same thing that was already presenting itself. I see more of the same thing, in a way I would not if I looked at the tree out the window or the book on my desk. Note, moreover, that the identity-consciousness is not the *mere thought* that the object seen at one time is identical with another. Rather, in continuous synthesis the identity is *given*. Husserl even claims that whether two perceptions $p_1$ and $p_2$ have the same object can only be known "with evidence" if we actually carry out such a continuous synthesis (*TS* §44: 132; also §10: 24 and A. D. Smith 2008b: 326–7). Otherwise, what strikes us as an "identity of sense" might turn out only to be a "similarity of sense" (*TS* §44: 131).

The perceptual manifold of an object does not consist solely of veridical perceptions. Some of them can be illusory (A. D. Smith 2008b: 329). But they are all of the same object, and the distinctive kind of conflict that arises when one experience of a thing conflicts with another is only intelligible when the two experiences present what is recognizably the same object, or are synthesizable via a string of experiences some members of which present what is recognizably the same object. The moon illusion would not be an illusion if the perception of the horizon moon and the zenith moon were not of the same object, and to that extent harmonious. And despite conflicting, the experiences of the moon are synthesizable into a continuous identity-consciousness. It would be absurd, on the other hand, to suppose that there could be a moon illusion in which it looks just the way it actually does while on the horizon, and three hours later looks exactly like an empty bag of chips.

Two perceptual acts belong to the same manifold if, and only if, they are of the same object. And two perceptual acts are of the same object if, and only if, they have the same (perceptual) X-component as part of their content. Now obviously not just any old contents, with just any old phenomenological character, can belong to the same manifold, as the previous example shows. However, the experience of the back or inside of a house can belong to the same manifold as an experience of its front, and the experience of an acorn can belong to the same manifold as an experience of an oak, even though those experiences differ radically. So having the same phenomenological character is not a necessary condition for being of the same object. And it's not sufficient either, as the example of balls A and B shows.

What, according to A. D. Smith's interpretation of Husserl, is necessary for any two acts to belong to the same manifold is "that each be synthesisable with any of the others in a unity of identification" (A. D. Smith 2008b:329). I am not sure that's right. Since at any time there are infinitely many possible perceptual experiences of an object, the manifold of an act will include all of those acts as well. But it's not at all obvious to me that those acts are synthesizable in a continuous synthesis, since perception presents its objects as being a certain way at a time, and synthesis takes place over time. Viewing the ball from here at t1, I cannot synthesize my perception of it with an act which presents it from over there at t1, since by the time I get over there, it will no longer be t1. Perhaps, then, any two perceptual experiences on the same spatiotemporal "line" proceeding from a given starting point – from my present perception of ball A, say – must be, at least in principle, synthesizable. And any two experiences on different lines, even if not synthesizable, must be harmonious enough to qualify as of the same object. They must, to put it in terms that will be more familiar in the next chapter, fulfill judgments that are about the same object, even if they don't fulfill precisely the same judgments. Harmoniousness with any other member of A's manifold, and synthesizability with the perceptual experiences belonging to some line L of that manifold, are good candidates for necessary conditions for belonging to A's manifold.

I don't have a conclusive argument for this claim, except that it seems extremely plausible, and that it tracks our intuitions about the identity of material objects over time rather closely. Beginning with the first point, suppose that one had an experience or sequence of experiences that was not synthesizable with any others belonging to A's manifold, and was disharmonious with a wide number of them. For instance, suppose that I hallucinate what seems to be ball A when I am in France and it is in Boston. In virtue of what is this experience supposed to count as of A rather than of B, an uninstantiated bundle of qualities making up a sensible profile (Johnston 2009), or some particular that does not even exist? What possible evidence would compel us to say that it is of A? It is not enough to stipulate that it just is of A, without any criteria whatsoever for determining that it is. Nor, as we have seen, is it enough that the subject thinks it is of A, since that's just the sort of thing a subject can be wrong about. A natural suggestion is that there is a causal connection between A and my present hallucination; it's of A because A is the causal source of the content I am now entertaining. But there are other candidates for serving the same role, including ball B, a picture of A, or the qualities that help constitute A's sensible profile. If we have a good reason to think that A could not be the object of this perceptual state – and we do, since A is thousands of miles away – then we also have a good reason to think that content of the mental state is not about A.

The synthesizability requirement also seems to harmonize with our widespread beliefs about the identity of objects over time. The sapling is the oak, and there are many possible lines of continuous syntheses of identification that, beginning with a perception of the sapling, terminate in a perception of the oak. What about more bizarre cases, like time travel? Well, if an object travels through time, there's a possible series of perceptions in which it can be given, namely the series that would occur if a perceiver were to travel along with it. Or teleportation? Again, it would be at least possible to travel along with it. But note that the farther we get from the possibility of a continuous synthesis, the more tenuous is our grip on the conviction that the objects at t1 and t2 are identical. In the case of, say, an amoeba that splits in two, there doesn't seem to be any obvious answer to the question of which, if either, of the resulting amoebae is identical with the original. But the synthesizability requirement tracks that intuition precisely: in the continuous perception of an amoeba from the time before to after the split, the synthesis of identification is interrupted. What was a harmonious identity-consciousness breaks up into confusion.

We can now make good phenomenological sense of the claim that the experiences of ball A and ball B are different. First, obviously, the two objects have different manifolds. If I perceive A while ball B is out of sight, then the experience I have is part of A's manifold but not part of B's. Second, any experience belonging to A's manifold fails to belong to B's, and vice versa, since any experience that belonged to both manifolds would harbor an X-component that was of both. And we can see this phenomenologically as well. For suppose that there were some perceptual experience $p_1$ that belonged to both manifolds. In order to be of A, it would have to be synthesizable with every experience on some line $L_A$ of A's manifold. And in order to belong to B's it would have to be synthesizable with every experience on some line $L_B$ of B's manifold. But those two requirements cannot be met. An identity-consciousness, proceeding along $L_A$, will track A through space continuously. If B were in the same general region of space as A such that it were visible along with A, then a difference-consciousness would be established; A and B would be seen located in different locations within that region of space. If B were not in the same region of visible space, then there would be no way to track A continuously until one becomes aware of B. Twin earth objects and earthly objects also have different manifolds. There is no continuous series of experiences that will ground an identity-consciousness of my house with my house's *Doppelgänger*. I would have to leave my house and travel there. Or I could bring my house there, and see it and its *Doppelgänger* at the same time, which would establish their difference. This account can even be extended to twin earth differences of natural kinds, as Steven Crowell has argued. As he puts it, "because the water I perceive is not an inert datum but an element within a normative space of intentional implications (teleological interconnections), it adumbrates avenues along which further aspects can become given – if/then structures that indicate a course of possible empirical investigation that could eventually disclose something like molecular structure" (Crowell 2008: 346).

Now we can return, finally, to the topic of hallucination. Obviously all nonhallucinatory experiences of a single object A belong to A's manifold. But can any hallucinatory experience belong to A's manifold? Take some possible line L of synthesis in A's manifold, and suppose that $p_1$ were a hallucination belonging to L. In that case, it must be synthesizable with every act belonging to L, and harmonious with every act in A's manifold. But how could all of these conditions be satisfied? They cannot be satisfied by p1 radically misrepresenting A, for if the representation were radical enough to be more than an illusion, it would not be able to be a member of such a synthesis. For example, $p_1$ might occur while I am in France and A is in Boston. Or $p_1$ might present A, not as a steel ball, but as a table or a sunset or a rabid dog. But if $p_1$ is that grossly mistaken about A, then we lose our grounds for claiming that it is even of A at all. Not only is it difficult to see how an identity-consciousness could be instituted between $p_I$ and the non-hallucinatory members of A's manifold, but $p_I$ fails to harmonize at all with many of what undeniably are members of A's manifold. So, it appears, (1) if any experience is of A, it is synthesizable with other experiences along some line L of A's manifold, and (2) if any experience is synthesizable in that way, then it must be non-hallucinatory experience of A (in which case synthesizability is also a sufficient condition for being of A) from which follows (3) there can be no hallucinatory experience of A.

I am not absolutely confident that this argument works. Suppose, for instance, that evil neuroscientist 1 has manipulated my brain such that, as I run through a continuous synthesis of perceptions of A along line L, he periodically flips a switch that shuts down my relevant sense organs and induces an experience that is subjectively indistinguishable from the one I would have had had he not flipped the switch. Unlike Tye's (2009: 83) evil neuroscientist, ours does not produce indistinguishable experiences "serendipitously." He is trying very hard to refute a premise in my argument, and is therefore trying to produce experiences that are synthesizable with the veridical members of A's manifold. He is very good at doing this, and can track the right line of synthesis depending on my own bodily movements. (We can even suppose that he periodically induces these movements, and a sense that they are done voluntarily.) If, for instance, I move right, he induces the appropriate experience, one that not only is indistinguishable from the one that I would have had, but which, like that experience itself, harmonizes in the right way with the kinesthetic sensations I have. Since this experience is synthesizable with the other phases of L, and is therefore harmonious with all of the other members of A's manifold, it is of A. But since my sense organs are not functioning, it is not a veridical perception of A.

This argument depends on the claim that if my sense organs are not functioning and my brain state is brought about through the neuroscientist's manipulations, then I am not perceiving A. I am not entirely convinced. If the neuroscientist, in a bid to trick me, has actually succeeded in producing experiences just like the one I would have had, and does so, as he presumably must, by tracking the actual layout of my environment and my engagement with it, then perhaps this evil neuroscientist has just outwitted himself. In giving me all of that, of what has he deprived me? He has put me in a position, not only to form true beliefs about the world, but to play tennis and go swimming and have conversations. I am tempted to say that he has become, like a sense organ, something by whose means I am able to *perceive* my environment. For not only does he make it the case that I have an experience of the right character when I actually follow along line L, but makes sure that had I chosen to pursue line L* instead – by standing still rather than moving, say – he would have induced an appropriately different experience in me as well. If someone were to develop a technology like this, he should be hailed for granting the blind the ability to see and the deaf the ability to hear.

Let us, then, consider another example. Suppose that evil neuroscientist 2 is just out to trick me. He doesn't have any intention of producing experiences in me that correspond to what I would have had had he not flipped the switch or refute any key premise in some philosophical argument. He just whimsically flips it on and off in his lab, without so much as bothering to determine where I am, confident that the experiences he induces will not cohere with my veridical ones. However, every time he flips his switch, just by chance, I wind up having an experience indistinguishable from the one I would have had had he not flipped it. Now, I think, we have a strong counterexample to the claim that synthesizability along some line L of A's manifold is sufficient for being a nonhallucinatory veridical perception of A. For these experiences match up with those which come before and after only by chance. They do not come about as a result of the nature of my environment and my bodily condition, and had things been radically different at the time he flips his switch, my experience still would have been the same. They are, in other words, not *perceptual* experiences of A. But since they are synthesized with other perceptions of A, they are *of A*.

I think the best response is to say that synthesizability with the other experiences constituting a manifold simply is not sufficient for belonging to that manifold – that is, for being of A. Rather, an experience must also belong to a "stable system" of experiences, a "stable all-inclusive regularity for all the possible perceptions which could synthetically connect with the given perception" (*PP* §36: 142) – and which *would have* connected with appropriately different perceptions had circumstances been otherwise. Incorporating an idea from Sosa's virtue epistemology, we can understand stability along the lines of the safety of a performance, where a performance is safe just in case "not easily would it have failed, not easily would it have fallen short of its aim" (E. Sosa 2007: 25). What makes my experiences stable, or safe, is the familiar idea that in situations not too remote from the actual one, had things been different, my experiences would have been correspondingly different as well. That condition is satisfied in the first evil neuroscientist example, but not in the second. In the second, the experiences induced do not belong to a stable system, but to an intolerably precarious one: had things been different, even radically so, it's quite likely that I still would have had the experience and thereby fallen short of being in perceptual and cognitive contact with the world.

When things are going well, the character of my present experience depends, broadly, on the nature of the object and my surrounding environment and on the movements of my own body, with their characteristic kinesthetic sensations. If I am genuinely in touch with my environment and the objects in it, then my experiences will vary, in complex but systematic ways, on the condition of the environment itself and the kinesthetic series that I initiate or undergo. So, for instance, if I perceive A, then, had A not been there, I would not have had an experience of A. And if A had been moving rather than standing still, I would have had to track A by moving my eyes, head, or body. And if I had decided to initiate a different kinesthetic series, I would have had appropriately different experiences. Of course, the visual experiences I have don't have to change with every change in kinesthetic series (Drummond 1979: 26). To borrow an example from Michael Shim (2010), the visual experience of watching a tennis match might be the same whether I follow the ball by moving my whole head or only my eyes. (But even in this case, my auditory experiences would differ.) In perceiving A, it must not only be true that my experience in fact synthesizes with those on some line L, but that if I had pursued line L* instead – because of changes in either the object or my own bodily movements – my experiences would have synthesized with the experiences lying on *it*. There must, in other words, be a functional relationship among the character of the object perceived, the condition of one's body and its kinesthetic sensations, and the character and content of one's experience. This is obviously not the case when evil neuroscientist 2 is on the job. On the side of the world, my experiences are just a function of him flipping a switch and whatever that entails – and it does not entail that my environment will be any particular way.

On Husserl's view, at least while we are doing pure phenomenology, we cannot appeal to the object itself in explaining how and why an experience does belong to such a stable system. But I believe in impure phenomenology: *part* of what makes an experience belong to a stable system is the fact that it occurs in a context in which the object itself plays a decidedly important causal role. I would even partially agree with Johnston's claim that perceiving an object is not the final link in a causal chain that, when things go well, begins with some event involving the perceived object, but "is an event materially constituted by the *long physical process* connecting the object seen to the final state of the visual system" (Johnston 2009). But as we've seen, a lot more is involved: my visual system's being in a certain state because of a causal link with an object is not sufficient for perceiving that object. Perception also requires that I entertain the proper horizonal contents that will provide a framework for possible courses of continuous synthesis. It is, in part, an achievement.

Now, I think, we can say something about the relationship between IA, PS, and OD. I am tempted to say that being a phase in a possible continuous synthesis of identification along line L of an object A's manifold belongs to the phenomenological character of an experience. I also think that some experiences which belong to different manifolds are, under certain conditions, introspectively indistinguishable. So I think IA is likely false, and that PS and OD are both true. The important point, however, is that just as we have strong reasons for denying that a perception of A could possibly have the same intentional content as an experience of B, we have strong reasons for thinking that a perception of A could not have the same intentional content as any hallucination. Perception and hallucination do not differ insofar as the former takes place in favorable contexts and the latter does not; they differ intrinsically.

I don't have a firm view on the nature of hallucinations themselves. However, I do think that while singular contents directed towards actual individuals cannot belong to the content of hallucination, contents directed towards properties can. This is largely because, as Johnston (2009) points out, hallucination can be a source of the ability to think about properties. I can acquire the concept 'red' or 'square', for instance, through a hallucinatory experience. And, as in the case of imagination, I can acquire knowledge of properties and their relationships through hallucination. If I have a hallucination that is indistinguishable from a perception of my new couch fitting through my doorway, then I am in a position to know that my couch will fit through my doorway. Nothing, however, instantiates the properties that are made manifest to me in such an experience. There isn't a little mental couch somewhere fitting through a little mental doorway – and that answer is awful anyway since the objects I seem to see are rather large things out there in space – nor is there another, immaterial couch out in front of me fitting through an immaterial doorway. I have a veridical experience of uninstantiated sense-perceptible properties, just as I can in the case of imagination. What makes my experience an error, a hallucination, is that, unlike an imagination, it presents those properties as though they are instantiated in some particular objects – *those* particular objects, in fact – and there are no such objects. Hallucinations have X-components which fail to refer to anything actual.

## 6.5 CONCLUSION

Since perceptual states do not have conceptual content, and since the relational view is false, they must have nonconceptual content. More specifically, they have two kinds of nonconceptual content. One kind, as we've seen, is horizonal content. The other kind is intuitive content. The singular intuitive contents belonging to veridical perceptual experiences, moreover, could not also belong to indistinguishable hallucinations. The task before us now is to make sense of how nonconceptual contents can stand in reason-giving relations with conceptual states like belief and judgment. I will argue in the next chapter that Husserl's account of fulfillment, appropriately modified, holds the answer.

# CHAPTER 7

# To the things themselves

There are three main and interrelated tasks involved in spelling out the role of perception in knowledge. The first is to determine *whether* perceptual experiences justify beliefs. The second is to say *why* they do (or do not do) so. The third, assuming that experiences justify beliefs, is to specify *how* they do so. In the present chapter I will attempt to do all three, with special emphasis on the last. More specifically, I will present and defend a modified version of Husserl's theory of fulfillment, which I believe is the best available account of how perceptual and other intuitive experiences relate to thoughts.

In light of the results of the previous chapters, we have some idea what form the answers to these questions will take. Most importantly, we know that while perceptual experiences have the same sorts of objects as some thoughts, they have a radically different kind of intentional content. Perception is not thought with a sprinkling of qualia. And it is not, as the relational view contends, the sheer, content-free awareness of physical objects. Perception, rather, harbors "interwoven masses of intentions" (*LI* 6, §16: 721), whose contents are either intuitive, horizonal, or both – but not conceptual. And because the contents of perception are so different from those of thought, we can expect that the relation between perceptual states and beliefs will be quite different from that among beliefs (Mulligan 1995, §10.2).

Before going further, it's worth reminding ourselves of a point touched upon in Chapter 3, namely that this is no reason whatsoever for philosophical anxiety. Consider what Michael Huemer and Michael Thau have to say:

> If experiences did not have propositional content, it would be difficult to understand how a perceptual experience could be the basis for a belief, which does have propositional content, for there would be no logical relations between them. (Huemer 2001: 74)

Many of our beliefs are based on our perceptions. If perception relates subjects to propositions, then this process is no more mysterious than the process of beliefs leading us to other beliefs. However, if perception isn't a relation to a proposition, it is hard to see how there could be inferential relations between perception and belief. (Thau 2002: 75)

Both Huemer and Thau are asking for an explanation where none is needed. There is no need to explain how nonconceptual states can stand in *inferential* or *logical* relations with beliefs. They don't and can't. This doesn't mean we're in the presence of a mystery, however. What, in the theory of knowledge, could be *less* mysterious than that my belief can become epistemically justified when I manage to perceive, to come into the direct presence of, its truth-maker? There is nothing at all mysterious or problematic about the fact that perceptual experiences justify beliefs. That it does appear mysterious in light of this or that theory of epistemic justification is a powerful indictment of any such theory. Of course, someone might find it mysterious that beliefs about physical objects can be justified on the basis of perception, but that is a completely different worry. Provided perceptual experiences actually manage to "get at" a certain class of objects, they can provide warrant for beliefs about those objects. The fact that they can, moreover, is more obvious, by a long shot, than any theory according to which all reason-giving relations are inferential. "Experiences can provide foundations without being premises" (Conee 2004: 42).

So what is it about perception that makes it reason-giving? And how are the fleeting deliverances of perception transformed into the abiding products of knowledge – contents that can be retained, relived, transmitted, and documented? For the answers to those questions, we turn, with Husserl's assistance, to the experiences in which coming to know on the basis of perception actually happens.

## 7.I EPISTEMIC FULFILLMENT

The simplest way to introduce the phenomenon of epistemic fulfillment is to describe a simple case of it. Suppose that, shortly after we have left home, my wife asks me whether I have turned off the kitchen light. I believe that I have, and say so. I do not see the light, or my kitchen; what I see is the sidewalk, my neighbors' homes, and so forth. Here, "an act of meaning is performed . . . but nothing is thereby known, recognized" (*LI* 6, §8: 694). My wife is skeptical; she knows I often forget to do such things, and that I often forget that I've forgotten to do them. Her skepticism rubs off on me, since I know that she's often right, especially about my own unreliability. So we turn around, I unlock the door, and proceed to the kitchen. Now I have an experience that is as remarkable as it is familiar: I *find* the light to be as I thought (and think) it to be. I "experience how *the same* objective item which was 'merely thought of' in symbol is now presented in intuition, and that it is intuited as being precisely the determinate so-and-so that it was at first merely thought or meant to be" (*LI* 6, §8: 694). This is an experience of epistemic fulfillment. Such experiences happen all the time.

The fulfillment of propositional contents is parasitic upon simpler acts of fulfillment, acts of recognition (*Erkennen*) and identification. I can merely think about the color yellow. But I can also perceive it and recognize it, classify it, as yellow. Similarly, I can merely think about my house. But when I see it, I can then identify the thing I see as my house. If I cannot recognize my house or the color yellow, I cannot have the thought that my house is yellow fulfilled. Epistemic fulfillment is easy to confuse with perception itself, and even Husserl, as we'll see, sometimes conflates them. But although epistemic fulfillment – or primary epistemic fulfillment – essentially involves perception, it is not identical with it.[1] Rather, all acts of epistemic fulfillment, including simple acts of identification and classification, are internally complex. In order for epistemic fulfillment to occur, at least three conditions must be fulfilled:

(1) The intuitive condition: the object A must be perceived or otherwise intuitively presented.

(2) The conceptual condition: A must be conceived of, judged about, or otherwise conceptually represented.

(3) The synthesis condition: the intuitive and conceptual acts of perceiving and cognition must enter into an appropriate synthesis.

That is, fulfillment is a founded act that has, as its constituents, at least two acts with *different contents* but the *same object*. Finally, as we'll see, an act of fulfillment is a distinct act in its own right, whose content and quality differ from those of its underlying acts.

The intuitive condition and the conceptual condition are obviously necessary for fulfillment. I cannot find something to be as I think it to be if I do not find it and think of it.[2] For instance, the content of my belief that my wife is home is *supported* by a perception of her coat on the hook, but that experience does not *fulfill* the thought. Rather, that experience fulfills the thought that her coat is on the hook, which, together with my belief that if her coat is on the hook, then she is home, supports my belief that she is

---

[1] A point made clearly by Willard (1995, §IV) and Bernet (2003: 155).

[2] "In all cases an intention comes into coincidence with the act which offers it fullness, i.e. the object which is meant in it is the same as the object meant in the fulfilling act" (*LI* 6, §14b: 715).

home. This would be true, moreover, even if my belief that my wife is home were *psychologically* noninferential. To take a more far-fetched example, suppose that I have very good reasons for thinking that whenever it visually appears to be raining to me, it is in fact sunny, and vice versa. After a short time adjusting to this bizarre situation, I learn to make automatic, psychologically noninferential judgments that it is sunny every time it appears rainy, and vice versa. Nevertheless, the sunny-experience does not *fulfill* the thought that it is rainy. The experience is not of rainy weather, but of sunny weather, and does not present me with the very state of affairs that I believe to obtain, but with something else entirely.

What might not be obvious is that fulfillment is a higher-order act involving a synthesis between at least two different acts with different contents. We can, however, discover the complexity of epistemic fulfillment by appreciating how the constituent acts can be independently varied. Keeping the conceptual content of an act constant, we can vary its intuitive content drastically, even within the context of fulfillment. My thought that my desk is rectangular can remain constant, and constantly fulfilled, as it appears differently while I move around it. Keeping the intuitive content of an act of epistemic fulfillment constant, we can vary its conceptual content as well. Staring straight ahead at my couch, all sorts of thoughts can be fulfilled: that there is a couch over there, that the couch is tan, that the couch is next to the table, that someone is sitting on the couch, and so on (see section 4.3 above and *LI* 6, §4). But not all of those thoughts are, on any given occasion, fulfilled. Most perceptual experiences present us with far more than we think about.

A thought might not be fulfilled on the basis of an appropriate perceptual experience for a number of reasons. First, one might not have the required concepts to think the thought in question. A squid can (presumably) have a stinging sensation in its tentacle, but it cannot (I think) have the thought "I have a stinging sensation in my tentacle" fulfilled.

Second, one might perceive something only marginally while performing other acts of judgment directed towards focally perceived objects. Suppose, for instance, that I have been dealt a hand consisting of ten cards, and want to find out whether I have the ten of diamonds. I go through the hand card by card and discover that it is at the very bottom. In doing this, I manage to fulfill the thought that the ten of diamonds is in my hand. I also manage to perceive ten distinct cards. But I have not, for all that, verified the thought that there are ten cards in my hand. Again, I may thumb through the hand, counting each card, in order to verify that my hand is complete. In this case, my thought that there are ten cards in the hand is fulfilled. In doing this,

I may perceive the ten of diamonds. But I may not have the thought that the ten of diamonds is in my hand fulfilled.

Third, fulfillment might not occur if one's thoughts are directed towards unperceived objects and states of affairs. If I'm thinking about philosophy while commuting, I don't typically *think about* the road, the cars around me, my bike's handlebars, and so forth, and so don't typically have thoughts about them fulfilled. Yet at any given time, I perceive many of those objects, and am poised to have thoughts about them fulfilled should the need arise.

Finally, one might be paying attention to a perceived object and not have a judgment P fulfilled simply because one is entertaining some other fulfilled judgment Q. Someone might see an alizarin vase but only think that it's a red vase, even though he possesses the concept 'alizarin'. The thought that it is an alizarin vase is not fulfilled, even though it could be, given the situation and the perceiver's conceptual repertoire. Or, to take another example, someone might not have the thought "That is black" fulfilled because he is too busy fulfilling other thoughts on the same perceptual basis, like "That is a bird" or "Its wing span looks to be about 3 feet." This is surely the case most of the time. Of the many thoughts that could be fulfilled on the basis of perception, only a fraction ever are.

These four types of cases demonstrate that the intuitive condition can be met without the conceptual condition being met, and that, therefore, perception is not identical with fulfillment. But none of the examples thus far points to the importance of the synthesis condition. Its importance becomes clear when we realize that even when the intuitive and conceptual conditions are met, fulfillment might not take place. Before turning to such cases, a few words are in order about some trivially necessary conditions for the synthesis condition to be met. First, the acts must belong to the same subject. My perceiving that the light is off does not fulfill my wife's thought that it is off. Second, the two acts must occur at, or nearly at, the same time. My present perception of my rectangular desk cannot fulfill the thought that it is rectangular that I had last week – though it can fulfill a present thought with that same content (Willard 1984: 225–6).

Meeting these two conditions is not sufficient for satisfying the synthesis condition. As Husserl himself points out, a perceptual and a conceptual act trained on the same object might occur simultaneously without any fulfillment taking place (*LI* 6, §7: 690–1). I might think that Jim is in the café, and look right at Jim, but not have the thought that Jim is in the café fulfilled. This can happen for a variety of reasons. I might simply not be paying proper attention. Or I might fail to recognize him. Perhaps I've forgotten or misremembered what he looks like. Or his appearance might have changed, so that my thought is in fact fulfilled by a different sort of experience from the kind I thought would fulfill it. When I do discover that Jim is the person I'm looking at, a new experience, with its own phenomenological character, arises. A recognition or a knowing takes place on the basis of two (or more) acts, neither of which is an act of recognition or knowing.

These possible failures point to further necessary conditions of fulfillment, and, specifically, for satisfying the synthesis condition. One is that one's attentional resources must be distributed in the right way. I can get so lost in thought that the perceived world "fades" into a barely heeded background. If so, then I can fail to have my thought about O fulfilled, even when I see O, because I am not attending to my perceived environment and allowing it to guide my thinking. A further necessary condition, and a much more interesting one, is that I possess the relevant concept or concepts *authentically*. Following Wayne Davis and Jerry Fodor, I think that the criteria for possessing a concept are not incredibly demanding. Basically, possessing a concept amounts to being able to entertain thoughts about the thing or things to which the concept refers (Davis 2003: 429; Fodor 1998). The blind can think and know all kinds of things about colors, just as I can think and know all kinds of things about atoms and black holes. A huge amount of what we know is known by means of concepts that we do not grasp authentically. Possessing a concept authentically is another matter entirely.[3] A person possesses a concept authentically just in case she has sufficiently reliable, nondeferential capacities to identify its object over a sufficiently wide range of conditions and environments. I will, for ease of exposition, refer to this as "concept authenticity," with the understanding that what is authentic is not the concept, but one's mode of possessing the concept. I take it that concept authenticity, like the authenticity of selves but unlike the authenticity of dollar bills, is something that comes in degrees.[4]

So, to give some examples, given what muons are and what our current perceptual capacities are, everyone possesses the concept 'muon' inauthentically. I possess the concept of alizarin, which is a shade of red. But I possess it

---

[3] Those who have more demanding conditions for concept possession could see this as a difference between authentic and inauthentic concepts. So, while on my view Mary the neuroscientist, upon seeing a red object, would come to possess the concept 'red' authentically, it could plausibly be argued that she acquires a new, authentic concept of red. I don't think this is right. If, for instance, I were granted perfect pitch, my thought that a piece is in the key of A minor would be just what it was before. Or so it strikes me.

[4] Of course instantiation doesn't come in degrees. There's only one way for an experience to instantiate an intentional property. But what can vary are the other intentional properties with which it is or could be coinstantiated. The concepts I possess authentically can link up, in specifiable ways, with other, intuitive intentional contents, and thereby give rise to distinctive sorts of experiences.

inauthentically. This isn't because I cannot see alizarin, nor is it because I cannot perceptually discriminate it from other shades of red. I can do all of those things. But I cannot recognize it – at least not without deferring to a caption below a sample or an expert. Because I don't have perfect pitch or broad musical knowledge, this is also true of the note C, a B minor chord, and a counter-fugue. But I can perceive all of those things. Because I lack concept authenticity, my thoughts about them will go unfulfilled, even if I am both thinking of them and perceiving them. My thought "This is alizarin" is not fulfilled even when I am attentively and veridically perceiving an alizarin object in standard conditions.

Concept authenticity can be acquired and lost. Whether it is acquired depends on several factors. One necessary condition for acquiring concept authenticity with respect to some concept of A is that one be able to perceptually distinguish A from other objects. I cannot recognize that something is exactly 100 feet long or weighs 26 pounds without the assistance of tape-measures and scales, for instance, because, to me, a 100-foot-long object is, under most circumstances, perceptually indistinguishable from one that is one inch longer, and a 26-pound object feels just like an object that weighs a few ounces more. Being able to perceptually distinguish some object from others is not, however, a sufficient condition for concept authenticity. I can perceptually distinguish the note A from the note B, but, lacking perfect pitch, I cannot *recognize* an A or a B when I hear one. Another necessary condition is that one associate the concept with the sorts of experiences that present the object. This can happen passively or by actively impressing something on oneself. It may require more or less training, and depend more or less heavily on the power of one's memory.

Acquiring concept authenticity can be especially difficult, and losing it especially easy, when one type of object is highly similar to others. Being able to identify the various species of cichlid fish in the rift lakes of Africa is demanding because almost any given species of fish closely resembles some other, but perceptually distinguishable, species of fish from another lake. What sorts of concepts humans are best at authentically acquiring, and why we are best at acquiring them, are empirical questions. Plainly we are better at, say, recognizing people than recognizing musical chords, and this seems to be related, in part, to the fact that recognizing people is more important for our physical and social well-being than recognizing chords. If we found musical chords as fascinating as other people, or if the cost of lacking perfect pitch were as high as the cost of lacking the ability to recognize people, I suspect perfect pitch – which is a recognitional, not a merely perceptual, ability – would be a rather widespread phenomenon. We do, however, find various musical entities, such as melodies, quite interesting, and our ability to recognize their characteristic Gestalts, which are of course preserved across key signature changes, is highly reliable.

Concept authenticity can be lost in a number of ways. A fading memory is often a culprit. I no longer authentically possess many of the concepts I deployed when I passed lab practicals in biology, even though I could, if presented with a specimen, still see all of the same organs and structures I did before. When you lose concept authenticity relative to concepts of properties and kinds, this is often due to some change in you. Sometimes, however, one can lose concept authenticity relative to concepts of individual, changeable objects like people, cities, ski runs, and restaurants, for other reasons. They can become unrecognizable, and when that happens, the loss of concept authenticity is a Cambridge loss. The Rome of today would be hardly recognizable to Aurelius, even if he were in his cognitive and perceptual prime, just as you are quite likely unrecognizable to someone who last saw you when you were a small child. One of the many benefits of revisiting places and people is that it preserves concept authenticity.

Concept authenticity can also be lost because one finds oneself in an environment which differs substantially from the ones in which one's recognitional abilities were learned and mastered. As Alan Millar puts it, recognitional abilities are indexed to environments (Millar 2007, 2008). In some environments, recognitional abilities cannot be exercised because the relevant objects don't perceptually appear at all, or because they appear quite differently from normal. You might be unable to recognize Mount McKinley from the air, even if you have learned to identify it by sight from the ground. Millar also points out that one's recognitional abilities might fail even in environments where the relevant objects look, perceptually, the same way they do in one's home environment. Barn Country (Goldman 1976), which is full of both barns and papier-mâché facsimiles of barns, is one such environment, because there it is a *relevant* possibility that what I take to be a barn is a facsimile. To take an example from real life, one might be able to recognize a certain species of cichlid fish in Lake Tanganyika, but be unable to recognize it in an aquarium in which cichlids from Lakes Nyasa and Victoria swim alongside the members of the Tanganyika species.

These examples need to be handled with some care. First, there is a distinctive phenomenological character to fulfillment – there's something it's like to find the world to be as one thinks it to be – and even in environments in which one's recognitional abilities are compromised, experiences with that same phenomenological character can persist. If I don't know that I'm in Barn Country, the characteristic experience of fulfillment will persist – it's just that those experiences won't, in many cases, actually *be* experiences of fulfillment. But if I discover that I am in Barn Country, or that many cichlid species are in the aquarium, this will modify the phenomenological character of my experiences themselves. The characteristic "That's it!" sort of experience typical of fulfillment will no longer take place. So, while *being* in certain unfavorable environments will (often) prevent actual cases of fulfillment from occurring, it is only *knowing* (or justifiably believing) that one is in such an environment that will prevent the characteristic experience as-of-fulfillment from occurring.

Second, the two examples I used to illustrate unfavorable environments – Barn Country and an aquarium – are quite different. We know that physical objects have many modes of presentation, and that most perceptual encounters with them reveal only a fraction of what they have to offer. It is simply not true that one doesn't have the ability to recognize barns in Barn Country. Rather, one doesn't have the ability to recognize barns on the basis of a relatively superficial perceptual experience of them, for instance by seeing their fronts while driving by. But given further exploration, the difference between a barn and a barn façade becomes readily apparent. The difference between Barn Country and a normal barn-filled environment, then, is that in Barn Country one's recognitional abilities require a more complete perceptual encounter with barns. If, on the other hand, I have a relatively superficial recognitional ability with respect to a species of Lake Tanganyika cichlids, such that even upon further exploration I cannot tell whether a given fish is a Tanganyika cichlid or a Nyasa cichlid, then my recognitional abilities are environmentally indexed in the way Millar describes.

Many of the examples discussed above powerfully illustrate both the dual intentionality involved in fulfillment, and the fact that it is a higher-order act in its own right, with properties possessed by neither of its constituents. To return to a previous example, my thought that Jim is in the café is true, and my perception of him in the café is veridical. But this is insufficient for fulfillment. As a consequence, a distinctive sort of deficiency is taking place; I am failing to find the world to be as I think it to be, even though the world is present to me as I think it to be. What's lacking, in this case, is the requisite consciousness of the identity of the object that is given with the object that is meant. Fulfillment, as Willard puts it,

> is an additional act in its own right. An act of knowing [fulfillment] consciously incorporates that relation between thought and intuition, along with the related acts of conceptualization and intuition, in the distinctive manner of its own direction upon the same object. (Willard 1995: 150–1)

It is that conscious incorporation of the relation between thought and intuition that is missing in the cases above. "In the unity of fulfillment, the fulfilling content coincides with the intending content, so that, in our experience of this unity of coincidence, the object, at once intended and 'given' stands before us, not as two objects, but as one alone" (*LI* 1, §14: 291).

Acts of epistemic fulfillment, then, have a different content from that of either perception or judgment. In fulfillment, the object is not only given, and not only meant, and not only given and meant. Rather, it is *given as it is meant.* "The synthesis of recognition, of 'knowing', is the consciousness of a certain agreement" (*LI* 6, §11: 701) – namely, the agreement between the world as represented and the world as given. Acts of epistemic fulfillment are founded, in the sense discussed in section 2.4. That is, they (1) contain other acts as parts, (2) could not exist if those founding acts did not, and (3) are intentionally directed upon an object O which is not the object of any of their founding acts. The founding acts, when I find that my light is off, both have my light's being off as their object. In fulfillment, not only is that object intended, but the *identity* of what is given and meant is also given. What I'm thinking about is seen to be identical with what is given to me, and I am thereby conscious of an identity. As Husserl puts it,

A more or less complete identity is the objective datum which corresponds to the act of fulfillment, which 'appears in it'. This means that, not only signification and intuition, but also their mutual adequation . . . can be called an act, since it has its own peculiar intentional correlate, an objective something to which it is directed.[5]

In fulfillment, "we gain an evidence-consciousness, a consciousness that exactly the same [object] that was meant in an empty manner is there in intuition in a genuine way, as the same [object] actually presented" (*APS*: 114).

This is part of what sets the experience of fulfillment apart from mere recognition and concept authenticity apart from a recognitional ability. A recognitional ability can be exercised without any distinctive phenomenological experience taking place. A blindsighter might reliably recognize squares, and a chicken sexer might reliably recognize female chicks. Perhaps even zombies could have recognitional abilities. But the ability to do that does not entail that the requisite conscious synthesis, which accounts for the fact that the object is given as it is meant, takes place. Fulfillment is an essentially conscious experience.

Acts of fulfillment also differ from both perception and belief along the dimension of quality or attitude-type. Husserl maintains that perceptual

---

[5] *LI* 6, §8: 696. Also see §12: 705.

states are assertive or positing, that is, they present objects as existing, but admits the possibility that they can fulfill a "mere presentation" – that is, a mere thought. He adds, however, that when an "adequate percept (*ange-messene Wahrnehmung*)" fulfills a mere presentation, the latter will acquire an "assertive tone," that is, be transformed into belief or judgment (*LI* 6, §38: 764). When an *adequate* intuition is in question, this is probably correct. However, perceptual acts are not adequate to their objects, and though the vast majority of perceptual experiences result in corresponding beliefs about the existence and character of what they present – thoughts with empirical content receive their "original legitimizing basis" in sense perception (*Ideas 1*, §136: 328) – this is not necessary. My thought that the kitchen light is off is fulfilled by my perceptual experience of the light, even if, for whatever reasons, I fail to believe that it is off. Even if I don't believe that the kitchen light is off on the basis of such an experience, however, I will be "rationally motivated" to believe that it is off (*Ideas 1* §136: 328).

As the distinction between adequate and inadequate intuitions suggests, a further noteworthy feature of epistemic fulfillment is that it comes in degrees (*LI* 6, §16: 720). That is, the object can be more or less given as one thinks it to be. The highest possible degree is adequacy, in which each part and property of the thing is given exactly as it is meant to be. When that occurs, "the genuine *adequatio rei et intellectus* has been brought about. The object is actually 'present' or 'given', and present as *just what we have intended it*" (*LI* 6, §37: 762). This is typically not the case. When I think about my couch, I'm thinking of the *whole* couch. But my perception of the couch is inadequate; more of it exists than shows itself perceptually, and even some of the parts that do show themselves might prove to be otherwise on a closer or superior viewing. Accordingly, the object isn't given exactly as it is meant, and, in the case of physical objects, this ideal is unachievable (*Ideas 1* §138). Part of what explains the fact that empirical knowledge has something less than absolute warrant is that this ideal cannot be met: the object perceived, or allegedly perceived, might always prove, in the further course of thought and experience, to have properties other than those it appeared to have, or even not to exist at all. It would be a mistake, however, to peg the degree of warrant of an act of fulfillment to the degree to which there is a complete coinciding between what is given and what is meant. An act in which only a smallish fraction of an object's properties and parts is perceived does not necessarily, or even normally, provide only a very small degree of warrant for beliefs about it. I can be practically certain that a basketball exists and that it is orange on the basis of an extremely incomplete perceptual encounter with it, and become only marginally more certain of these things after exploring the basketball perceptually for an hour or a week. The degree of epistemic warrant of a belief within the context of fulfillment does not line up in any neat way with the degree to which it is perceptually given.

## 7.2 OTHER KINDS OF FULFILLMENT

Epistemic fulfillment, as we have seen, is a distinctive sort of higher-order act in which an intuitive and a conceptual act are directed upon the same object. Furthermore, the intuitive and conceptual act must be part of a larger synthesis or fusion that enables one to become conscious, whether explicitly or marginally, that the object is given as it is meant:

> What the intention means, but presents only in more or less inauthentic and inadequate manner, the fulfillment . . . *sets directly before us*, or at least more directly than the intention does. In fulfillment our experience is represented by the words: *'This is the thing itself'*. (*LI* 6, §16: 720)

This having of the thing itself, however, needs to be understood broadly to include not only perceptual consciousness, but other forms of intuition as well.

The paradigmatic case of fulfillment is *primary epistemic fulfillment*. In primary epistemic fulfillment, the intuitive act is *self-giving* with respect to its object; that is, it presents the object itself *in person*. With respect to empirical objects and states of affairs, only perception is self-giving and, therefore, only acts of epistemic fulfillment whose intuitive components are *perceptual* are primary. Thoughts with empirical content can, however, also be intuitively fulfilled in non-self-giving acts such as imagination, memory, and image-consciousness, and in such cases the sort of fulfillment will either be merely illustrative or derivatively epistemic.[6]

I begin with the former. My thought that my light is off can be fulfilled imaginatively, but this type of fulfillment is merely illustrative, not epistemic. In it, I don't confront my light in person, and such an experience does not rationally motivate any belief that my light is off. We can appreciate the non-self-giving character of imagination by examining some of the respects in which it differs from perception. First, imaginative acts are not positing with respect to empirical objects – they don't present their objects as actual. I don't run away from imagined tigers, and I don't dodge imagined projectiles. They

---

[6] Husserl (*APS*: 122 ff.) distinguishes between two modes of "bringing to intuition": the "merely disclosive" and the "genuinely confirming."

are not even positing with respect to mental objects; the imagined tiger simply is not presented as existing, not even in my or anyone else's mind. If what I were imagining were something real and mental, something "in my mind," I would, for that reason, not be *imagining*, but introspecting, and I would not be imagining a *tiger*, since there are no mental tigers (see *PICM* §10). Second, the contents of imagination don't vary systematically with those of positing acts; they do not implicate what I take to be real. I can simultaneously imagine a rainy day while perceiving a sunny scene, with no felt conflict. And my actual body is not among the cast of characters in imagined scenarios. No matter how loud I imagine a sound to be, it does not hurt my ears. No matter how bright I imagine a light to be, it doesn't hurt my eyes. Imagined pain is not painful. Imagined visual and auditory contents do not vary systematically with movements of my actual head, eyes, torso, and legs. Finally, in the case of perception, the intuitive fulfillment of a thought is almost always, at the same time, a way of determining the object and its immediate environment more closely. When I think that my office is messy, and then perceive it as such, my perceptual experience presents me with the precise way in which the office is messy, and its content can fulfill further, more determinate thoughts about my office. When, on the other hand, I merely imagine my office as messy, whatever intuitive content overflows the mere thought does not have the character of telling me how the office is. It is "mere filling" (*APS*: 122).

This doesn't, it should be noted, mean that imagination cannot primarily epistemically fulfill certain kinds of thoughts, nor that it is unable to contribute to empirical knowledge. Imagination can epistemically fulfill thoughts about *properties* and their possible relationships. Imagination can inform me that the properties *square* and *red* can be coinstantiated, for instance – all I have to do is imagine a red square. This shows that an intuitive act is self-giving relative to certain kinds of objects. Relative to empirical states of affairs, imagining is merely illustrative; relative to (some) properties and relations, it is self-giving.

Unlike imaginings, memories with intuitive content can epistemically fulfill empirical thoughts, but only in a derivative way.[7] So can image-consciousness – that is, the consciousness of an object by means of a perception of an image of it. Both involve an intuitive act that is (1) positing – it purports to say how things are – (2) *not* self-giving, and (3) dependent in

---

[7] This is not the same as Husserl's distinction between primary and secondary fulfillment in *APS*, part 2, §19, which is a distinction between the fulfillment of a prefigured intention and the fulfillment that results from the overabundance of intuition when we determine an object more closely.

some way upon an act that is or was self-giving. This third condition, however, is differently met in the case of straightforward memory and image-consciousness.[8] In the case of straightforward memory, the self-giving act upon which it is dependent is a *past perception* whose object is the *same* as the memory's itself. In the case of image-consciousness, the non-self-giving intuition is dependent upon a *present* self-giving intuition – a perception, in most cases – of a *different* object from the object of the image-consciousness, namely the *image of* that object. Accordingly, memory is a *direct* (though not self-giving) kind of consciousness, since it isn't founded on any present act that presents a different object than its own. Image-consciousness, on the other hand, is *indirect*, because it does: I can only be image-conscious of the Eiffel Tower in virtue of being conscious of something else, such as a photograph of it. Memories can also, however, be indirect: I might fulfill a thought about the Eiffel Tower by remembering an image of it. In that case, the fulfillment is derivative twice over; it is based on a previous experience which was itself a mere image-consciousness. This doesn't, however, necessarily make it an inferior form of fulfillment to straightforward memory or image-consciousness. A clear and distinct memory of a clear and distinct image of the Eiffel Tower is better than a vague and confused memory of a perception of it or an image-consciousness founded on the perception of a dirty, obscure, or doctored image of it.

A straightforward memory is experienced as the reliving of a previous perceptual experience, and is therefore, as part of its very sense, dependent upon it (*FTL* §59: 158). (It is not, however, a *representation of* a perceptual experience (*PCIT* §27)). Its non-self-giving character, furthermore, shows up in interesting ways. First, the possibilities for resolving conflicts are much more limited. If I am unsure what color Smith's shirt was, and in two rememberings I picture him wearing two differently colored shirts, there is not much I can do to resolve this conflict. I cannot take a closer look at the past. It holds me at an always-increasing distance from itself. Second, while virtually *nothing* counts as "mere filling" in perception, plenty of contents do in remembering (*APS*: 124–6). I might intuitively present Smith as wearing a shirt with a determinate color and speaking at a very determinate volume, but this need not rationally motivate beliefs to the effect that he was

---

[8] Husserl sometimes characterizes remembering as a self-giving experience, one which presents the *past* in the flesh, but this seems wrong (*APS*: 140–1). The past – or at least a portion of the past that lies outside of the cone of *retentional* consciousness that partly constitutes perceptual awareness itself – could only be presented in person by going back to it and perceiving it. This cannot, as far as we know, happen, in which case the past cannot be presented in person. Elsewhere Husserl acknowledges as much. See *PCIT* §17.

wearing a shirt with precisely that color and speaking at just that volume. I might represent him as though no one was near him or walked behind him during our conversation; neither need motivate any belief that no one was near him or walked behind him. Third, the order and duration of rememberings do not always, or even typically, track the order and duration of events remembered. I can always "replay" or revise my rememberings mid-stream, and in many cases cannot help doing so. And unless you're *really* good at reliving experiences, their duration doesn't match the duration of the remembered event itself. Try, for instance, to remember the most recent walking excursion you took – down the hall to get a coffee, for instance. How sure are you, at the end of your remembering, that the experience of remembering that walk took as long as the walk itself? In perception, on the other hand, you are extremely confident that the walk took as long as your experience of it.

Derivative epistemic fulfillment can and does occur – but need not occur – through image-consciousness. I can learn what the Eiffel Tower looks like via photographs, learn what different species of cichlids look like through illustrations, and learn about the current conditions at Arapahoe Basin by viewing its webcams. Image-consciousness is phenomenologically peculiar. It is not a matter of being conscious of something that just happens to be an image; it is the consciousness of something as an image. When I am image-conscious of the Eiffel Tower, I must be directly conscious of something else, namely an image of the Eiffel Tower. I must, that is, be directly conscious of the image-object (the picture) in order to be indirectly aware of the image-subject (the Eiffel Tower) (*PICM* §9). Of course, the fact that my consciousness of the Eiffel Tower is indirect does not entail that I am not attending to it. Precisely the opposite is the case: in my awareness of the Eiffel Tower, the image-object becomes partly transparent. If I attend too closely to it, my experience will become merely a straightforward perception of something that happens to be an image. But it's still always there for me, and its being there for me is part of what explains the fact that image-consciousness is not, even phenomenologically, self-giving. In fact, if an image resembles its object too closely, image-consciousness falls away and becomes straightforward perception of the image. A photograph of a painting of the Sierras can support an image-consciousness whose image-subject is the painting. But an exact duplicate of that painting does not support a sustained image-consciousness of the original painting, but only of the Sierras – the same image-subject of the original. Furthermore, not all of the features of an image-object are themselves representational. I trust images to depict relative sizes faithfully, but not, except in rare cases, absolute ones. I don't take Texas to be blue just because its image on a map is. A coffee stain on a picture does not have any pictorial significance. Far from it: if it is poorly placed, it will interfere with good image-consciousness.

Whether image-consciousness is epistemic or merely illustrative depends, in large measure at least, on how that image is taken – whether, in other words, the image-consciousness is positing or not. If it is taken to be a faithful representation of something, then it can ground an epistemic fulfillment of how that object is or was. I trust the webcams at Arapahoe Basin, and trust them to tell me how things are on the mountain. I don't trust Bierstadt's depictions of the Sierras, because I know that they don't, and did not, look that similar to the Alps. And with regard to some images, there is no question of trusting them. An image of floppy watches draped over tree branches doesn't epistemically fulfill any thoughts about any things at any particular place.

All of the forms of fulfillment discussed so far – primary epistemic fulfillment, direct and indirect forms of derivative epistemic fulfillment, and merely illustrative fulfillment – have a complex structure, and all of them essentially involve intuitive and conceptual contents. But there is another type of fulfillment that occurs wholly within the sphere of intuition itself, one at the level, as Husserl says, of "mere receptivity" (*APS*: 107). As we've seen, one of the characteristics of perceptual consciousness is that each phase in the streaming flow of perception has both intuitive and empty, horizonal contents. And as we have also seen, those empty horizonal contents are nonconceptual, and at least some of them anticipate further properties and features of the perceived object or environment, and the experiences in which they would come to intuition. As a piece of music unfolds, anticipatory intentions find their fulfillment or frustration when later phases of the piece are intuited. The piece unfolds as I expected, or not as I expected. This is not a matter of my verifying judgments on the basis of experience. It is not a matter of me comparing the world as it is given with the world as it is thought to be, as is the case in epistemic fulfillment. Rather, this is a process of fulfillment (or frustration) occurring at the level of perception itself. It is a process whereby empty contents belonging to the fabric of perception give way to intuitive contents that present the same objects – or not. This is *intuitive fulfillment*.[9]

---

[9] Donn Welton (1983: 248) draws a similar distinction in language closer to Husserl's own: "The relationship between implicated sense and fulfilled sense is completely different from the relationship between signifying meaning and perception. For in the dialectic of fulfillment and implication and of perception and apperception the objective sense is discovered as a sense found in perception."

Phenomenologically, intuitive fulfillment differs substantially from epistemic fulfillment. As I become absorbed in a piece of music, I am not, typically, in the business of making and verifying judgments. Nevertheless, anticipatory intentions are fulfilled, and sometimes frustrated, as when a note is missed. The fulfillment of my thought that the piece will end with a crescendo is *not* the fulfillment of the predelineated consciousness of the crescendo that is part of the perceptual act itself, the one that I anticipate with a felt tension running throughout my entire body. And when I lose a ski edge and begin to fall, I anticipate my imminent pain viscerally, not intellectually. Moreover, the syntheses of intuitive fulfillment have a different temporal structure from the syntheses of epistemic fulfillment. In epistemic fulfillment, the thoughtful apprehension of the object and the intuitive apprehension can be, and perhaps must be, simultaneous. I fulfill the thought that there is a crescendo *at the same time* that I hear the crescendo. In intuitive fulfillment, on the other hand, the fulfilling experience only comes *after* the empty one. There is not an overlap of *present* empty horizonal contents and intuitive ones, since the very same part or moment cannot be simultaneously intended via an empty *horizonal* content and a presenting, intuitive one. Rather, there is an overlap between past, and presently *retained*, empty horizonal contents and present intuitive ones. What makes a continuous perceptual series harmonious is just this continuous, flowing fulfillment of horizonal contents by intuitive ones.

### 7.3 DEPARTURES FROM HUSSERL

Although my interest is principally philosophical rather than interpretive, I should point out that while parts of my account of epistemic, illustrative, and intuitive fulfillment follow some of Husserl's discussions rather closely, my account differs from his in important ways. First, Husserl almost always speaks as though the fulfillment of a thought or any other "meaning-intention" is either contemporaneous with or subsequent to that thought. Dallas Willard, quite plausibly, interprets him as holding that "In general, fulfillment occurs only where there is a self-conscious realization of the enhancement of the degree to which what was (in some measure) merely thought of becomes intuitively present *as* it was thought to be."[10]

---

[10] Willard (1984: 226). Also see Dwyer (2007: 92): "every filled intention fulfills what was previously only emptily meant, as it was emptily meant."

This, it seems to me, is not the case. While finding the world to be as one thought or currently thinks it to be is a familiar enough experience, so is thinking of it as one already found it to be. The curled up cat on the sofa is already perceived before I recognize it as a cat; Jim is already perceptually given when I realize that it's him. And, as Husserl himself insists, when in the course of perception I determine objects more closely, thoughts become fulfilled which I had not entertained before. What distinguishes epistemic fulfillment from everything else is that in it, we both perceptually and thoughtfully apprehend the world. Epistemic fulfillment is knowledge, or at least something that approaches knowledge. Which order the intuitive and conceptual acts occur in is irrelevant, provided that the appropriate synthesis between them takes place. We wouldn't want to insist that some-one doesn't know that his house is on fire simply because the temporal progression went from finding to thinking rather than from thinking to finding, especially when the former progression is the rule in empirical knowledge.

It is, however, noteworthy that in intuitive fulfillment, the temporal order does go from empty intention to intuition, and this brings us to a second, related issue. I have insisted that in epistemic fulfillment, the fulfilling and the fulfilled acts have the same objects but different contents. Husserl himself provides the key argument in §§4–5 of the sixth *Logical Investigation*. There he argues, on the basis of arguments to which I've already appealed, that because we can vary the conceptual and perceptual content of a perceptual judgment independently of one another,

we must locate no part of the meaning in the percept [*Wahrnehmung*] itself. The percept, which presents the object, and the statement which, by way of the judgement . . . thinks and expresses it, must be rigorously kept apart. (*LI* 6, §5: 685, emphases omitted)

This is exactly the view I have defended.

However, in later sections Husserl claims that the fulfilling and fulfilled acts *do* have the same matter or intentional content. Sometimes Husserl says that the two acts have the same intentional or semantic essence (matter + quality). In fulfillment "the semantic essence of the signitive (or expressive) act reappears *identically* in corresponding intuitive acts" (*LI* 6, §28: 744). Elsewhere, he merely insists that they have the same matter:

Our comparison of meaning-intentions with their correlative intuitions . . . showed us . . . that the very thing that we marked off as the 'matter' of meaning, reappeared once more in the corresponding intuition, and furnished the means for an identi-fication. Our freedom, therefore, to add to or take away intuitive elements, and

even all correspondent intuitions ... was based on the fact that the whole act
attaching to the sound of our words had the same 'matters' on the intuitive as on
the meaning side.[11]

Since the matter of a signitive act is a conceptual content, it follows that the
matter of a perceptual act is a conceptual content as well.

What accounts for the intuitiveness of an act, on this rival view, isn't any
distinctive kind of intentional content, but intrinsically nonintentional
sensory or "hyletic" content, which borrows whatever intentionality it has
by means of "interpretation," "apprehension," or "apperception." In perception sensory data are "in a certain manner 'interpreted' or 'apperceived',
and ... it is in the phenomenological character of such an animating
interpretation of sensation that what we call the appearing of the object
consists."[12] Without interpretation, sensations would be "dead matter."
Thanks to interpretation, they "are able to present an object" (*TS* §15:
39–40). Whatever else interpretation is, moreover, it is clear that it involves
the sensory components being united, in the right way, with meanings or
concepts. "The perceptual presentation," Husserl writes, "arises in so far as
an experienced complex of sensations gets informed by a certain act-
character, one of conceiving or meaning."[13] If there's any doubt that
perception involves an act of meaning, on Husserl's account, he also writes
that it is "analytically true" that "everything that is intuitively present is also
meant" (*LI* 6, §23: 732). On the view I have defended, this is far from
analytically true.

   This account of perception is obviously at odds both with the arguments
presented in previous chapters and Husserl's own arguments that perception is not a carrier of meaning. That is, Husserl himself appears to be
committed to an inconsistent triad:
(1) Perceptual acts are not carriers of meaning (content ≠ meaning).
(2) Signitive or conceptual acts are carriers of meaning (content  meaning).
(3) In epistemic fulfillment, the intuitive and conceptual acts have identical
    matters or contents.
The conjunction of (2) and (3) – call it the bad theory – together with
Husserl's claim that all perceptual acts can fulfill some conceptual act (*LI* 6,

---

[11]  *LI* 6, §25: 738. Husserl makes similar points throughout his discussions of fulfillment. See the rest of
     *LI* 6, §25; *LI* 6, §30: 749; *Ideas 1* §136: 327 and *APS*: 445–9. Also see Willard (1995: 152); Rosen (1977:
     27); and Bernet (2003: 155).
[12]  *LI* 5, §2: 539. See also all of *LI* 5, §14, as well as *LI* 6, §6: 688. This theory is still present much later. See
     *APS*: 55.
[13]  *LI* 1, §23: 310. Also see *LI* 5, §15: 567–8.

§21: 728), entails that every perceptual act has conceptual content. On this view, perception is thinking in presence – that is, epistemic fulfillment.[14]

I have discussed Husserl's own motivations for holding the bad theory, as well as the problems it faces, elsewhere (Hopp 2008a). Interestingly, however, he sometimes seems to reject it. He says, for instance, that

the way in which I earlier discussed "evidence" was vague. I often used "evidence" in a sense equivalent to the givenness of something itself. But surely we must distinguish: evidence as insight that belongs to judgment, <to the> judgment that <something> is there itself that exists and that is given again <as> that – and, on the other hand, the being-given itself'. (*PCIT*: 305)

Again:

Perception has its own intentionality that as yet does not harbor anything of the active comportment of the ego and of its constitutive accomplishment. For the intentionality of perception is rather presupposed in order for the ego to have something for which or against which it can decide. (*APS*: 94)

But none of this is very decisive, since these passages occur before or at the same time as other passages in which Husserl seems to endorse the bad theory.

One final noteworthy point is that by distinguishing perception, and the intuitive fulfillment taking place in it, from epistemic fulfillment, we can make sense of a difficult passage in §8 of the sixth *Logical Investigation*. There Husserl argues, as I have, that the object of an act of epistemic fulfillment is the identity of what is given and what is meant. In an addendum to that section, however, he writes that it is not an act of identification. As he says, "where a name is actually applied to an object of intuition, we refer to the intuited and named *object*, but not to the identity of this object, as something at once intuited and named" (*LI* 6, §8: 697). From this he appears to conclude that in fulfillment there is "no intentional consciousness of identity, in which identity, as a unity referred to, first gains objective status" (*ibid.*). Rather, in fulfillment "an identifying consciousness has been *experienced*, even if there is no *conscious intention* directed at identity" (*ibid.*). But this doesn't follow. From the fact that a name, whose sense is a conceptual content, refers to the object intuited rather than to "identity" – and here Husserl presumably means not the relation of identity as such, but the identity of what is meant and what is

[14] Husserl's commentators disagree whether he's committed to some version of conceptualism, and each side has considerable textual evidence in its favor. Kevin Mulligan (1995) is the chief advocate for anti-conceptualism, while Richard Cobb-Stevens (1990) has advocated a conceptualist reading. See Mooney (2010) for an excellent overview of the debate.

given – it does not follow that we are not *also* conscious of an identity. The whole point of characterizing fulfillment as a founded act was to recognize that its total object differs from any of the objects of its founding members, not that its founding members no longer have their proper objects or that we are not also conscious of them too. Indeed, in fulfillment the worldly object might be the focal object of attention, and the consciousness of the identity of the given and the meant might be marginal, poised to become an object of attention (see Willard 1995: 191). What is more plausible, however, is that in *intuitive* fulfillment there is no such objective awareness of an identity, but that, instead, what we called an "identity-consciousness" in the last chapter is simply the seamless continuity of acts in which the same object is presented. We might say that epistemic fulfillment is an act of "relational identification," an act that *registers* an identity, namely the identity of the objects of two already constituted acts. Intuitive fulfillment, on the other hand, *constitutes* an identical object – that is, it builds up our consciousness of the object in the first place. Obviously not all identity-consciousness can be relational, since without becoming aware of objects in the first place by means of identity-constituting acts, one could not then go on to relate them (it) in thought or experience. If I can think that A = B, I must already have the ability to think of A and of B.

As we have seen, Husserl characterizes fulfillment as an "evidence-consciousness" (*APS*: 114), and it's not difficult to see why. If you are really serious about knowing about something, you will want to perceive it, if possible (Bernet 2003). If I really want to know about the Sonora Desert, and if that desire outweighs, say, my fear of venomous reptiles and my desire to stay cool, I will go there and see if for myself. If I really want to know about ancient Rome, I will bemoan the fact that I cannot perceive it. My claims to really want to know about these things would be difficult to sustain if, given the opportunity to see them, I refused. To imagine a different scenario, if I am unsure whether I left the light on, and really want to find out, it would, in the absence of serious countervailing considerations, be crazy for me to refuse the opportunity to perceive it. This conversation appears fantastic even by philosophical standards:

ME: "I really need to know whether I left the light on."
YOU: "Well, just go inside and check."
ME: "No, no, that won't help at all."

What makes this conversation so absurd is that seeing does, and *obviously* does, have an enormously important role to play in the production of knowledge. In any context that is even approximately normal, having one's thought that the light is off epistemically fulfilled by seeing the light which is off settles the question whether it's off, and settles it decisively. "Precisely because it gives its objective affair as the affair itself, any consciousness that gives something-itself can establish rightness, correctness, for another consciousness" (*FTL* §59: 159).

That perception can justify beliefs follows from what beliefs aim at and what perception delivers. A huge amount of what each of us believes and knows is derived from our knowledge of other propositions. I know that Moscow is a cold place in January, and I know that the moon has no atmosphere. But I don't know these things because I have verified them experientially. I have learned them in the way that I learn most things of consequence: through the testimony of authoritative witnesses and experts, reasoning, and other epistemically founded modes of acquiring knowledge. Nevertheless, each of my beliefs is directed towards or intentionally aimed, not at its own propositional content or the propositional contents that support it, but at the world. Believing is world directed. It aspires to represent the world as it is. It aims at truth.[15] But in mere thought or belief I am not conscious of the match between the world, on the one hand, and my belief, on the other. I am conscious of the world, but *emptily*. The intention to reach the object, to relate to it in person, is unrealized (*LI* 1, §9).

In order to grasp the object in person, I need to perceive it; perception is the only sort of experience in virtue of which empirical states of affairs present themselves in person. In perception, "the object stands . . . as there in the flesh" or "as actually present" (*TS* §4: 12). "Every perception is characterized by the intention of grasping its object as present, and *in propria persona*" (*LI* 5, §5: 542). And yet perception is not sufficient for knowledge. As we have seen, it isn't justified. And because its intentional content is essentially experiential rather than detachable, it cannot persist beyond the experience itself. The content of a perceptual experience is unfit to be an "abiding possession" (*EJ* §47: 198). It's simply not true, for instance, that "Perception constructs perceptual representations of our surroundings, and these are passed to our system of epistemic cognition to produce beliefs about the world" (Pollock and Oved 2005: 325). "Perceptual representations" – the contents of perception – cannot be "passed" to any nonintuitive act. I don't believe things from a spatial

---

[15] For a good defense, see Alston (1996: 253 ff.).

perspective, for instance, but perceptual presentations are always perspectival. Nor is perceptual content linguistically communicable. Talking to someone is not sufficient to place her in a perceptual state identical with your own, nor is being in such a state necessary for someone to understand what you have said (Hopp 2009a). I can *state* a belief. I cannot state a perception. Nevertheless, although the content of perception can't figure in judgments or beliefs, its objects are just the things beliefs aim at. In fulfillment, what the belief merely represents is presented. The term 'fulfillment', then, has a dual sense: it doesn't just register the fact that an empty intention gets filled out with intuitive content, but that a certain end inherent in believing itself has been achieved. Beliefs aim at the truth but, with equal immediacy, the direct consciousness of truth, and that is what fulfillment is. In epistemic fulfillment, we ratify a truth-bearer by consulting its truth-maker, and are directly aware of the match between them. Just in virtue of having beliefs, that is what you want to happen to them – though, of course, you might want other things a lot more.

In light of what's already been said, it is also clear that justifying a belief by fulfilling it perceptually is totally different from justifying a belief on the basis of other beliefs or judgments. First, if my belief B is supported by other beliefs B*, B**, etc., and if B is justified, then those beliefs must themselves be justified. If, however, B is justified in virtue of being fulfilled by a perceptual experience, the perceptual experience is not itself warranted. Perceptual experiences aren't the kinds of things that could be justified or unjustified (*IL* §3: 9). A person isn't stupid in virtue of perceiving or failing to perceive something. Keen hearing is not a sign of intelligence, and hallucinating is not a form of irrationality. Second, the constituent acts in fulfillment *must* have the same objects. If a belief B is epistemically supported on the basis of B*, B**, etc., however, it is rarely the case that any of those supporting beliefs has the same object as the belief it supports, and never the case that all of them do. Finally, because perceptual experiences do not have conceptual or propositional content, they do not stand in inferential relations with other mental states. The content of my perceptual state is not a premise from which I infer anything, and believing on the basis of perception is not a species of reasoning.[16] In reasoning, I come to believe that the world is a certain way by thinking of the *other* ways I take it to be; reasoning is a matter of determining what is the case given that something

---

[16] Burge (2003: 528). Unlike Burge, however, I don't have any qualms about characterizing nonconceptual contents as *reasons*. I don't regard reasons as consisting solely of the kinds of things that can be exploited in reasoning.

else is the case. In fulfillment, I come to believe that the world is a certain way because I find it to be just that way.

Fulfillment not only differs from inferential justification, but it is typically superior. It's the only context in which I can become intuitively aware of the correspondence between what I mean and the world itself. In fulfillment, I don't consult my own beliefs, other propositions, or the authority of my peers. I turn, instead, to the things themselves. I become directly aware of a state of affairs through perception, and become aware that my belief corresponds with that state of affairs in fulfillment. That is just what perceptual knowledge at its best is. There is, moreover, no mystery as to why perception is relevant to belief. The fact that the intuitive content presents, in a positing way, a given state of affairs makes it intrinsically suited to stand in reason-giving relations with other contents about that state of affairs. A perception of a barn is intrinsically of a barn – it wouldn't be this experience if it were of something else – and, in virtue of that, has an obvious connection with propositions about that barn. Moreover, because perception *presents* the state of affairs that the thought is about in the flesh, in fulfillment a belief or judgment acquires epistemic justification immediately and noninferentially. It is able to stand over against its own truth-maker, and we are conscious of that. To borrow Mark Johnston's (2006) phrase, sensory awareness – or rather epistemic fulfillment – is "better than mere knowledge."

In characterizing fulfillment as a kind of immediate justification, I am thereby rejecting state internalism (section 3.2) – that is, the view that "there is no first-order knowledge unless there is also higher-order knowledge with respect to the factors that make first-order knowledge possible" (Van Cleve 2003: 45). It's undoubtedly true that my belief that the light is off is justified because it is perceptually fulfilled. But in order for my belief to be justified, that claim only has to be true, not believed or known. No one needs to know a theory of fulfillment in order to have thoughts fulfilled, any more than anyone needs to know a theory of thought to think or perception to perceive. As Husserl puts it, "If I call this intuited object a 'watch', I complete, in naming it, an act of thought and knowledge, but I know the watch, and not my knowledge" (*LI* 6, §67: 837).

This sort of state externalism follows from the idea, endorsed by Husserl, that the having of evidence and knowledge is a possibility inherent in any thinking and perceiving consciousness, not something that depends upon higher-order acts directed at those first-order acts of thinking and perceiving. Knowing is just what thinking, at its best, is. As Husserl puts it, "The concept of any intentionality whatsoever . . . and the concept of evidence, that intentionality that is the giving of something-itself, are essentially correlative" (*FTL*, §60: 160). Since acts of perceiving and thinking, including acts of fulfillment, do not depend for their existence or their whatness on reflective intentional acts directed upon them, but are, rather, presupposed by the latter, so knowing, which is just what all thinking potentially is and what successful thinking actually is, does not depend upon such reflection either. When, as epistemologists, we come to regard certain acts as epistemically privileged, this isn't a matter of us making them so. It is a matter of discovering that they are, and were already, so. Epistemologists don't have better reasons for believing that dinosaurs died out 65 million years ago than paleontologists do, or better reasons for believing that they have hands than a five-year-old does, just because they have some second-order story to tell about epistemic justification.

Furthermore, I am not committed to the claim, endorsed by the myth-makers that Sellars attacks (1997), that acts of fulfillment do not presuppose the possession of concepts or other knowledge. Fulfillment does depend on having concepts – you cannot have the thought that P fulfilled if you can't think that thought. However, as Alston (1989) and Pryor (2000) have pointed out, the fact that my ability to know something presupposes a great deal of knowledge does not entail that it is inferentially supported by that knowledge. A piece of knowledge might depend on others for either its existence or its "epistemization" (Alston 1989: 58). Only the second sort of dependence is incompatible with a belief's being immediately justified. My belief that I am wearing shoes might depend on all sorts of knowledge for its existence. It doesn't thereby depend on that knowledge for its justification. Once I have the concept of shoes, I am in a position to have thoughts about shoes immediately verified on the basis of experience.

The claim that fulfillment is better than mere knowledge, however, deserves some care. If every perceptual experience were adequate to its object, defending the claim that fulfillment is an immediate and superior form of justification would be much easier. Unlike mere knowledge – i.e. empty knowledge – this sort of knowledge would always take its measure from the things themselves, and it would always have at least as high a degree of justification as any mere knowledge. And here it is worth pointing out that although I am committed to the view that we perceive physical objects and states of affairs, the theory of fulfillment does not depend on that. If you have been convinced by various arguments that you couldn't possibly perceive a tree, you could still endorse the theory of fulfillment by merely restricting its scope of possible application. However, we do, I am convinced, perceive physical objects, and things are more complicated. Just as what seems to be a perceptual experience might turn out to be an indistinguishable hallucination, so can what seems to be an episode of fulfillment turn out to be pseudo-fulfillment. And just as perception is inadequate to its object, so that its object might always turn out to be otherwise than it appears to be, so beliefs epistemically founded on such imperfect experiences might turn out to be false.

Let me begin with illusions. If I have an experience that presents a wall W as being blue, when it is in fact green, the experience nevertheless epistemically fulfills the thought that W is blue. The experience's object in this case is W's being blue, as is the thought's, and the two are synthesized in the right way. So, epistemic fulfillment can occur even when the perceptual experience involved is illusory. Fulfillment, then, does not guarantee truth. It is important to note that this really is the experience's object. It is of the wall, and presents it as being blue. In particular, we must reject the claim, often made on behalf of those pleading for sense data, that if an object perceptually appears to have a certain property, then there is some object that *does* have that property. Since, by hypothesis, the wall does not have that property, we would have to conclude that the experience's object was not W, but something else. But this constitutes a massive distortion of the phenomenology. It is not a veridical perception of something which is blue. It's a nonveridical perception of something that is not in fact blue. And the sense datum inference underlying this argument is objectionable on other grounds as well. Something can, for instance, appear to be a barn. By this I don't just mean that something can intellectually seem to be a barn, in the way that, say, something can intellectually seem to be very old or stars can intellectually seem to be very far away. I mean that it perceptually appears to be a barn – that the empty horizons bound up with and partially constituting the intuitive contents point towards avenues of fulfillment that only become fulfilled in the experience of a barn. But if I'm in fact seeing a barn façade, it doesn't follow that something else, much less a sense datum, is a barn. There's just no barn around at all. The sense datum inference even fails with less controversial examples. Something can appear to be ten feet in front of me, or larger than my body, or on top of a table. But sense data can't, as far as I can tell, have those properties. And virtually everything appears to have more to it, to have parts and features that could be disclosed upon further inspection. But sense data don't have more to them.

If the perceptual experience is hallucinatory, on the other hand, it cannot epistemically fulfill thoughts about any actual object; in these cases we have mere pseudo-fulfillment. This is because (section 6.4) no hallucination can have the same particular object as a veridical perception, and so the intuitive and the conceptual conditions cannot both be met. I can think about my friend Dave and I can also perceive him. I'm also able to recognize Dave; I know what he looks like, how he behaves, and so forth. This provides me with the materials to have thoughts about Dave fulfilled perceptually. But if I am hallucinating, the experience does not epistemically fulfill the thought that Dave is talking. It only seems to. However, hallucinations do present the world as being a certain way, and can epistemically fulfill thoughts whose contents exploit the seeming presence of the object they are about. The thought "That is a barn" is epistemically fulfilled by a hallucination that presents me with a barn. In presenting me with barn-properties as instantiated, the hallucinatory experiences presents them as instantiated in some particular thing, and it is that particular thing that I purport to refer to by means of the demonstrative "that." Of course this demonstrative fails to refer to anything – there's just no barn at all, least of all a mental or "intentional" one. But that's just what makes this hallucination the distinctive kind of mistake that it is; it presents the world as though it contains a particular barn in it, the one in the region of space before me, and there is none.

The susceptibility of a putative act of fulfillment to defeat is not simply a function of the inadequacy of the perceptual experience underlying it, but of its conceptual content as well. The proposition that *he is talking* is easier to fulfill, and less liable to defeat, than the proposition that *Dave is talking*, because it is easier to possess demonstrative concepts authentically than it is to possess detachable concepts of individuals authentically. Demonstratives give us concept authenticity on the cheap: we simply exploit the presence of the thing they refer to. But like most cheap things, they wear out quickly. Possessing a detachable concept of Dave authentically is more difficult, but more worthwhile. Detachable concepts enable one to re-identify an object without tracking it continuously. It makes one's experiences more vulnerable to defeat, but the payoff is greater too. Similar remarks hold for various sorts of properties and kinds. The fulfilled belief that something is an animal is less liable to defeat than is the fulfilled belief that it's a cat, and the fulfilled belief that something is a red thing is less liable to defeat than that it is a barn.

Beliefs grounded in fulfillment or pseudo-fulfillment are, then, defeasible, and the justification they possess is *prima facie*. Such a belief that P can be defeated directly by a rebutting defeater, where a rebutting defeater is any evidence that provides one with a reason to believe something contrary to P, or by an undercutting defeater, which defeats the connection between one's evidence and one's belief that P (Pollock 2001: 235; Schellenberg 2008: 77).

So, my belief that the wall is blue will be rebutted if I have another set of experiences that present it as green. My belief that Dave is talking will be undercut if I learn that I am hallucinating, or if I learn that he has been cloned and there are now hundreds of look-alikes in the area.

The fact that my seemingly fulfilled beliefs can be undermined in all of these ways does not compromise my claim that they are immediately justified. In particular, even though there are plenty of propositions and possible experiences which, if true or veridical, would undermine my justification for believing that my light is off, I don't need to first rule them out in order to justifiably believe that my light is off (Pryor 2000). My justification for believing that the light is off rests on an experience that presents that very light as being off. That is my evidential basis. And just in virtue of that, I am justified in believing that it is off, provided that I don't have positive reasons to believe that any defeating states of affairs actually obtain. Indeed, seeing that my light is off provides me with a reason to reject any potential defeaters, unless and until evidence points in their favor. Granted, in virtue of being defeasible, my belief's justification is negatively epistemically dependent on the truth of other propositions, some of which I believe. But it is not positively epistemically dependent on them. My fulfilled belief doesn't derive its justification from them, and I don't use them as premises which, together with my experience, make my belief justified (Audi 2003: 205). In the same way, the fact that a bridge is structurally sound is negatively dependent on its not having been jolted by an earthquake. But its soundness doesn't positively depend on that. What positively supports the bridge is not the absence of earthquakes – or evil demons, since they could destroy bridges as easily as they could destroy knowledge – but the presence of beams, girders, and foundations.

This claim is supported by phenomenological considerations. Reflecting on what we do when we come to know things on the basis of experience, it doesn't seem that our beliefs depend on anything more sophisticated than consulting the world itself, as it reveals itself in perception, and accommodating our beliefs to it. "An experience of there being hands seems to justify me in believing there are hands in a perfectly straightforward and immediate way" (Pryor 2000: 536). If, on the other hand, one had to antecedently rule out every possible defeater of a belief's content in order to justifiably believe it, virtually no one, with the possible exception of trained epistemologists, would have any justified beliefs – and even they probably wouldn't have many.

One of the most fundamental facts about conscious life is the inequality of evidential worth of different types of mental acts. When I imagine or just think that there is a lion in my living room, this gives me no reason whatsoever to believe that there is, and does not jeopardize whatever positive evidence I have that there is not. I am not an irresponsible parent for allowing my children to play there without first verifying that there's no lion in there. I would, rather, be an irresponsible epistemic agent – and parent – if I refused to allow them to go to the living room without first ruling out every merely imagined possible state of affairs that might endanger them. Similarly, a team of engineers would not be acting responsibly as thinkers or engineers if, on the basis of the merely imagined possibility that an evil demon might undermine their bridge upon completion, they were to fail to build the bridge. What they need is a positive reason to believe that, and mere imagination doesn't provide it. On the other hand, if I were actually to see a lion in my living room, I would be insane to send my children in there. Perception has an evidential worth that merely conceiving and imagining don't. Furthermore, I don't first need to rule out every merely imagined defeater in order to be perfectly justified in believing that there's a lion in there and acting accordingly. It would be a symptom of insanity to say, "Well, I just imagined that an evil demon could be causing us to hallucinate a lion. That defeats my evidence that there's a lion in there. Go ahead!"

Still, the vulnerability of fulfillment to defeat might prompt one to argue that the sorts of beliefs I think can be fulfilled really cannot be. For instance, rather than claiming that my belief that the wall is blue is fulfilled, why not say instead that (1) my belief that it appears to me as though the wall is blue is fulfilled? Then I can conclude that it is probably true that the wall is blue on the basis of (1) together with (2): if it appears to me that the wall is blue, then the wall is (probably) blue. Fulfillment, then, will be confined to (1), and will be much less liable to defeat.

There are several problems with this proposal. For one thing, we need some story about how I can be justified in believing (2) which does not appeal to ordinary perceptual experiences. But as Plantinga points out, "it is at best extremely unlikely that there are any decent (noncircular) arguments" for a claim like that (Plantinga 1993b: 97). Moreover, this approach butchers the phenomenology of the experience with no discernable epistemic gain. I'm not any closer to knowing that the light is off in virtue of performing this little exercise, since whatever epistemic vulnerabilities the original act of fulfillment had will now accrue to the conjunction of (1) and (2). Finally, not only does (1) fail to provide a more faithful description of my experience, it completely falsifies it. When I have an illusory experience of a blue wall, it's certainly true that it appears to me that the wall is blue.

But the latter claim is not part of the experience's own *content*. Rather, the experience says that the wall *is* blue. If my experience were not of a blue wall, if it did not in fact "say" that the *wall is blue*, it would be false to claim that it perceptually appears to me that the wall is blue. If my experience only "says" that a cloud appears like Elvis, it is false that it appears to me that the cloud is Elvis. Rather, it appears to me that the cloud appears like Elvis. Statements about how things appear to me, or how I am appeared-to, are made on the basis of reflection. Such statements are not fulfilled by the perceptual experiences themselves, but on the basis of reflective experiences which have those very experiences as their objects. The experience itself purports to depict how things are. Failing to align one's beliefs with its content is a way of muting it.

Again, it falsifies the experience itself if, in the presence of a barn, you describe your experience as being of only an array of colors and shapes. That claim is easier to fulfill, but is, at the same time, unfaithful to the experience: it's a way of treating an inadequate presention of a barn as a more adequate presentation of something else. Speaking for myself, I have to force myself to try to believe that my experiences aren't of ordinary physical objects as being this way and that, and I never succeed. I don't seem to be reading things into my experiences when I characterize them as being of my house or of a car. Rather, I seem to be censoring them when I try to depict them as being of anything less. Construing my experiences as of something less than the world because they are inadequate and vulnerable to defeat is rather like concluding that because shooting free throws often goes awry, I wasn't really trying to make free throws, but only trying to hit the rim – or, since that's a risky undertaking too, to release the ball. In both cases, a risky activity directed towards one kind of thing is falsely reinterpreted as a safe activity directed at something completely different.

These remarks are immediately relevant to Anil Gupta's views on experience. Gupta is the first to acknowledge that experiences contribute to knowledge. The "insight of empiricism," as he puts it, is that "experience is our principal epistemic authority and guide" (Gupta 2006: 1). This is the principal truism about experience. The second is that experiences are multiply factorizable. That is: "The subjective character of experience – how things seem to be in experience – is a product of two factors: how things are and our state and position in the world" (5). Any "total experience" can be the result of several world–self combinations, and, "given only the experience, we cannot recover the world–self combination" that generated it (7). The experience E I have when looking at a pink rabbit under normal lighting could also have resulted from looking at a white rabbit under red light, or from being deceived by an evil neuroscientist. Perhaps unicorns and elves are performing a magical dance around me and have left me beguiled. By itself, E provides no justification for any ordinary judgment (7). It only justifies me in believing one thing rather than something else in conjunction with my "view," which consists in "my concepts, conceptions, and beliefs" (76).

Let us pause here and consider why my experience, by itself, does not provide me with "any justification" for making any determinate judgment (7). It could be because while my total experience E has a determinate content – it presents me with a situation in which my light is off, I am seeing it, my body is upright, the light is a certain distance and direction from me, and so forth – it positively depends on my having justification for believing that conditions are normal, that my nervous system is working properly, that I am not surrounded by enchanted unicorns, and so forth. Gupta seems to suggest, at times, that this is his view (7). On this view, my experience has a determinate content, and its content does present me with a determinate world–self combination. It's just that an experience with just this determinate content could have been brought about by other factors. Since, that is, the world–self combination could have been quite different from how my experience presents it as being, I require independent reasons for ruling those possible veridicality-defeating world–self combinations out.

I don't think this is a plausible view, for reasons already discussed: having a thought perceptually fulfilled provides me with *prima facie* justification for endorsing it. But the position above isn't Gupta's position. Rather, Gupta denies not only that my experience relies upon my view for its epistemic force, but that it relies upon my view for its intentional content. As he puts it, multiple-factorizability "points to the multiplicity of possible objects for any given experience" (Gupta 2006: 9). And if experiences can have a multiplicity of different possible objects – if my total experience E could present me with something besides my light's being off, my standing up, my being a certain distance from it, etc. – then it could have a different total *content*. And if it can have a different content, then it could have had different conditions of satisfaction. Had my view included the conviction that, for instance, every time I have an experience with this "phenomenal character," then unicorns are dancing around me, then the experience would have pointed towards unicorns dancing around me. It would not have presented my light as being off and so forth and had its epistemic force overruled by the counter-force of my belief. Rather, it just would have had a different world–self combination as its object, and been right.

This clearly doesn't follow from multiple-factorizability by itself. That any total experience can be brought about by a multitude of world–self combinations does not entail that the *content* of the experience is compatible with any more than one of them. It is perfectly consistent to claim that my experience E is veridical if and only if my light is off, I am standing up, and so on, but that there are a number of objective world–self combinations in which this experience would have been generated. It just would have been nonveridical in most of them. Rather, what helps generate Gupta's astonishing conclusion is his claim, which he calls "reliability," that what he calls the "given" in an experience "does not yield anything false or erroneous; in particular, it does not yield a false proposition" (Gupta 2006: 27). So whatever is given in my experience E, it's not a light that is turned off, since there are plenty of possible situations in which E would have yielded a false proposition if that were so.

The real issue, then, is with reliability: what reasons do we have for supposing that experiences are reliable in this strict sense? Gupta offers us two. First, he writes, "Experience is passive, and it is always a good policy not to assign fault to the passive" (Gupta 2006: 28). He goes on: "The experience is bound to be the way it is, given the circumstances, and it is useless to blame it for my false belief" (*ibid.*). What we ought to do, in the face of an experience which is bound to be the way it is, is assume responsibility for our false beliefs and try to change ourselves, not it.

I am not persuaded. One might as well argue that the sentence "Only five people live in New York" isn't false because, after all, it's passive and can't help be what it is, given the way the world is. The assumption here is that to characterize an experience as nonveridical is to "assign fault" to it. But that's no more true than saying that in characterizing a sentence as false, one is assigning fault to it. Furthermore, this would require us to conclude that none of our passively held beliefs, of which there are many, is false, since they're bound to be the way they are too. Of course we might negatively evaluate things which are false and nonveridical. But negatively evaluating something is not always a matter of holding it blameworthy; I don't think cancer and earthquakes are blameworthy. And if I negatively evaluate a perceptual experience E, that's because I believe that (1) E is nonveridical and (2) good experiences are veridical. But in characterizing an experience as nonveridical, I'm not *evaluating* it at all. That requires a further step.

Gupta's second reason for endorsing reliability is that "Only skeptics and rationalists can comfortably abandon it" (Gupta 2006: 29). Empiricists, on the other hand, cannot, since they "view experience as vested with the highest epistemic authority" (*ibid.*). Suppose, then, that some experiences are nonveridical. How, according to an empiricist, can we correct that error? Skeptics don't have to worry about this problem, and rationalists can appeal to "constraints that they deem to be truths supplied by reason" (*ibid.*). But empiricists will have to appeal to something else, namely coherence. Coherence can't just be a "purely logical" constraint, because even maximally coherent wholes can include false propositions. But if coherence is to be a substantive, rather than a merely logical, constraint, we have to explain from whence it derives its authority. "The empiricists," Gupta concludes, "are in danger of positing a sixth sense, the sense of coherence, as the ultimate seat of epistemic authority" (Gupta 2006: 29–30).

Again, I am not persuaded. First, the claim that "experience" has the "highest epistemic authority" is in many ways ambiguous. First, what is "experience"? Does this mean the sum total of a person's perceptual experiences? Relatively self-standing, temporally extended experiences, such as hearing of a piece of music or inspection of a painting? Or punctual sense impressions? And does having the "highest epistemic authority" consist in being absolutely indubitable? Does it consist in having a higher epistemic authority than any other source of justification, though possibly falling short of absolute indubitability? Or does "experience" have the highest epistemic authority insofar as it provides the most warrant for empirical beliefs that any source of empirical evidence could provide? Finally, does *each* experience have the *same* degree of authority?

On any of the above interpretations of "experience," it is highly dubious that it has either the highest conceivable epistemic authority or a higher authority than any other kind of knowledge. My knowledge that $1 = 1$ and that the color red is not middle C, are, I think, pretty close to absolutely indubitable. But I cannot think of any empirical belief that has that degree of justification. If empiricism entails something else, we should abandon empiricism.

On the other hand, the claim that "experience" is the highest epistemic authority with regard to beliefs about empirical objects and states of affairs can be made plausible, depending on what we mean by "experience." That the total sum of my experiences is my ultimate court of appeal for the sum total of my empirical beliefs sounds right, but this doesn't entail that the evidence it provides is absolutely immune from defeat, nor does it entail that each of the experiences and phases of experience constituting this web of experiences has equal epistemic authority. First, the authority of an experience depends on (1) the object that it is of, (2) the extent to which that object is given in the experience – the experience's adequacy – and (3) the beliefs about that object that it justifies. Suppose I see a house in a continuous perceptual experience A, whose partial acts include $a_1$–$a_{10}$. This experience is epistemically authoritative with regard to beliefs about the house, but not Ben Franklin or the weather in Moscow. Second, it is inadequate to the house, which partially explains the fact that it has less epistemic authority than other possible experiences. If, for instance, there is some possible experience A*, whose partial acts are $a_1$–$a_{20}$, A* will provide more justification for a number of propositions which A also fulfills, such as "That is a house." Both A and A* also have a greater epistemic authority than any of the partial acts making them up. So, provided experiences are more than punctual sense impressions – and how could we experience hearing a sentence or listening to a melody if they weren't? – we can rule out the claim that every experience has the same epistemic authority. We can see this in other cases as well. My belief that a wooden surface is smooth can be fulfilled by a visual experience VE, a tactual experience TE, or a combined visual-tactile experience VTE. The latter provides more justification for the belief than either of the other two. Finally, my experience A of the house provides more justification for some empirical beliefs about the house than others. The property of being a house is less adequately given than the property of having a window, and it is, accordingly, easier to fulfill the proposition that the structure has a window than that it is a house.

This gives us a clue for resolving conflicts: all else being equal, we trust the experiences that are more adequate to their objects, and hold on more firmly to beliefs which have been more adequately fulfilled than others. Furthermore, we can certainly be sensitive to issues of coherence without treating it as a sufficient condition for justification or as "the ultimate seat of epistemic authority" (Gupta 2006: 29–30). If in experience A the house appears yellow, but upon closer inspection via A* appears green, I will, if I'm rational, detect an inconsistency, and, all else being equal, trust A* rather than A. Finally, if two equally adequate experiences conflict, and there is no other way of resolving that conflict, why shouldn't we be skeptical about the propositions that they each fulfill and withhold judgment? If empiricism cannot accommodate considerations of coherence to influence our belief formation or allow for local skepticism when experiences are inadequate or conflict, then just what are we supposed to find attractive about empiricism? Finally, do we really have to choose between being empiricists, skeptics, or rationalists? I think I'm all three: an empiricist about a great deal of knowledge about the physical world, a rationalist about logic, mathematics, and philosophy, and a skeptic about the precise height in nanometers of my house, the existence of extra-terrestrial life, and the date on which the sun will go supernova.

Virtually every perceptual experience has the ability to justify some empirical proposition. Each "has its right to proclaim, as it were, Being" (*TS* §84: 251). If I have an experience that presents me with a sunny day, that rationally motivates and justifies the belief that it is sunny outside. But, as Husserl puts it, "this rational positing within perception is not an absolute positing; it is like a force that can be overwhelmed by stronger counter-forces" (*ibid*). If I have become rationally convinced that each time it appears to be sunny, it is actually raining, my experience doesn't thereby lose its justificatory power. Rather, its justificatory power has been over-whelmed by something else. And this is just how things seem from the point of view of experience itself. That the evidence of experience is never absolute, that the absolute givenness of reality is not achievable, is no reason for despair. As Husserl puts it, if the task of acquiring knowledge

lies in the production of absolutely complete givenness, then it is *a priori* unsolv-able; it is an unreasonably posited task. What we will conclude from this is therefore in the first instance the fact that the knowledge of reality cannot have this ideal, insofar as we may have confidence that knowledge accomplishes some-thing actually rational and does so because it posits rational goals. (*TS* §39: 114–15)

Elsewhere he writes, "To reduce evidence to an insight that is apodictic is to bar oneself from an understanding of any scientific production" (*FTL* §60: 161). The "insight of empiricism" is not that experiences are infallible, but that we are entitled to endorse the propositions that they fulfill unless there is evidence to the contrary. And that evidence will almost always derive from further experience.

### 7.5 CONCLUSION

I have, with the aid of Husserl and many others, attempted to spell out the outlines of an account of what mental content is, its various types, and how the nonconceptual contents constitutive of perceptual experiences can justify the contents of ordinary beliefs about the extra-mental world. There are, no doubt, many holes in my account, and much further epis-temological and phenomenological work to be done. For instance, I haven't dealt with the problem of skepticism. This is, in part, because I think several compelling responses to the skeptic have been proposed (Pryor 2000; Huemer 2001). If that strikes one as problematic, then the account above can be read as an account of what perceptual justification and knowledge look like if skepticism is false. Nor have I addressed the critical topic of intersubjectivity and the role of others in helping constitute our consciousness of the world (see Zahavi 2001). And there is much more to be said on every topic I have discussed. There are plenty of reasons to suppose that consciousness is among the most complex phenomena in the world, and very few reasons for doubting that the study of it is anything less than the infinite task Husserl took it to be. But if knowledge and epistemic justification are within our ken, and if perception does in fact make the world itself available to us, then, I think, something along the lines of the present account stands a decent chance of being the case.

# Bibliography

Alston, William. 1988. "The Deontological Conception of Epistemic Justification."
  *Philosophical Perspectives* 2: 257–99.
  1989. "What's Wrong with Immediate Knowledge?" In *Epistemic Justification:
  Essays in the Theory of Knowledge*. Ithaca: Cornell University Press.
  1996. *A Realist Conception of Truth*. Ithaca: Cornell University Press.
  1999. "Back to the Theory of Appearing." *Philosophical Perspectives* 13: 181–203.
  2002. "Sellars and the 'Myth of the Given'." *Philosophy and Phenomenological
  Research* 65: 69–86.
Audi, Robert. 1983. "Foundationalism, Epistemic Dependence, and Defeasibility."
  *Synthese* 55: 119–35.
  2003. *Epistemology*, 2nd edn. New York: Routledge.
Austin, J. L. 1964. *Sense and Sensibilia*. New York: Oxford University Press.
Bach, Kent. 2007. "Searle Against the World." In S. L. Tsohatzidis, ed., *John
  Searle's Philosophy of Language*. Cambridge University Press.
Balog, Katalin. 2009. "Phenomenal Concepts." In B. McLaughlin, A. Beckermann,
  and S. Walter, eds., *Oxford Handbook in the Philosophy of Mind*. Oxford
  University Press.
Barber, Michael. 2008. "Holism and Horizon: Husserl and McDowell on
  Non-conceptual Content." *Husserl Studies* 24: 29–97.
Bell, David. 1990. *Husserl*. New York: Routledge.
  1996. "The Formation of Concepts and the Structure of Thought." *Philosophy
  and Phenomenological Research* 56: 583–96.
Bennett, M. R. and P. M. S. Hacker. 2003. *Philosophical Foundations of
  Neuroscience*. Malden: Blackwell Publishing.
Bergmann, Hugo. 1908. *Untersuchungen zum Problem der Evidenz der inneren
  Wahrnehmung*. Halle: Verlag von Max Niemeyer.
Bermudez, José Luis. 2003. "From Perceptual Experience to Subpersonal
  Computational States." In Y. H. Gunther, ed., *Essays on Nonconceptual
  Content*. Cambridge, MA: The MIT Press.
Bernet, Rudolph. 2003. "Desiring to Know Through Intuition." *Husserl Studies* 19:
  153–66.
Bernet, Rudolph, Iso Kern, and Eduard Marbach. 1993. *Introduction to Husserlian
  Phenomenology*. Evanston, IL: Northwestern University Press.
Blackburn, Simon. 1984. *Spreading the Word*. Oxford: Clarendon Press.

Block, Ned. 2007. *Consciousness, Function, and Representation*. Cambridge, MA: The MIT Press.

Bonjour, Laurence. 1985. *The Structure of Empirical Knowledge*. Cambridge, MA: Harvard University Press.

    1999. "Foundationalism and the External World." *Philosophical Perspectives* 13: 229–49.

Brandom, Robert. 2002. "Non-Inferential Knowledge, Perceptual Experience, and Secondary Qualities: Placing McDowell's Empiricism." In N. H. Smith, ed., *Reading McDowell: On Mind and World*. London: Routledge.

Brewer, Bill. 1999. *Perception and Reason*. Oxford: Clarendon Press.

    2004. "Realism and the Nature of Perceptual Experience." *Philosophical Issues* 14: 61–77.

    2005. "Perceptual Experience Has Conceptual Content." In M. Steup and E. Sosa, eds., *Contemporary Debates in Epistemology*. Malden: Blackwell.

    2006. "Perception and Content." *European Journal of Philosophy* 14: 165–81.

    2007. "Perception and Its Objects." *Philosophical Studies* 132: 87–97.

    2008. "How to Account for Illusion." In A. Haddock and F. Macpherson, eds., *Disjunctivism: Perception, Action, Knowledge*. Oxford University Press.

Briscoe, Robert. 2008. "Vision, Action, and Make-Perceive." *Mind and Language* 23: 457–97.

Broad, C. D. 1925. *The Mind and Its Place in Nature*. London: Routledge and Kegan Paul.

Burge, Tyler. 1977. "Belief *De Re*." *The Journal of Philosophy* 74: 338–62.

    1991. "Vision and Perceptual Content." In E. Lepore and R. Van Gulick, eds., *John Searle and His Critics*. Cambridge: Blackwell Publishers.

    2003. "Perceptual Entitlement." *Philosophy and Phenomenological Research* 67: 503–48.

    2005. *Truth, Thought, Reason: Essays on Frege*. Oxford University Press.

Byrne, Alex. 2001. "Intentionalism Defended." *Philosophical Review* 110: 199–240.

    2003. "Consciousness and Conceptual Content." *Philosophical Studies* 113: 261–74.

    2005. "Perception and Conceptual Content." In M. Steup and E. Sosa, eds., *Contemporary Debates in Epistemology*. Malden: Blackwell.

Camp, Elisabeth. 2009. "Putting Thoughts to Work: Concepts, Systematicity, and Stimulus Independence." *Philosophy and Phenomenological Research* 78: 275–311.

Campbell, John. 1996a. "Molyneux's Question." *Philosophical Issues* 7: 301–18.

    1996b. "Shape Properties, Experience of Shape and Shape Concepts." *Philosophical Issues* 7: 351–63.

    1999. "Immunity to Error through Misidentification and the Meaning of a Referring Term." *Philosophical Topics* 26: 89–104.

    2002. *Reference and Consciousness*. Oxford: Clarendon Press.

Carnap, Rudolph. 1967. *The Logical Structure of the World*. R. A. George, trans. Berkeley, CA: University of California Press.

Casullo, Albert. 2003. *A Priori Justification*. Oxford University Press.

Chalmers, David J. 1996. *The Conscious Mind*. Oxford University Press.

Child, William. 1994. *Causality, Interpretation and the Mind*. Oxford: Clarendon Press.

Chisholm, Roderick. 1942. "The Problem of the Speckled Hen." *Mind* 51: 368–73.

   1957. *Perceiving: A Philosophical Study*. Ithaca: Cornell University Press.

   1965. "The Theory of Appearing." In R. J. Swartz, ed., *Perceiving, Sensing, and Knowing*. Garden City, New York: Anchor Books.

   1988. "The Evidence of the Senses." *Philosophical Perspectives* 2: 71–90.

Christensen, Carleton B. 1993. "Sense, Subject and Horizon." *Philosophy and Phenomenological Research* 53: 749–79.

Chuard, Philippe. 2006. "Demonstrative Concepts without Re-Identification." *Philosophical Studies* 130: 153–201.

Cobb-Stevens, Richard. 1990. *Husserl and Analytic Philosophy*. Dordrecht: Kluwer Academic Publishers.

   2003. "Husserl's Fifth Logical Investigation." In D. O. Dahlstrom, ed., *Husserl's Logical Investigations*. Dordrecht: Kluwer Academic Publishers.

Conee, Earl. 2004. "The Basic Nature of Justification." In E. Conee and R. Feldman, *Evidentialism*. Oxford University Press.

Crane, Tim. 1992. "The Nonconceptual Content of Experience." In T. Crane, ed., *The Contents of Experience*. Cambridge University Press.

   2006. "Is There a Perceptual Relation?" In T. S. Gendler and J. Hawthorne, eds., *Perceptual Experience*. Oxford: Clarendon Press.

Crimmins, Mark and John Perry. 1989. "The Prince and the Phone Booth: Reporting Puzzling Beliefs." *The Journal of Philosophy* 86: 685–711.

Crowell, Steven. 2008. "Phenomenological Immanence, Normativity, and Semantic Externalism." *Synthese* 160: 335–54.

Crowther, T. M. 2006. "Two Conceptions of Conceptualism and Nonconceptualism." *Erkenntnis* 65: 245–76.

Cussins, Adrian. 2003. "Content, Conceptual Content, and Nonconceptual Content." In Y. H. Gunther, ed., *Essays on Nonconceptual Content*. Cambridge, MA: The MIT Press.

Dahlstrom, Daniel. 2006. "Lost Horizons: An Appreciative Critique of Enactive Externalism." In A. Ferrarin, ed., *Passive Synthesis and Life-World*. Pisa: Edizioni ETS.

   2007. "The Intentionality of Passive Experience: Husserl and a Contemporary Debate." *The New Yearbook for Phenomenology and Phenomenological Philosophy* 7: 25–42.

Davidson, Donald. 1984. "On the Very Idea of a Conceptual Scheme." In *Inquiries Into Truth and Interpretation*. Oxford: Clarendon Press.

   2001. "A Coherence Theory of Truth and Knowledge." In *Subjective, Intersubjective, Objective*. Oxford: Clarendon Press.

Davies, Martin. 1992. "Perceptual Content and Local Supervenience." *Proceedings of the Aristotelian Society* 92: 21–45.

Davis, Wayne A. 2003. *Meaning, Expression, and Thought*. Cambridge University Press.

2005a. *Nondescriptive Meaning and Reference: An Ideational Semantics.* Oxford University Press.

2005b. "Concepts and Epistemic Individuation." *Philosophy and Phenomenological Research* 70: 290–325.

Dennett, Daniel. 1991. *Consciousness Explained.* New York: Little, Brown and Company.

De Warren, Nicolas. 2006. "The Archaeology of Perception: McDowell and Husserl on Passive Synthesis." In A. Ferrarin, ed., *Passive Synthesis and Life-World.* Pisa: Edizioni ETS.

Dretske, Fred I. 1969. *Seeing and Knowing.* The University of Chicago Press.

2000a. "Entitlement: Epistemic Rights without Epistemic Duties?" *Philosophy and Phenomenological Research* 60: 591–606.

2000b. "Simple Seeing." In *Perception, Knowledge, and Belief.* Cambridge University Press.

Dreyfus, Hubert L. 1982. "The Perceptual Noema." In H. L. Dreyfus with H. Hall, eds., *Husserl, Intentionality, and Cognitive Science,* 97–123. Cambridge, MA: The MIT Press.

Drummond, John J. 1979. "On Seeing *a* Material Thing *in* Space: The Role of Kinaesthesis in Visual Perception." *Philosophy and Phenomenological Research* 40: 19–32.

1990. *Husserlian Intentionality and Non-Foundational Realism.* Dordrecht: Kluwer Academic Publishers.

1991. "Phenomenology and the Foundationalism Debate." *Reason Papers* 16: 45–71.

Dubois, James M. 1995. *Judgment and Sachverhalt.* Dordrecht: Kluwer Academic Publishers.

Dummett, Michael. 1973. *Frege: Philosophy of Language.* London: Gerald Duckworth.

1994. *Origins of Analytical Philosophy.* Cambridge, MA: Harvard University Press.

2006. *Thought and Reality.* Oxford: Clarendon Press.

Dwyer, Daniel J. 2007. "Husserl's Appropriation of the Psychological Concepts of Apperception and Attention." *Husserl Studies* 23: 83–118.

Evans, Gareth. 1982. *The Varieties of Reference.* Oxford University Press.

Fales, Evan. 1996. *A Defense of the Given.* New York: Rowman & Littlefield.

Farkas, Katalin. 2003. "What is Externalism?" *Philosophical Studies* 112: 187–208.

Feldman, Richard. 2004a. "Authoritarian Epistemology." In E. Connee and R. Feldman, *Evidentialism.* Oxford University Press.

2004b. "The Ethics of Belief." In E. Connee and R. Feldman, *Evidentialism.* Oxford University Press.

Findlay, J. N. 1963. *Language, Mind, and Value: Philosophical Essays.* London: George Allen & Unwin.

Fish, William. 2009. *Perception, Illusion, and Hallucination.* Oxford University Press.

Fodor, Jerry A. 1998. *Concepts: Where Cognitive Science Went Wrong.* Oxford University Press.

2007. "The Revenge of the Given." In B. P. McLaughlin and J. Cohen, eds., *Contemporary Debates in the Philosophy of Mind*. Malden: Blackwell.

Føllesdal, Dagfinn. 1969. "Husserl's Notion of Noema." *The Journal of Philosophy* 66: 680–7.

1982. "Husserl's Theory of Perception." In H. L. Dreyfus with H. Hall, eds., *Husserl, Intentionality, and Cognitive Science*. Cambridge, MA: The MIT Press.

Forrai, Gabor. 2001. *Reference, Truth and Conceptual Schemes*. Boston: Kluwer Academic Publishers.

Foster, John. 2000. *The Nature of Perception*. Oxford University Press.

Frege, Gottlob. 1994. "The Thought: A Logical Inquiry." In R. M. Harnish, ed., *Basic Topics in the Philosophy of Language*. Englewood Cliffs, NJ: Prentice Hall.

1997a. "On *Sinn* and *Bedeutung*." In M. Beaney, ed., *The Frege Reader*. Oxford: Blackwell.

1997b. "Logic." In M. Beaney, ed., *The Frege Reader*. Oxford: Blackwell.

1997c. "A Brief Survey of My Logical Doctrines." In M. Beaney, ed., *The Frege Reader*. Oxford: Blackwell.

Friedman, Michael. "Exorcising the Philosophical Tradition: Comments on John McDowell's *Mind and World*." *The Philosophical Review* 105: 427–67.

Fumerton, Richard. 1995. *Metaepistemology and Skepticism*. Lanham, MD: Rowman & Littlefield.

2001a. "Epistemic Justification and Normativity." In M. Steup, ed., *Knowledge, Truth, and Duty*. Oxford University Press.

2001b. "Brewer, Direct Realism, and Acquaintance with Acquaintance." *Philosophy and Phenomenological Research* 63: 417–22.

2002. "Critical Study: Bill Brewer's Perception and Reason." *Noûs* 36: 509–22.

Gallagher, Shaun. 2005. *How the Body Shapes the Mind*. Oxford: Clarendon Press.

Gallagher, Shaun and Dan Zahavi. 2007. *The Phenomenological Mind: An Introduction to Philosophy of Mind and Cognitive Science*. New York: Routledge.

Geach, Peter. 1957. *Mental Acts: Their Content and Their Objects*. London: Routledge & Kegan Paul.

Gendler, Tamar Szabo and John Hawthorne, eds. 2006. *Perceptual Experience*. Oxford: Clarendon Press.

Gibson, James J. 1986. *The Ecological Approach to Visual Perception*. London: Lawrence Erlbaum.

Goldman, Alvin. 1976. "Discrimination and Perceptual Knowledge." *The Journal of Philosophy* 73: 771–91.

2001. "Internalism Exposed." In H. Kornblith, ed., *Epistemology: Internalism and Externalism*. Malden: Blackwell.

Grice, H. P. 1994 (1975). "Logic and Conversation." In R. M. Harnish, ed., *Basic Topics in the Philosophy of Language*. Englewood Cliffs, NJ: Prentice Hall.

Gupta, Anil. 2006. *Empiricism and Experience*. Oxford University Press.

Gurwitsch, Aron. 1964. *The Field of Consciousness.* Pittsburgh: Duquesne University Press.

1966. *Studies in Phenomenology and Psychology.* Evanston, IL: Northwestern University Press.

Hacker, P. M. S. 1987. *Appearance and Reality.* Oxford: Basil Blackwell.

Hamlyn, D. W. 1994. "Perception, Sensation, and Non-Conceptual Content." *Philosophical Quarterly* 44: 139–53.

Hanna, Robert. 1993. "Logical Cognition: Husserl's Prolegomena and the Truth in Psychologism." *Philosophy and Phenomenological Research* 53: 251–75.

2008. "Kantian Non-conceptualism." *Philosophical Studies* 137: 41–64.

Hanson, Norwood Russell. 1961. *Patterns of Discovery.* Cambridge University Press.

Harman, Gilbert. 1990. "The Intrinsic Quality of Experience." *Philosophical Perspectives* 4: 31–52.

Heck, Richard G. Jr. 2000. "Nonconceptual Content and the 'Space of Reasons'." *The Philosophical Review* 109: 483–523.

2007. "Are There Different Kinds of Content?" In B. P. McLaughlin and J. Cohen, eds., *Contemporary Debates in the Philosophy of Mind.* Malden: Blackwell.

Heffernan, George. 1997. "An Essay in Epistemic Kuklophobia: Husserl's Critique of Descartes' Conception of Evidence." *Husserl Studies* 13: 89–140.

1999. "A Study in the Sedimented Origins of Evidence: Husserl and His Contemporaries Engaged in a Collective Essay in the Phenomenology and Psychology of Epistemic Justification." *Husserl Studies* 16: 83–181.

2009. "On Husserl's Remark That '[S]elbst Eine Sich als Apodiktisch Ausgebende Evidenz Kann Sich als Täuschung Enthüllen …' (XVII 164:32–33): Does the Phenomenological Method Yield Any Epistemic Infallibility?" *Husserl Studies* 25: 15–43.

Heidegger, Martin. 1962. *Being and Time.* J. Macquarrie and E. Robinson, trans. New York: Harper and Row.

1985. *History of the Concept of Time.* T. Kisiel, trans. Bloomington: Indiana University Press.

Higginbotham, James. 1998. "Conceptual Competence." *Philosophical Issues* 9: 149–62.

Hilbert, David. 2004. "Hallucination, Sense-Data, and Direct Realism." *Philosophical Studies* 120: 185–91.

Hintikka, Jaakko. 1975. *The Intentions of Intentionality and Other New Models for Modalities.* Dordrecht: D. Reidel.

1989. "The Cartesian Cogito, Epistemic Logic and Neuroscience: Some Surprising Interrelations." In J. Hintikka and M. B. P. Hintikka, *The Logic of Epistemology and the Epistemology of Logic.* Boston: Kluwer.

1995. "The Phenomenological Dimension." In B. Smith and D. W. Smith, eds., *The Cambridge Companion to Husserl,* 78–105. Cambridge University Press.

2003. "The Notion of Intuition in Husserl." *Revue Internationale de Philosophie* 224: 169–91.

Hintikka, Jaakko and John Symons. 2007. "Systems of Visual Identification in Neuroscience: Lessons from Epistemic Logic." In J. Hintikka, *Socratic Epistemology*. Cambridge University Press.

Hinton, J. M. 1967. "Experiences." *The Philosophical Quarterly* 17: 1–13.

1973. *Experiences: An Inquiry into Some Ambiguities*. Oxford: Clarendon Press.

Hopp, Walter. 2008a. "Husserl on Sensation, Perception, and Interpretation." *Canadian Journal of Philosophy* 38: 219–46.

2008b. "Husserl, Phenomenology, and Foundationalism." *Inquiry* 51: 194–216.

2009a. "Husserl, Dummett, and the Linguistic Turn." *Grazer Philosophische Studien* 78: 17–40.

2009b. "Conceptualism and the Myth of the Given." *European Journal of Philosophy* 17: 363–85.

Horgan, Terence and John Tienson. 2002. "The Intentionality of Phenomenology and the Phenomenology of Intentionality." In D. Chalmers, ed., *Philosophy of Mind: Classical and Contemporary Readings*. Oxford University Press.

Huemer, Michael. 2001. *Skepticism and the Veil of Perception*. Lanham, MD: Rowman & Littlefield.

Hume, David. 1955. *An Enquiry Concerning Human Understanding*. C. W. Hendel, ed. New York: The Liberal Arts Press.

1978. *A Treatise of Human Nature*. P. H. Nidditch, ed. Oxford: Clarendon Press.

Hurley, S. L. 1998. *Consciousness in Action*. Cambridge, MA: Harvard University Press.

Husserl, Edmund. 1969. *Formal and Transcendental Logic*. D. Cairns, trans. The Hague: Martinus Nijhoff.

1970a. *Logical Investigations*, 2 vols. J. N. Findlay, trans. London: Routledge & Kegan Paul.

1970b. *The Crisis of European Sciences and Transcendental Phenomenology: An Introduction to Phenomenological Philosophy*. D. Carr, trans. Evanston, IL: Northwestern University Press.

1973. *Experience and Judgment*. L. Landgrebe, ed., J. S. Churchill and K. Ameriks, trans. Evanston, IL: Northwestern University Press.

1977a. *Cartesian Meditations*. D. Cairns, trans. The Hague: Martinus Nijhoff.

1977b. *Phenomenological Psychology*. J. Scanlon, trans. The Hague: Martinus Nijhoff.

1982. *Ideas Pertaining to a Pure Phenomenology and to a Phenomenological Philosophy. First Book: General Introduction to a Pure Phenomenology*. F. Kersten, trans. The Hague: Martinus Nijhoff.

1989. *Ideas Pertaining to a Pure Phenomenology and to a Phenomenological Philosophy. Second Book. Studies in the Phenomenology of Constitution*. R. Rojcewicz and A. Schuwer, trans. Dordrecht: Kluwer Academic Publishers.

1991. *On the Phenomenology of the Consciousness of Internal Time (1893–1917)*. J. B. Brough, trans. Dordrecht: Kluwer Academic Publishers.

1997. *Thing and Space*. R. Rojcewicz, trans. Boston: Kluwer Academic Publishers.

2001. *Analyses Concerning Passive and Active Synthesis*. A. J. Steinbock, trans. Boston: Kluwer Academic Publishers.

2005. *Phantasy, Image Consciousness, and Memory*. J. Brough, trans. Dordrecht: Springer.

2008. *Introduction to Logic and Theory of Knowledge: Lectures 1906/07*. C. O. Hill, trans. Dordrecht: Springer.

Hylton, Peter. 1990. *Russell, Idealism, and the Emergence of Analytic Philosophy*. Oxford: Clarendon Press.

James, William. 1922. *Essays in Radical Empiricism*. New York: Longmans, Green.

1952. *The Principles of Psychology*. Chicago: Encyclopedia Britannica, Inc.

Johnson, Bredo C. 1986. "The Given." *Philosophy and Phenomenological Research* 46: 597–613.

Johnson, Kent. 2004. "On the Systematicity of Language and Thought." *The Journal of Philosophy* 101: 111–39.

Johnston, Mark. 2006. "Better than Mere Knowledge? The Function of Sensory Awareness." In T. S. Gendler and J. Hawthorne, eds., *Perceptual Experience*. Oxford: Clarendon Press.

2009. "The Obscure Object of Hallucination." In A. Byrne and H. Logue, eds., *Disjunctivism: Contemporary Readings*. Cambridge, MA: The MIT Press.

Kant, Immanuel. 1965. *Critique of Pure Reason*. N. K. Smith, trans. New York: Macmillan.

Kaplan, David. 1994. "Demonstratives." In R. M. Harnish, ed., *Basic Topics in the Philosophy of Language*. Englewood Cliffs, NJ: Prentice Hall.

Kelly, Sean. 2001a. "Demonstrative Concepts and Experience." *The Philosophical Review* 110: 397–420.

2001b. "The Non-conceptual Content of Perceptual Experience: Situation Dependence and Fineness of Grain." *Philosophy and Phenomenological Research* 62: 601–8.

2004a. "Reference and Attention: A Difficult Connection." *Philosophical Studies* 120: 277–86.

2004b. "Seeing Things in Merleau-Ponty." In T. Carmen and M. B. N. Hansen, eds., *The Cambridge Companion to Merleau-Ponty*. Cambridge University Press.

Kind, Amy. 2003. "What's So Transparent About Transparency?" *Philosophical Studies* 115: 225–44.

King, Jeffrey C. 2007. *The Nature and Structure of Content*. Oxford University Press.

Klein, Colin. 2007. "An Imperative Theory of Pain." *The Journal of Philosophy* 104: 517–32.

Kornblith, Hilary. 1980. "Beyond Foundationalism and the Coherence Theory." *The Journal of Philosophy* 77: 597–611.

Kuhn, Thomas. 1970. *The Structure of Scientific Revolutions*, 2nd edn. University of Chicago Press.

Kvanvig, Jonathan. 2007. "Propositionalism and the Metaphysics of Experience." *Philosophical Issues* 17: 165–78.

Langsam, Harold. 2009. "The Theory of Appearing Defended." In A. Byrne and H. Logue, eds., *Disjunctivism: Contemporary Readings.* Cambridge, MA: The MIT Press.

Levin, Janet. 2008. "Molyneux's Question and the Individuation of Perceptual Concepts." *Philosophical Studies* 139: 1–28.

Levinas, Emmanuel. 1973. *The Theory of Intuition in Husserl's Phenomenology.* A. Orianne, trans. Evanston, IL: Northwestern University Press.

Lewis, C. I. 1929. *Mind and the World Order.* New York: Daver Publications.

Liebesman, David. 2010. Review of Jeffrey C. King's *The Nature and Structure of Content. Philosophical Review* 119: 246–50.

Loar, Brian. 1990. "Phenomenal States." *Philosophical Perspectives* 4: 81–108.

——— 2003. "Phenomenal Intentionality as the Basis of Mental Content." In M. Hahn and B. Ramberg, eds., *Reflections and Replies: Essays in the Philosophy of Tyler Burge.* Cambridge, MA: The MIT Press.

Locke, John. 1975. *An Essay Concerning Human Understanding*, P. H. Nidditch, ed. Oxford: Clarendon Press.

Lohmar, Dieter. 2002. "Husserl's Concept of Categorial Intuition." In D. Zahavi and F. Stjernfelt, eds., *One Hundred Years of Phenomenology.* Dordrecht: Kluwer Academic Publishers.

——— 2006. "Categorial Intuition." In H. L. Dreyfus and M. A. Wrathall, eds., *A Companion to Phenomenology and Existentialism.* Malden: Blackwell.

Lyons, Jack C. 2008. "Evidence, Experience, and Externalism." *Australasian Journal of Philosophy* 86: 461–79.

——— 2009. *Perception and Basic Beliefs.* Oxford University Press.

Majors, Brad and Sarah Sawyer. 2005. "The Epistemological Argument for Content Externalism." *Philosophical Perspectives* 19: 257–80.

Margolis, Eric. 1998. "How to Acquire a Concept." *Mind and Language* 13: 347–69.

Markie, Peter J. 2006. "Epistemically Appropriate Perceptual Belief." *Noûs* 40: 118–42.

Martin, M. G. F. 2003. "Perception, Concepts, and Memory." In Y. H. Gunther, ed., *Essays on Nonconceptual Content.* Cambridge, MA: The MIT Press.

——— 2006. "On Being Alienated." In T. S. Gendler and J. Hawthorne, eds., *Perceptual Experience.* Oxford: Clarendon Press.

——— 2009a. "The Reality of Appearances." In A. Byrne and H. Logue, eds., *Disjunctivism: Contemporary Readings.* Cambridge, MA: The MIT Press.

——— 2009b. "The Limits of Self-Awareness." In A. Byrne and H. Logue, eds., *Disjunctivism: Contemporary Readings.* Cambridge, MA: The MIT Press.

Martin, Wayne M. 1999. "Husserl's Relapse? Concerning a Fregean Challenge to Phenomenology." *Inquiry* 42: 343–70.

——— 2006. *Theories of Judgment.* Cambridge University Press.

Matthen, Mohan. 2005. *Seeing, Doing, and Knowing.* Oxford: Clarendon Press.

McDowell, John. 1982. "Criteria, Defeasibility, and Knowledge." In McDowell, 1998d.

1984. "De Re Senses." *The Philosophical Quarterly* 136: 283–94.

1986. "Singular Thought and the Extent of Inner Space." In McDowell, 1998d.

1991. "Intentionality De Re." In McDowell, 1998d.

1994. *Mind and World*. Cambridge, MA: Harvard University Press.

1998a. "Having the World in View: Sellars, Kant, and Intentionality." *The Journal of Philosophy* 95: 431–91.

1998b. "Précis of *Mind and World*." *Philosophy and Phenomenological Research* 58: 365–8.

1998c. "Reply to Commentators." *Philosophy and Phenomenological Research* 58: 403–31.

1998d. *Meaning, Knowledge, and Reality*. Cambridge, MA: Harvard University Press.

2009. "Avoiding the Myth of the Given." In *Having the World in View*. Cambridge, MA: Harvard University Press.

McGinn, Colin. 1982. *The Character of Mind*. Oxford University Press.

McIntyre, Ronald. 1987. "Husserl and Frege." *The Journal of Philosophy* 84: 529–35.

1999. "Naturalizing Phenomenology? Dretske on Qualia." In J. Petitot, F. J. Varela, B. Pachoud, and J. Roy, eds., *Naturalizing Phenomenology*. Stanford University Press.

Merleau-Ponty, Maurice. 1962. *Phenomenology of Perception*. C. Smith, trans. London: Routledge & Kegan Paul.

Millar, Alan. 1991a. *Reasons and Experience*. Oxford: Clarendon Press.

1991b. "Concepts, Experience and Inference." *Mind* 100: 495–505.

2007. "The State of Knowing." *Philosophical Issues* 17: 179–96.

2008. "Perceptual-Recognitional Abilities and Perceptual Knowledge." In A. Haddock and F. Macpherson, eds., *Disjunctivism: Perception, Action, Knowledge*. Oxford University Press.

Miller, Izchak. 1984. *Husserl, Perception, and Temporal Awareness*. Cambridge, MA: The MIT Press.

Miller, Jared. 2009. "Phenomenology's Negative Dialectic: Adorno's Critique of Husserl's Epistemological Foundationalism." *Philosophical Forum* 40: 99–125.

Millikan, Ruth Garrett. 1990. "The Myth of the Essential Indexical." *Noûs* 24: 723–34.

2004. *The Varieties of Meaning*. Cambridge, MA: The MIT Press.

Mohanty, J. N. 2008. *The Philosophy of Edmund Husserl*. New Haven: Yale University Press.

Montague, Michelle. 2007. "Against Propositionalism." *Noûs* 41: 503–18.

Mooney, Timothy. 2010. "Understanding and Simple Seeing in Husserl." *Husserl Studies* 26: 19–48.

Moore, G. E. 1951. "The Refutation of Idealism." In *Philosophical Studies*. London: Routledge & Kegan Paul.

1959. "Proof of an External World." In *Philosophical Papers*. London: George, Allen and Unwin.

1965. "Some Judgments of Perception." In R. J. Swartz, ed., *Perceiving, Sensing, and Knowing*. Garden City, New York: Anchor Books.

Moran, Dermot. 2005. *Edmund Husserl: Founder of Phenomenology*. Cambridge: Polity Press.

Moser, Paul K. 1988. "Foundationalism, The Given, and C. I. Lewis." *History of Philosophy Quarterly* 5: 189–204.

Mulligan, Kevin. 1995. "Perception." In B. Smith and D. W. Smith, eds., *The Cambridge Companion to Husserl*. Cambridge University Press.

Nenon, Thomas. 1997. "Two Models of Foundation in the *Logical Investigations*." In B. C. Hopkins, ed., *Husserl in Contemporary Context*. Dordrecht: Kluwer Academic Publishers.

Noë, Alva. 2002. "On What We See." *Pacific Philosophical Quarterly* 83: 57–80.

2004. *Action in Perception*. Cambridge, MA: The MIT Press.

O'Shaughnessy, Brian. 2000. *Consciousness and the World*. Oxford University Press.

Papineau, David. 2002. *Thinking About Consciousness*. Oxford University Press.

Peacocke, Christopher. 1983. *Sense and Content: Experience, Thought, and Their Relations*. Oxford University Press.

1992. *A Study of Concepts*. Cambridge, MA: The MIT Press.

1998. "Nonconceptual Content Defended." *Philosophy and Phenomenological Research* 58: 381–8.

2001. "Does Perception Have a Nonconceptual Content?" *The Journal of Philosophy* 98: 239–64.

Perry, John. 1979. "The Problem of the Essential Indexical." *Noûs* 13: 13–21.

2001. *Reference and Reflexivity*. Stanford: CSLI Publications.

Philipse, Herman. 1995. "Transcendental Idealism." In B. Smith and D. W. Smith, eds., *The Cambridge Companion to Husserl*. Cambridge University Press.

Pietersma, Henry. 1973. "Intuition and Horizon in the Philosophy of Husserl." *Philosophy and Phenomenological Research* 34: 95–101.

2000. *Phenomenological Epistemology*. Oxford University Press.

Plantinga, Alvin. 1993a. *Warrant: The Current Debate*. Oxford University Press.

1993b. *Warrant and Proper Function*. Oxford University Press.

Pollock, John L. 2001. "Defeasible Reasoning with Variable Degrees of Justification." *Artificial Intelligence* 133: 233–82.

Pollock, John L. and Joseph Cruz. 1999. *Contemporary Theories of Knowledge*. New York: Rowman & Littlefield.

Pollock, John L. and Iris Oved. 2005. "Vision, Knowledge, and the Mystery Link." *Philosophical Perspectives* 19: 309–51.

Porter, Steven L. 2006. *Restoring the Foundations of Epistemic Justification*. New York: Lexington Books.

Price, H. H. 1950. *Perception*. London: Methuen.

Prichard, H. A. 1909. *Kant's Theory of Knowledge*. Oxford: Clarendon Press.

Prinz, Jesse. 2002. *Furnishing the Mind: Concepts and Their Perceptual Basis*. Cambridge, MA: The MIT Press.

Pryor, James. 2000. "The Skeptic and the Dogmatist." *Noûs* 34: 517–49.

2005. "There is Immediate Justification." In M. Steup and E. Sosa, eds., *Contemporary Debates in Epistemology*. Malden: Blackwell.

Putnam, Hilary. 1981. *Reason, Truth and History*. Cambridge University Press.
    1994. "The Meaning of 'Meaning'." In R. M. Harnish, ed., *Basic Topics in the Philosophy of Language*. Englewood Cliffs, NJ: Prentice Hall.
Quine, Willard Van Orman. 1961. *From a Logical Point of View*. New York: Harper & Row.
Reid, Thomas. 1969. *Essays on the Intellectual Powers of Man*. B. Brody, ed. Cambridge, MA: The MIT Press.
Reinach, Adolf. 1982. "On the Theory of the Negative Judgment." B. Smith, trans. In B. Smith, ed., *Parts and Moments: Studies in Logic and Formal Ontology*. Munich: Philosophia Verlag.
Rey, Georges. 1999. "Concepts and Stereotypes." In E. Margolis and S. Laurence, eds., *Concepts*. Cambridge, MA: The MIT Press.
Robinson, Howard. 1994. *Perception*. London: Routledge.
Rollinger, Robin D. 2009. "Brentano's Psychology and Logic and the Basis of Twardowski's Theory of Presentations." *The Baltic International Yearbook of Cognition, Logic, and Communication* 4: 1–23.
Rorty, Richard. 1972. "The World Well Lost." *The Journal of Philosophy* 69: 649–65.
    1979. *Philosophy and the Mirror of Nature*. Princeton University Press.
Rosen, Klaus. 1977. *Evidenz in Husserls deskriptiver Transzendentalphilosophie*. Meisenheim am Glan: Verlag Anton Hain.
Runzo, Joseph. 1982. "The Radical Conceptualization of Perceptual Experience." *American Philosophical Quarterly* 19: 205–17.
Russell, Bertrand. 1984. *Theory of Knowledge: The 1913 Manuscript*. E. R. Eames in collaboration with K. Blackwell, eds. London: George Allen & Unwin.
    1985. *The Philosophy of Logical Atomism*. D. Pears, ed. Peru, IL: Open Court Publishing Company.
    1999. *The Problems of Philosophy*. Mineola: Dover Publications.
Salmon, Nathan. 1986. *Frege's Puzzle*. Cambridge, MA: The MIT Press.
    1989. "Illogical Belief." *Philosophical Perspectives* 3: 243–85.
Sartre, Jean-Paul. 1956. *Being and Nothingness*. New York: Washington Square Press.
Scheler, Max. 1973. *Formalism in Ethics and Non-Formal Ethics of Values*. M. S. Frings and R. L. Funk, trans. Evanston, IL: Northwestern University Press.
Schellenberg, Susanna. 2007. "Action and Self-Location in Perception." *Mind* 116: 603–31.
    2008. "The Situation-Dependency of Perception." *The Journal of Philosophy* 105: 55–84.
Schlick, Moritz. 1959. "The Foundation of Knowledge." D. Rynin, trans. In A. J. Ayer, ed., *Logical Positivism*. Glencoe, IL: The Free Press.
Schuhmann, Karl and Barry Smith. 1985. "Against Idealism: Johannes Daubert vs. Husserl's *Ideas I*." *Review of Metaphysics* 39: 763–93.
Schwitzgebel, Eric. 2006. "Do Things Look Flat?" *Philosophy and Phenomenological Research* 72: 589–99.

238 *Bibliography*

Searle, John R. 1983. *Intentionality*. Cambridge University Press.
Sellars, Wilfrid. 1963. *Science, Perception, and Reality*. London: Routledge and Kegan Paul.

   1975. "The Structure of Knowledge." In Hector-Neri Castandeda, ed., *Action, Knowledge, and Reality: Critical Studies in Honor of Wilfrid Sellars*. Indianapolis: Bobbs Merrill.

   1997. *Empiricism and the Philosophy of Mind*. Cambridge, MA: Harvard University Press.

Shim, Michael K. 2005. "The Duality of Non-conceptual Content in Husserl's Phenomenology of Perception." *Phenomenology and the Cognitive Sciences* 4: 209–29.

   2010. "Representationalism and Husserlian Phenomenology." Presented at the *Workshop in Phenomenological Philosophy*, Seattle University.

Siegel, Susanna. 2002. "The Role of Perception in Demonstrative Reference." *Philosopher's Imprint*, vol. 2, no. 1, philosophersimprint.org/002001.

   2006. "Which Properties are Represented in Perception?" In T. S. Gendler and J. Hawthorne, eds., *Perceptual Experience*. Oxford: Clarendon Press.

Siewert, Charles P. 1998. *The Significance of Consciousness*. Princeton: Princeton University Press.

   2004. "Is Experience Transparent?" *Philosophical Studies* 117: 15–41.

   2005. "Attention and Sensorimotor Intentionality." In D. W. Smith and A. L. Thomasson, eds., *Phenomenology and Philosophy of Mind*. Oxford: Clarendon Press.

   2006. "Is the Appearance of Shape Protean?" *Psyche* 12.

   2007. "In Favor of (Plain) Phenomenology." *Phenomenology and the Cognitive Sciences* 6: 201–20.

Smith, A. D. 2001. "Perception and Belief." *Philosophy and Phenomenological Research* 62: 283–309.

   2002. *The Problem of Perception*. Cambridge, MA: Harvard University Press.

   2008a. "Disjunctivism and Discriminability." In A. Haddock and F. Macpherson, eds., *Disjunctivism: Perception, Action, Knowledge*. Oxford University Press.

   2008b. "Husserl and Externalism." *Synthese* 160: 313–33.

Smith, Barry. 1987. "On the Cognition of States of Affairs." In K. Mulligan, ed., *Speech Act and Sachverhalt: Reinach and the Foundations of Realist Phenomenology*. Dordrecht: Kluwer Academic Publishers.

   1989. "Logic and Formal Ontology." In J. N. Mohanty and W. McKennna, eds., *Husserl's Phenomenology: A Textbook*. Lanham, MD: University Press of America.

   1999. "Truth and the Visual Field." In J. Petitot, F. J. Varela, B. Pachoud, and J. Roy, eds., *Naturalizing Phenomenology*. Stanford University Press.

Smith, David Woodruff. 1982a. "What's the Meaning of 'This'?" *Noûs* 16: 181–208.

   1982b. "Husserl on Demonstrative Reference and Perception." In H. L. Dreyfus with H. Hall, eds., *Husserl, Intentionality, and Cognitive Science*. Cambridge, MA: The MIT Press.

   1989. *The Circle of Acquaintance*. Dordrecht: Kluwer Academic Publishers.

2004. *Mind World*. Cambridge University Press.

2007. *Husserl*. New York: Routledge.

Smith, David Woodruff and Ronald McIntyre. 1982. *Husserl and Intentionality: A Study of Mind, Meaning, and Language*. Dordrecht: D. Reidel.

Snowdon, Paul. 2005. "The Formulation of Disjunctivism: A Response to Fish." *Proceedings of the Aristotelian Society* 105: 129–41.

Soames, Scott. 2002. *Beyond Rigidity: The Unfinished Semantic Agenda of Naming and Necessity*. Oxford University Press.

Soffer, Gail. 2003. "Revisiting the Myth: Husserl and Sellars on the Given." *The Review of Metaphysics* 57: 301–37.

Sokolowski, Robert. 1971. "The Structure and Content of Husserl's *Logical Investigations*." *Inquiry* 14: 318–50.

1981. "Husserl's Concept of Categorial Intuition." *Phenomenology and the Human Sciences*, Supplement to *Philosophical Topics* 12: 127–41.

2000. *Introduction to Phenomenology*. Cambridge University Press.

2003. "Husserl's Sixth Logical Investigation." In D. Dahlstrom, ed., *Husserl's Logical Investigations*. Boston: Kluwer Academic Publishers.

Sosa, David. 2007. "Perceptual Friction." *Philosophical Issues* 17: 245–61.

Sosa, Ernest. 1995. "The Raft and the Pyramid: Coherence versus Foundations in the Theory of Knowledge." In P. K. Moser and A. Vander Nat, eds., *Human Knowledge*, 2nd edn. Oxford University Press.

2007. *A Virtue Epistemology*. Oxford University Press.

Speaks, Jeff. 2005. "Is There a Problem about Nonconceptual Content?" *The Philosophical Review* 114: 359–98.

2009. "Transparency, Internationalism, and the Nature of Perceptual Content." *Philosophy and Phenomenonological Research* 79: 539–73.

Stanley, Jason. 1997. "Names and Rigid Designation." In B. Hale and C. Wright, eds., *A Companion to the Philosophy of Language*. Oxford: Blackwell.

Thau, Michael. 2002. *Consciousness and Cognition*. Oxford University Press.

Thompson, Evan. 2007. *Mind in Life: Biology, Phenomenology, and the Sciences of the Mind*. Cambridge, MA: Harvard University Press.

Travis, Charles. 2004. "The Silence of the Senses." *Mind* 113: 57–94.

Tugendhat, Ernst. 1967. *Der Wahrheitsbegriff bei Husserl und Heidegger*. Berlin: Walter de Gruyter.

Twardowski, Kasimir. 1977. *On the Content and Object of Presentations*. R. Grossmann, trans. The Hague: Martinus Nijhoff.

Tye, Michael. 1992. "Visual Content and Visual Qualia." In T. Crane, ed., *The Contents of Experience*, Cambridge University Press.

1995. "A Representational Theory of Pains and their Phenomenal Character." *Philosophical Perspectives* 9: 223–39.

2000. *Consciousness, Color, and Content*. Cambridge, MA: The MIT Press.

2006. "Nonconceptual Content, Richness, and Fineness of Grain." In T. S. Gendler and J. Hawthorne, eds., *Perceptual Experience*. Oxford: Clarendon Press.

2007. "Intentionalism and the Argument from No Common Content." *Philosophical Perspectives* 21: 589–613.

2009. *Consciousness Revisited: Materialism without Phenomenal Concepts.* Cambridge, MA: The MIT Press.

Van Cleve, James. 1979. "Foundationalism, Epistemic Principles, and the Cartesian Circle." *The Philosophical Review* 88: 55–91.

1985. "Epistemic Supervenience and the Circle of Belief." *The Monist* 68: 90–104.

1999. *Problems from Kant.* Oxford University Press.

2003. "Is Knowledge Easy – or Impossible? Externalism as the Only Alternative to Skepticism." In S. Luper, ed., *The Skeptics: Contemporary Essays.* Burlington: Ashgate Publishing Company.

Veblen, Thorstein. 1994. *The Theory of the Leisure Class.* New York: Dover Publications.

Vesey, G. N. A. 1965. "Seeing and Seeing As." In R. J. Swartz, ed., *Perceiving, Sensing, and Knowing.* Garden City, New York: Anchor Books.

Walton, Roberto J. 2003. "On the Manifold Senses of Horizonedness: The Theories of E. Husserl and A. Gurwitsch." *Husserl Studies* 19: 1–24.

Welton, Donn. 1977. "Structure and Genesis in Husserl's Phenomenology." In F. Elliston and P. McCormick, eds., *Husserl: Expositions and Appraisals.* Notre Dame: Notre Dame Press.

1983. *The Origins of Meaning.* The Hague: Martinus Nijhoff Publishers.

Wettstein, Howard. 1986. "Has Semantics Rested on a Mistake?" *The Journal of Philosophy* 83: 185–209.

Wiggins, David. 2001. *Sameness and Substance Renewed.* Cambridge University Press.

Willard, Dallas. 1967. "A Crucial Error in Epistemology." *Mind* 76: 513–23.

1977. "The Paradox of Logical Psychologism: Husserl's Way Out." In F. Elliston and P. McCormick, eds., *Husserl: Expositions and Appraisals.* Notre Dame: Notre Dame Press.

1984. *Logic and the Objectivity of Knowledge.* Athens, OH: Ohio University Press.

1988. "A Critical Study of *Husserl and Intentionality.*" *Journal of the British Society for Phenomenology* 19: 186–98 (part 1); 311–22 (part 2).

1992. "Finding the Noema." In J. J. Drummond and L. Embree, eds., *The Phenomenology of the Noema.* Dordrecht: Kluwer Academic Publishers.

1994. "The Integrity of the Mental Act: Husserlian Reflections on a Fregean Problem." In L. Haaparanta, ed., *Mind, Meaning, and Mathematics.* Boston: Kluwer Academic Publishers.

1995. "Knowledge." In B. Smith and D. W. Smith, eds., *The Cambridge Companion to Husserl.* Cambridge University Press.

1999. "How Concepts Relate the Mind to Its Objects: The God's Eye View Vindicated?" *Philosophia Christi* 2: 5–20.

Williams, Michael. 1977. *Groundless Belief: An Essay on the Possibility of Epistemology.* New Haven: Yale University Press.

1988. "Epistemological Realism and the Basis of Scepticism." *Mind* 97: 415–39.

2005. "Doing Without Immediate Justification." In M. Steup and E. Sosa, eds., *Contemporary Debates in Epistemology*. Malden: Blackwell.

Williamson, Timothy. 2000. *Knowledge and Its Limits*. Oxford University Press.

Williford, Kenneth. 2006. "The Self-Representational Structure of Consciousness." In U. Kriegel and K. Williford, eds., *Self-Representational Approaches to Consciousness*. Cambridge, MA: The MIT Press.

Wittgenstein, Ludwig. 1958. *Philosophical Investigations*. G. E. M. Anscombe, trans. Englewood Cliffs, NJ: Prentice-Hall, Inc.

Wolterstorff, Nicholas. 1987. "Are Concept-Users World-Makers?" *Philosophical Perspectives* 1: 233–67.

Yolton, John W. 1953. "Linguistic and Epistemological Dualism." *Mind* 62: 20–42.

Yoshimi, Jeffrey. 2009. "Husserl's Theory of Belief and the Heideggerean Critique." *Husserl Studies* 25: 121–40.

Zahavi, Dan. 2001. *Husserl and Transcendental Intersubjectivity*. Athens, OH: Ohio University Press.

2003. *Husserl's Phenomenology*. Stanford University Press.

2004. "Husserl's Noema and the Internalism-Externalism Debate." *Inquiry* 47: 42–66.

# Index

Alston, William, 88, 154, 214
Audi, Robert, 217
Austin, J. L., 178

beliefs
  basic, 99
  epistemic status of, 106–7
Bermudez, José Luis, 131
Blackburn, Simon, 48
body, 167–9
  as bearer of intentionality, 169
  body-as-subject and, 168, 169
  body image and, 168
  body schema and, 168
Bonjour, Laurence, 95
Brandom, Robert, 86
Brewer, Bill, 106
  on the demonstrative theory of perception,
    118–19, 124, 125–6
  epistemological argument, 92
  on perceptual error, 156
  on rational intelligibility, 93–4
  on the relational view, 149
  on space, 167
Burge, Tyler, 145, 175

Camp, Elisabeth, 142
Campbell, John, 18, 51, 74, 123, 149, 162
Carnap, Rudolf, 61
Casullo, Albert, 175
categorial intuition, 68–73
Chisholm, Roderick, 162
coherence, 222, 223
coherentism, 91, 99, 109
concepts
  authentic possession of, 195–7
  effects on perceptual experience, 53, 59–60
  intentional contents and, 38–9, 141
  linguistically expressible contents and, 39, 122,
    138, 144
  objectivity of, 144, 146

phenomenal, 143
properties and, 38–9
sortal, 51–2, 74
conceptual condition, 192
conceptual content, 38–40
  conceptualized objects and, 39–40
  defined, 142
  detachability thesis and, 105
  intuitive character and, 142, 145
  radically parasitical, 143
conceptualist principle, 107
Conee, Earl, 191
content
  of books, 27–9
  demonstrative see demonstrative contents
  detachable, 105
  empty, 24, 54, 76, 104, 211
  Husserl's theory of, 29–33
  intentional properties and, 31–2, 35, 36, 37
  intuitive, 24
  real vs. ideal, 28–9, 31
Crane, Tim, 131, 136
  on content, 11–12
Crowell, Steven, 184
Cruz, Joseph, 107
Cussins, Adrian, 9, 134, 145, 179
  on nonconceptual content, 134–5

Dahlstrom, Daniel, 147
  on horizons, 147–8
Davidson, Donald, 61, 81, 89, 101
Davis, Wayne, 15, 21, 195
defeaters
  rebutting, 216
  undercutting, 216
delineation thesis, 74
demonstrative contents, 118
  concept authenticity and, 216
  determinate perceptual experiences
    and, 121
  founded on perception, 124, 175

linguistic expressibility of, 122
not sufficient for perception, 120
demonstratives, 74
concepts and, 74–6
senses of, 121–3
detachability thesis, 105, 145
disjunctivism, 153
moderate, 172
radical, 153, 156–7
weird object, 154–6, 157–8
doxastic assumption, 107, 108
doxastic voluntarism
falsity of, 88
irrelevance for epistemic justification, 88
Dretske, Fred, 48, 51
Drummond, John, 187
dualism, 6
duck–rabbit, 49
Dummett, Michael, 145

empiricism, 221
epistemic duties, 87
epistemic principles, 95
Evans, Gareth, 18, 19, 21, 127, 137
on dynamic Fregean thoughts, 123
evil neuroscientist 1, 185–6
evil neuroscientist 2, 186, 187
experiential conceptualism, 2
strong, 37, 93, 115
weak, 37, 44, 47, 93, 118
explication, 70, 71
externalism, epistemic, 109
about states, 213

Feldman, Richard, 89
Fish, William, 153, 156
on the phenomenal character of hallucinations, 153
on the subjective character of experience, 163
Fodor, Jerry, 16, 34, 195
Forrai, Gabor, 49
foundationalism, 99, 109
founded acts, 69
Frege, Gottlob, 23, 33
on grasping thoughts, 33–4
fulfillment, 68, 72, 140
complexity of, 193–4
as consciousness of truth, 212
content of, 199
degrees of, 200–1
derivative epistemic, 202–5
illustrative, 201–2
immediate justification and, 213–14
inferential justification and, 212–13
intuitive, 205–6

intuitive condition, 192
perception and, 73
primary epistemic, 201
quality of, 199–200
recognition and, 199
susceptibility to defeat of, 215–17
synthesis condition, 192, 195

Gallagher, Sean, 42
on bodily awareness, 168, 169
Gendler, Tamar, 8
generality constraint, 127
given, myth of, 83, 85, 87
Goldman, Alvin, 197
Grice, Paul, 123
Grossmann, Reinhardt, 17
Gupta, Anil, 219
on the given, 219–21
on the reliability of experience, 221–2

hallucination
fulfillment and, 215–16
hallucinations
content of, 160
independence from beliefs, 158–60
objects of, 160
of properties, 188
unmasked, 158
veridical perception and, 188
Hanna, Robert
on content, 11
Hanson, Norwood, 49
Harman, Gilbert, 22
on content, 10–11
Hawthorne, John, 8
Heck, Richard, 108, 124, 136
on the demonstrative theory of perception, 125
Heffernan, George, 114
Heidegger, Martin, 48, 169
Hintikka, Jaakko, 119
horizons, 53, 165–6
concepts and, 59–60, 76, 80, 146–8
inner, 54, 55–7
manifold *see* manifold, perceptual
outer, 57–8
types of, in Husserl's work, 54–5
Huemer, Michael, 190
on content, 9–10
Hume, David, 40
Hurley, Susan, 146
Husserl, Edmund
on categorial intuition, 68–73
on the defeasibility of justification, 224
on the generality of concepts, 144–5
on fulfillment, 192, 199, 207

Husserl, Edmund (cont.)
    on horizons, 54–8
    on manifolds, 181
    on perception, 208
    on the relationship between intentionality
        and knowledge, 213–14
    theory of content, 29–33

idealism, 150
    transcendental, 3
illusion, 215
image-consciousness, 204–5
imagination, 103, 104, 202
    non-positing character of, 201
indexicals, 120
intentional essence, 31
intentionalism, 172
intentionality, 7–8, 35
    content view, 18
    lazy, 174
    nonexistent objects and, 13–18
    spotlight view, 13, 18, 22, 24, 140
internalism, content, 173
internalism, epistemic, 94, 109
    about reasons, 94, 159
    about states, 94, 95–7, 213
interpretation, 208
introspective access, 172
intuition
    direct, 203
    indirect, 203
    self-giving, 201
    types of, 103–4

James, William, 61
Johnston, Mark, 158, 187, 213
    on hallucinations, 188
justification
    defeasible, 216, 217
    immediate, 213–14
    normative conception of, 89–90
    positive and negative epistemic dependence
        and, 217
    role-oughts and, 89

Kant, Immanuel, 61, 167
Kelly, Sean, 53, 76, 133, 145
    on nonconceptual content, 133–4
King, Jeff, 16
knowledge
    empty, 214
    fulfillment and, 213
    indubitable, 222
    intentionality and, 213–14
    as thinking at its best, 213

Korblith, Hilary, 108
Kuhn, Thomas, 49
    on perception, 49–51
Kvanvig, Jonathan, 111
    on the self-representational character
        of perception, 111–12

Levin, Janet, 171
Lewis, C. I., 64
    on the given, 64–7
Locke, John, 27
Lyons, Jack, 94

manifold, perceptual, 181
    determinable X and, 182
    horizon and, 180
    illusion and, 181
    spatiotemporal lines of, 182, 184
    synthesizability and, 182–4, 186
manifolds, perceptual, 180
    hallucinations and, 184–7
    identity-consciousness and, 181
maps, 44
Martin, M. G. F., 8, 149, 153, 157
    on the nature of hallucinations, 153, 157
matter, intentional, 29, 176
    quality and, 29–31
McDowell, John, 106
    content, theory of, 10, 83–5
    on disjunctivism, 156
    on the space of reasons, 85–92
McIntyre, Ronald, 22, 177
memory, 103, 202–4
Merleau-Ponty, Maurice, 67
Millar, Alan, 8, 52
    on recognitional abilities, 197
Millikan, Ruth, 125
Molyneaux's question, 171
moon illusion, the, 181
Moore, G. E., 78

names
    descriptivism, 21–2
    direct reference theory of, 19–21
    Frege–Mill dichotomy, 21
    Husserl on, 20
Noë, Alva, 44, 45
    on conceptual content, 44–6
noema, 29, 176
noetic structure, 107
nonconceptual content, 37, 38, 84, 93, 131, 140; *see*
        conceptual content
    ambiguity of definitions of, 131–2
    animals and, 131
    content view, 132

of hallucinations, 160
intuitive and horizonal, 189
relative vs. absolute, 132
richness argument for, 131
state view, 132
nonconceptualism, absolute, 132
content interpretation, 138–40
object interpretation, 132–5
nonconceptualism, relative, 132
content interpretation, 136–8
object interpretation, 135–6
nonsense (*Unsinn*), 128
absurdity (*Widersinn*) and, 128–9

O'Shaughnessy, Brian, 124
object determination, 173

Papineau, David, 143
particularity, problem of, 173, 174
Peacocke, Christopher, 30, 134
on content, 11
perception
adequate, 79
conditions of satisfaction and, 43–6
content view of, 160
demonstrative theory of, 119
diversity of objects of, 41, 60–1
dual component theory of, 116
epistemic role of, 99–101, 210–12, 222–4
fineness of grain, 25–6
hallucination and, 188
inadequacy of, 43, 53–6, 79, 161, 166, 170–2, 200
indirect, 150–1
multiple factorizability of, 219, 221
positing character of, 200, 213
presentational character of, 48, 103, 150, 213
richness of, 25, 41
role of bodily awareness in, 167–9
safety and, 186
sign consciousness and, 151
of states of affairs, 67–8, 72
straightforward, 69, 71
synthesizability requirement, 182–4
Perry, John, 18, 32
phenomenal force, 113–15
phenomenological sameness, 172
phenomenology, 3–6
plain, 3
pure, 187
physicalism, 6
pictures, 44
Pietersma, Henry, 24
Plantinga, Alvin, 99, 107, 218
platonism, 91

Pollock, John, 107
presentification, 103
Price, H. H., 48
Prinz, Jesse, 8
propositions, 33, 93, 145
as contents of thought, 32
not objects of thought, 15–17
states of affairs and, 12, 17, 19, 84
proprioception, 168, 169
protention, 165
Pryor, James, 96, 108, 113, 214, 217
on the phenomenal force of perception, 113–15
psychologism, 34
pure internalism, 173
problems with, 173–5
Putnam, Hilary, 35

qualia, 5, 6
quality, intentional, 31
Quine, W. V. O., 74

recognition, 192
Reinach, Adolf, 147
relational view
problems with, 170–2
subjective character of experience and, 162–3
virtues of, 149–52
representational realism, 150
retention, 164
Russell, Bertrand, 13, 33, 42, 79

Salmon, Nathan, 20
*Salvia divinorum*, 158
scheme/content distinction, 67
Searle, John, 44, 110
on perceptual content, 174
Sellars, Wilfrid, 1, 86, 214
semantic essence, 31
sensations, 61–4, 101, 104, 142
awareness of, 62–3
in Husserl's theory of perception, 208
kinesthetic, 187
sense data, 77–8, 215
sense datum inference and, 215
sense datum theory, 77–8, 152, 155, 160, 161, 170
sense, Fregean, 19, 21, 33
cognitive significance and, 23
reference and, 30
sense, interpretive, 30
sensorimotor profile, 53
Shim, Michael, 187
Siewert, Charles, 3, 155

skepticism, 96–7, 222, 224
Smith, A. D., 43, 51, 116, 180, 181
  on the synthesizability of perceptual
    experiences, 182
Smith, David Woodruff, 122, 175
  on content, 9
  on the contents of perception, 176
  on the determinable X, 177
Snowdon, Paul, 161
Soames, Scott, 19
Sokolowski, Robert, 70
Sosa, Ernest, 108, 186
space
  allocentric, 26, 167
  egocentric, 26, 167
Speaks, Jeff, 132, 136
  on nonconceptual content, 133
speckled hen, 162
Stanley, Jason, 21
states of affairs, 9, 10, 11, 46
  as objects of thought, 13, 17, 32
  propositions and, 17

Thau, Michael, 190
  on content, 12
theory of appearing, 154
Thompson, Evan, 168
  on bodily awareness, 168–9

thought
  unboundedness of, 23–6
time-consciousness, 164–5
  longitudinal intentionality and, 165
  transverse intentionality and, 165
truth, 13
  consciousness of, 212
Twardowski, Kasimir, 15
twin earth, 173, 184
Tye, Michael, 139, 172, 185

Van Cleve, James, 66, 94, 99, 213
vehicle of thought, 32
virtue epistemology, 186

Willard, Dallas, 18, 34, 177, 194
  on fulfillment, 198, 206
Williams, Michael, 96
Williford, Kenneth, 147
Wittgenstein, Ludwig, 155, 179

X, determinable, 176
  unique to object, 177

Yoshimi, Jeffrey, 148
  on horizons, 147–8

Zahavi, Dan, 42

Made in the USA
Middletown, DE
10 July 2021